Outdoor Adventures:
San Francisco Bay Area

A Complete Guidebook to
All the Local Recreational Sports

Outdoor Adventures:
San Francisco Bay Area

By
Rick Blick

A Sports Resource Guidebook

ICS Books, Inc.
Merrillville, Indiana

OUTDOOR ADVENTURES: SAN FRANCISCO BAY AREA
Copyright © 1995
10 9 8 7 6 5 4 3 2 1

Published by:
ICS BOOKS, Inc.
1370 E. 86th Place
Merrillville, IN 46410
800-541-7323

recycled paper

All ICS titles are printed on 50% recycled paper from pre-consumer waste. All sheets are processed without using acid.

LIBRARY OF CONGRESS CATALOGING-IN-PUBLICATION DATA

Blick, Rick.
    Outdoor adventures, San Francisco Bay area: a sports resource guidebook / by Rick Blick.
        p.   cm. – (Outdoor adventures; 1) Includes bibliographical references (p.) and index.
        ISBN 1-57034-006-4
        1. Outdoor recreation – California – San Francisco Bay Area – Guidebooks. 2. Sports – California – San Francisco Bay Area – Guidebooks. 3. San Francisco Bay Area (Calif.) – Guidebooks.
    I. Title. II. Series.
    GV191.42.C2B55 1995
    796.5'09794'6--dc20
                                                                    95-5104
                                                                    CIP

Introduction

The enticing Bay Area playground.
Photo: Aero Photographs

Remember when you were growing up and all you ever heard from adults was "Why don't you go outside and play?" That's been the strategy of parents for generations to get rid of unruly kids (like you were) that were bouncing off the walls. So you ventured outside, perhaps a bit scared at first, and looked for adventure in your own backyard or at local playgrounds. You learned the hard way, with a lot of falls and tears in the beginning, to climb to the summit of the monkey bars or nearby trees. Other times, you would push the limit on the swing set till you almost went over the top, envisioning your first 360. You would usually finish off the day going for warp speed down the slippery slides of the local park. Every once in awhile, you even got to go to the beach, to frolic in the water and sand having more fun than you ever thought possible. Remember the thrill of body surfing your first shore break wave?

As the years passed you acquired your first bicycle, which opened all new adventurous possibilities and brought innumerable smiles to your face. All of a sudden, adventuring became so much fun that when your parents, or the sitter, would try to bring you back in the house rebellion set in. You would either beg or ignore them for at least thirty minutes before finally heading back to the boring house and another early bedtime. Life was great fun playing every day, except for the occasional wipe out that would bring scrapes, black and blues, or stitches to different parts of your body. These silly injuries might have put you back in the house for a short while, but after a few days of healing and restlessness, you were right back out there going for it.

Sadly, with time, we all grow a little older and start acting very mature, more and more serious, and boring. We stop carving out time for sports adventure because society tells us it's time to cease having fun. Adults aren't supposed to have fun. We're supposed to be responsible and entrenched in the establishment of society. Our stress levels start climbing off the chart, because we have no release, but it seems normal because everyone is stressed out. Welcome to the rat race.

You must grow up, of course, during your athletic prime, which seems such a waste. Any free time you have, which isn't much, is spent doing errands, paying bills, or shopping in some mall. Maybe you take a few hours on the weekend to watch sports on television, wash the car, pull weeds in the garden, or complain about work. You are lucky to sneak in an hour a week on an exercise bike or stair stepper at the health club.

Forget all that jazz and go out and play!
Keep that health club membership though, because you're going to need the weights and Jacuzzi to maintain those muscles for playing outside. There are so many great outdoor adventure sports available in the Bay Area that you will have trouble keeping up with all of them. It doesn't matter if you are just a beginner or an expert. This area offers world class sports for each. If you need to rationalize carving out some play time for these great sports, consider that they will be good for both your mental and physical health. And that is definitely true. For example, an afternoon of windsurfing, parachuting, or rock climbing will put you in a great mood by releasing any and all built-up tensions and frustrations. And you'll feel so much better than you would after pulling a two-hour stint pulling weeds in the garden.

All of us deep down long for adventure.
Every year, we save our hard-earned money to vacation in exotic locations for two short weeks that seem to fly by. Then, it's back to the salt mine for another fifty weeks, till the next vacation. Vacations are great, but what about those fifty other weeks? You need to seek some adventure fun, and you can get it right here on a daily basis. Conditions are so good in the Bay Area for these great sports that you can fit adventure playtime around any work, school, or parenting schedule!

The San Francisco Bay Area is the greatest urban playground in America, and probably the world.
Within a sixty-mile radius of downtown San Francisco, there are at least fifteen adventure sports you can get involved in, all with world-class conditions during the proper season. The fog may be a bit thick at times, and wetsuits are required for the water sports, but this is one great sports town. Where else, on a normal run-of-the-mill Saturday and within the confines of a large metropolis, could you surf some perfect five-foot waves under the Golden Gate Bridge, and then ride a mountain bike up the awesome single track and fire trails of Mount Tamalpais thirty minutes later. You'll actually be riding on the same trails where mountain bikes were invented some 20 years ago.

Or perhaps you'd rather spend your Saturday afternoon on a sailboat or windsurfer, enjoying some picturesque high-wind sailing on San Francisco Bay. How about a jaunt in a sea kayak around Alcatraz? Maybe a paraglide off Mount Diablo? How about a sky dive or bungee cord jump in the morning, then a great trail run out to Stinson Beach on the famous Dipsea Trail in the afternoon? Make sure to save some time for some challenging rock climbing in Berkeley, or road biking the many miles of scenic back roads this area offers.

Of course, you can't forget to fit in some open-water swimming in Aquatic Park to prepare for a swim race from Alcatraz to San Francisco in June. You can warm that body temperature back up by in-line skating the hills of the nearby Presidio. Are you tired yet? We haven't even covered the awesome local hang gliding or open-water rowing spots.

Sure, other cities have one or two great sports they are associated with. In the San Francisco Bay Area, you can do them all. But beware, this place can wear you out. Take each sport at your own pace, so you'll enjoy each one. Also, make sure to never get in situations over your head. That way you won't be prone to any silly injuries—that is, any injuries other than sore muscles or a bruised ego from a crash on the learning curve of these great sports.

To get involved in these adventure sports, you'd better get in good shape, both physically and mentally, because the adrenaline envelope of life is going to get pushed. Forget about trimming the rose bushes or mowing the lawn. Tape the 15 football games on television all weekend to watch later. You'll have to leave the car dirty, because you won't have time to wash it. Besides, you are just going to get sand in it from the beach anyway. Just pick a sport and get started. If you happen to be visiting to work or sightsee, let somebody else do the normal tourist stuff at Fisherman's Wharf. You've seen enough wax museums in your life. Go out and get some sports adventure. Every day you wait is a another thrill lost.

This guide book is definitely not like any others you'll see.

A quick browse through any bookstores' section on the Bay Area will offer you volumes on where to eat, shop and sightsee in this area. These tourist books are full of great information, but will ultimately leave you fat, broke and bored. There are also numerous books on all the different weekend escapes from the Bay Area. Why escape from a place as beautiful as San Francisco every weekend? Stay here and commit the travel money saved to learning a new sport. It might just change your life.

This book is about sports adventure only.

The pages that follow will show you an entirely different side of the Bay Area than typical guidebooks. Inside, you'll find all the detailed information you'll need to get involved in these great local adventure sports. Just picture yourself stepping out the plane door as you parachute from 10,000 feet, or trail running in the beautiful local redwood forests. All of these sports have very fast learning curves, thanks to the many local professional schools that welcome newcomers for basic lessons. A complete listing of local schools for each sport follows, along with rental equipment details. With the help of the professional instructors that staff these schools, the learning process is actually fun, while at the same time as safe as humanly possible.

Also outlined in this book are the costs associated with each sport—and the prices are way cheaper than you think. Each sport's learning curve is also explained in detail, so you know exactly what you are getting into. In addition, a load of information is supplied on how to find good deals on purchasing your own equipment (new and used). Finally, you will learn the best season to play at each sport. Detailed maps show the best local places to play at each sport. One of these hot spots is probably right outside the front door of your residence or hotel. All are within the boundaries of this adventure sports paradise known as the San Francisco Bay Area. So hang on, turn the page, and welcome to some really fun adventures.

Dedication

*This book is dedicated to all you
adrenaline junkies out there who have the courage
and perseverance to learn a new sport, no matter what
your age, or how many of your friends call you crazy.*

Disclaimer

The author and publishers do not endorse or promote the listed activities nor the places to undertake such activities. The participation in what is herein described as "Adventure Sports" carries with it the inherent risk for injury, or even death. As with all strenuous activities, it is recommended that you consult with your physician before undertaking any physically demanding sport. Additionally, in the interest of diminishing the risks associated with some of the sport activities that are the subject of this book, it is important that you gain the requisite expertise in each activity and familiarize yourself with the area in which you intend to participate in such activity.

Lastly, none of the retail shops, publications, organizations, or instructional schools have paid any compensation to be included in this guide. They are listed for informational purposes only.

Author's Note

We'd like to think we covered all sports in this informative guidebook, but alas, there were some great sports that got left out. No insult is meant to all you local and visiting scuba divers, skateboarders, BASE jumpers, land lugers, abalone divers, motorcycle racers, balloonists, or glider pilots. All these sports can be done in, or close to, the Bay Area, and surely qualify as adventuresome. It's just that there wasn't enough space to include these sports in this book.

Some other great sports, such as snow skiing, snow boarding, white-water rafting, and river kayaking didn't make the cut because they couldn't be done in the immediate area, although world-class conditions for each abound throughout the great state of California. Awesome skiing and snowboarding are available all winter only 175 short miles away in beautiful Lake Tahoe. For whitewater rafting and kayaking, there are some Class 5 rivers within a two-and-a-half hour drive of the Bay Area.

*The criteria for a recreational adventure sport to be included in **Outdoor Adventures: San Francisco Bay Area** were that you could learn the sport right here from scratch, and then be able to play locally in some world-class conditions. The playground had to fall within a 60-mile radius of downtown San Francisco.*

Within these limits, you can jam out after a full day of work, school, driving car pools, sightseeing, or business meetings, and still get in some great sports adventure. You can spend all weekend playing instead of dealing with the travel hassles of getting somewhere to play. If you happen to be visiting this area, most of these great sports can be found just minutes from your hotel room.

These are tough criteria for any sport to fit, but the fifteen sports outlined here all make it with flying colors. It is this proximity to a major city that makes these awesome recreational adventure sports so much fun, and so easily accessible to the more than 6 million people who call the San Francisco Bay Area home, or the 13 million visitors who come here every year. We are relatively sure that the 15 active sports outlined in detail in this guide will be more than enough to keep you busily entertained, challenged, thrilled, scared, jazzed and smiling. Good luck, you're going to need it.

Lastly, any suggestions you might have to make this a better guide are welcome. Please send any thoughts to:

Outdoor Adventures: San Francisco Bay Area
c/o ICS Books
P.O Box 10767
Merrillville, IN 46411

Contents

Look For These New Adventures
In The

Seattle Area, Denver
And New York

Excuses

Sailing the Bay.
Photo: Latitude 38 archives

L et's get the excuses out of the way first. The fact is, you will definitely get some strange looks when surfing on a chilly Winter morning around here. Ditto when you get spotted road biking in the pouring rain. Your friends, family and/or date might think you have lost it when you show up to functions late and have to change clothes in the car because you just couldn't pass up an afternoon of windsurfing off Crissy Field in 20-knot winds. Even if you are never late, some people that you hang around with that are less adventuresome than you will come up with ways to deter you from these great sports. They will blab on and on about how difficult, time consuming, expensive, and hard to learn they may be. This is just not the case. All these sports can be easily learned and played without spending a lot of money. These same so-called buddies will take up all your free time helping them move, shop, watch television, or do errands. It's easy to create excuses to wait yet another season before partaking in some of these exhilarating adventure sports. Another great sports season is missed while you hang around the house or shop in some stale mall.

Be especially aware of these lame excuses and don't fall for any of them:

The water is too cold.
Let's face it, the water here is freezing. This fact more than any other keeps most people from trying any water sports. Before you complain about how cold it is, think how crowded it would be if the water was as warm as it is in Los Angeles or San Diego. There would be so many surfers at every break it would look like rush hour traffic. The fact is, wetsuits made today will keep you more than adequately warm for the water temperature in and around the bay. The wetsuits are so good you will actually feel too warm a lot of the time. No kidding.

Wetsuits cost too much.
They are not cheap, but for around $200, a wetsuit will open up a whole new world for you. Wetsuits come in many different varieties and many prices. For Bay Area water sports, you'll need a suit with full-length arms and legs all year long. The thickness of the neoprene material directly relates to the warmth of the suit and the cost. A 3/2 wetsuit will have 3 millimeters of thickness of neoprene around the body and 2 millimeters of thickness around the arms. A better suit for the water conditions here would be a 4/3 wetsuit. The added neoprene on the arms and trunk translates directly to that much more warmth for you. This extra warmth will allow you to have fun in the water that much longer without getting cold. A 4/3 wetsuit will cost more that a 3/2, but it is worth every cent. Used suits can be found at surf shops in the area, but they are not as warm as new ones. The stitching begins to stretch as a suit get older, allowing heat to escape. Also, make sure to get a good wetsuit that fits right. "Tight is right," when fitting a wetsuit, according to Marin SurfSports owner Kevin Campion.

The water is polluted.
As of this writing, there is no reason not to do water sports in the Bay Area due to a water pollution problem. The water is definitely not as clean as it was a hundred and fifty years ago when the Gold Rush ships sailed into the Bay, but the tides are strong enough to keep the water pollution below any major health-hazard level. Surfers are advised to avoid Ocean Beach right after heavy rainstorms because storm drains dump raw sewage into these waters when sewage treatment facilities get too backed up (this only happens during extended rains). Otherwise, you'll be having too much fun to worry about the water you're swallowing. Help keep the San Francisco Bay as clean as possible. We encourage you to support the local and national environmental organizations listed in the back of this guide.

There are sharks out there.
Sharks are native to this area of the Pacific Ocean, but they are not out to get you, despite the media claims. In the last sixty years, there have been some seventy shark attacks on humans along the 800-mile coast of California, according to expert sources. These attacks did result in seven deaths, so always be careful, but there are a lot of miles of coastline, so the chances of a great white shark attack are slim. You have more chance of being struck by lightning than being bitten by a shark. Shark sightings in Northern California seem to be focused on the corners of the "red triangle;" the corners of the triangle are Point Reyes, the Farallon Islands and Ano Nueva. Be aware if you are in the water in any of these areas. Actually, you might want to stay out of the water at these three places, just to be safe. There has not been a reported shark attack on any swimmers, surfers, kayakers, or windsurfers inside San Francisco Bay, or at Ocean Beach. This is not to downplay the existence of sharks in these waters, but when you're crossing the Bay on a windsurfer going 25 knots, or surfing eight-foot walls off Ocean Beach, you'll have other things to think about. A shark should be the last thing on your mind.

I can't swim.
Weak excuse. You can learn to swim easily no matter what your age, and then all the water sports described here will be open to you. Every pool in town gives adult beginner swimming lessons all year. Call your local Department of Recreation or YMCA for information and class schedules. The phone numbers for your immediate area are in your local phone book.

I get seasick.
Nice try, but most sea sickness can be controlled through medicine; either ear patches or tablets. The newer medications usually do not have the negative side effects associated with the medications of just a few years ago. Give them a try. They really do work.

I don't know how to get started, or stay informed, in these sports.
It is true some of these sports look very hard to get into, but actually they are all very easy and can be taken by anyone no matter age or athletic ability. *This book will be able to tell you almost all you need to know.*

To stay up-to-date on current events around the Bay Area, you should read the following free magazine publications; they are full of local information for the sports they represent. The magazines are free, as they are supported by the advertisements of the local retail stores. The ads will keep you abreast of any equipment sales that might be going on. *Wind Tracks,* for the windsurfer, is available at any of the area windsurf shops. *CitySports* will keep you up-to-date on in-line skating, running and both road and mountain biking. This great monthly publication is usually available at health clubs in the area. At the same clubs, you can usually find *California Bicyclist*, which keeps the local bike world informed. *Latitude 38* will keep you current on the local sailing scene, and is available at all local marine stores. Lastly, *The Schedule* will keep you informed on the local running races; it is available at any local health club.

I'm not very athletic.

This is a feeble excuse. If you are a natural athlete, the steps of the learning curve might be easier, but natural athletes tend to give up sooner on sports they don't immediately grasp. Persistence is the key. Take the proper lessons and you can become an accomplished athlete. Plus, you don't have to be very athletic to ride a mountain bike, paddle a sea kayak, or bungee jump. You can leave the harder sports, like windsurfing and rock climbing, for later. Remember, this is about having fun, not becoming a star athlete.

These sports are too expensive.

This can be proven wrong. Sure, it can cost major dollars if you decide you need new top-of-the-line equipment every year, but you don't. You can rent equipment for all of these sports cheaply. A boogie board rents for about $10 per day. Windsurfers rent for about $20, and the same for mountain bikes. Four people can easily rent a sailboat for about $20 each. Getting your own equipment can be easy and inexpensive as well. There is an abundance of good, reasonably priced, used equipment all over the Bay Area if new stuff is too expensive for your budget. The sources for good used equipment include the classified sections of your local newspapers, local recreational sports magazine monthlies like *CitySports* (415-626-1600), as well as specialized sports publications like *The Sports Market Place* (415-924-4204). Each chapter in this book includes a cost breakdown for purchasing new and used equipment for each sport. An additional outlet for good reasonably priced used sporting equipment are the chain of stores called **Play It Again**. These stores are usually stocked with a very good inventory of used mountain and road bikes, in-line skates, hockey equipment, climbing gear, etc. **Play It Again** can be found in **Concord** (510-825-3396), **Pleasanton** (510-734-6750), **San Bruno** (415-952-6882), **Sunnyvale** (408-247-1234), **Los Altos** (415-988-6800) and **Campell** (408-371-4531). Most sports stores in the Bay Area encourage trade-ins to help you advance in your sport.

I don't have a car.

How about a bicycle? You can carry a surfboard on it using racks available at surf shops, or you can make a wheeled cart to haul a windsurfer. Plus, there are so many places to play in the Bay Area that one has to be close to your home. Therefore, a car is not a necessity. In addition, mass transit is so good in this area that you could, for example, take a BART train from San Francisco to Berkeley, rent some equipment and learn to windsurf at the marina, then take the train back home.

These sports take too much time to learn.
Not true. The learning curve is fast on most of these sports, especially bungee jumping and boogie boarding. For the sports that do take longer, like windsurfing, rowing and hang gliding, you'll be glad not to rush it. The learning process is a lot of the adventure, and it's fun right from the beginning.

The set-up and preparation takes too much time.
The prep work on most of these sports is quick. Preparing a sailboat for sailing can be done in as little as 15 minutes. You can rig a windsurfer in about 10 if you're in a hurry. With hang gliding, or paragliding, you might want to take a little extra time, just to be safe. Sports like in-line skating, trail running, and road or mountain biking require almost no preparation time at all.

I don't have anyone to do these adventure sports with.
Bad excuse, because a lot of these sports—road biking, trail running, in-line skating—can be great solo work outs. Sure, groups are fun, but so is the solitude of a good trail run by yourself. Most of these sports require instruction anyway. If you have to go to class by yourself, you will have the chance to make instant great friends by lunch of the first day, because you will all share the common interest of going for it. Just get out there and have some fun. There is also the option of joining one of the many local clubs in the area for every one of these sports.

I'm chicken.
This is actually a somewhat valid excuse but with the excellent professional athletic schools available here that are staffed by expert teachers in each sport, you will feel very safe. The hardest part is the decision to sign up for the class. You'll be very happy you did. Of course, you could always pick one of the calmer sports, like road biking, sea kayaking or trail running to get started. Pick up paragliding or windsurfing later.

Part 1
WATER

The Bay Area is quite simply a water wonderland. It offers some of the best sailing and windsurfing in the world from March through October, when classic west winds come funneling through the Golden Gate. This aquatic paradise then rolls into a serious surf season from September till February. By then, winter storm swells will be pumping waves at the local breaks as the winds turn off-shore. All year long the playground is open for sea kayaking, rowing a shell, or some great open-water bay swimming.

WETSUITS

The first purchase you have to make to use this local aquatic playground is a wetsuit.

The bay's water temperature ranges from 60° to 68° Fahrenheit in summer, and will drop as low as 48° F in winter. This is too cold for any human to survive for periods of an hour or more unless you have some serious protection. A good wetsuit is a necessity, not an option.

The improvements in wetsuit comfort, warmth and mobility over the last five to ten years have been phenomenal. Today's wetsuits are very versatile as well, so you only need one for all water sports you may participate in. Make sure it fits comfortably but snugly. Comfort is key, because you might be living in this suit when these sports get a hold of you.

Wetsuits come in different models, depending on the thickness of the neoprene rubber it is made from. This insulation is what keeps you warm. The thicker the suit the warmer it is. A 3/2 suit will have three millimeters thickness of neoprene in the trunk and legs, and two millimeters of thickness in the arms. A 3/2 suit will keep you warm in the summer months for periods of a couple of hours, but a 4/3 or a 5/4/3 suit will enable you to play in the water all day, and all seasons of the year, without ever getting cold. All you'll need is the addition of the neoprene hood, booties and gloves in the winter months to stay really warm all year long.

Today's wetsuits come in all sizes, styles and price ranges. They come with such crazy names as Bodyglove, O'neill, Hotline and Ripcurl to name just a few. The price of a new 4/3 suit will range from $220 to $380, and a 3/2 suit will cost anywhere from $99 to $200. Try to invest in a new one if your budget allows, to ensure the right fit and obtain the most warmth out of the suit. If the price is too steep for a new one, a selection of used suits are available at some surf shops when rental suit inventories are sold off. Used suits will definitely work, and save you considerable money, but the fit and warmth may not be as good you'd get with a new one.

HYPOTHERMIA

Hypothermia sets in when the body slips into a subnormal body temperature brought on by being exposed to the cold for too long a time. Basically, it means you are cold to the core. Hypothermia can lead to major health problems, and even death. Each person's body temperature reacts differently to cold water, so you may feel fine while your friend is freezing in the same water conditions. With the cold water of the bay and Pacific Ocean, hypothermia is something to always be aware of, and avoid.

Hypothermia sets in quickly and you usually are totally unaware it is happening. This is what makes it so dangerous. The core temperature of the body drops a few degrees in 10 to 15 minutes without a wetsuit, and the body pulls all the blood to the internal organs to keep them functioning. This pulls the blood away from the body's surface, and all of sudden you can't move your fingers. Lethargy sets in, your vision gets clouded, and uncontrollable shivering starts. If this ever happens to you, get out of the water immediately and get in a warm shower or sauna to warm up.

Wetsuits manufactured today will take the risk of hypothermia out of engaging in the recreational water sports as long as you use common sense and get out of the water when you start feeling really cold. Make sure to get a good, warm wetsuit and you will probably never come close to experiencing hypothermia.

TIDES

Most water sports in the bay are best done during certain tidal conditions. Basically, an ebb tide means water is moving out of the Golden Gate into the Pacific. A flood tide means thousands and thousands of gallons of sea water are ripping in through the gate. A slack tide is the no tidal condition; the water is not moving either way. Tidal charts or tide tables are useful for determining the conditions at a given time; they are available at most marine stores in the area. You also can follow the tides in the weather sections of local newspapers.

CHAPTER ONE

Surf

Season: Best September through March, but can be done all year.
Learning Curve: One full season for the basics.
A lifetime of fun to master.

Surfing was around long before the Beach Boys played a musical note. Historians place the Polynesians riding waves as far back as 1500 years ago. The first written description of surfing comes from the logbook of famous sea explorer Captain James Cook, who visited Hawaii in 1777. Surfing on the island was considered the sport of kings and queens (no wonder royalty was so important – they got the choice waves).

The introduction of surfing to America's mainland was fairly recent. In 1907, George Freeth brought riding waves to Redondo Beach from Hawaii and Californians have been hooked ever since. The sport has continued to grow in California and around the world since then, and remains one of the most challenging adventure sports you will ever find. The experience of picking your wave, then paddling like a maniac till you feel its back go up and propel you down the face is almost impossible to match. Give it a try.

These days, surfing is open to everyone. Surfers in the Bay Area often are considered a small club of dedicated fanatics. Not that many hardy souls do it (about 2,000 active surfers), and those who do are fairly hard-core, given the sometimes rough water and cold weather. The local surfers are easy to spot because of the boards on the car racks and big smiles on their faces. When most others are complaining about the winter weather bringing big storms, the surfers are pumped for the incoming swell. Wave riders here and the world over are convinced the experience of riding a wave is more than just sport. Surfing is a way of life. After you begin catching waves, you will totally agree. Since you never know when the waves will be good, you'll find yourself planning your life around the swells. This is not an activity you can plan on from 1 to 4 p.m. on a Saturday. You have to go when the waves are happening, so you don't plan too much during the surf season. The sport is well worth the uncertainty. Being in this beautiful ocean, paddling around on a sleek surfboard that allows you to ride mammoth swells will exhilarate your soul.

Although the Bay Area isn't considered a Mecca of surfing, like Santa Cruz, Hawaii or Southern California, this place offers many days of great surf, especially in the fall and winter months. One of the professional surf tours schedule a stop here every year, and you can bank on some 12 to 15 foot faces on the monster wall days at Ocean Beach when the big storms of winter arrive. The fact is, surfing is a lot of fun in small as well as big waves, and there are usually some kind of waves to ride almost every day of the year. Surfing is also quite a workout, so you'll get in great shape while you're getting "barreled." And once you get past the "barney" stage of wiping out on every takeoff, or dropping in on other surfers (a huge negative), you'll be accepted at any good break in the area. Till then, it might be best to learn and surf at some of the smaller, less-crowded spots, so you don't run into anyone. In surfing, as in any water sport, it's really easy to get in over your head as wind and wave conditions pick up. Always know your ability to ride the waves at the break you are planning to surf. If you think it's too big, don't paddle out. Come back when you know you are good enough to handle it, or the waves are smaller. A complete detailed explanation of the different breaks in this area can be found later in this chapter. The season for bigger surf runs from late September to March. The rest of the year usually offers smaller surf, so it's a great time to learn the basics. Be careful when starting out, because some of the breaks in this area have treacherous rip tides. Do not go surfing alone. Make sure there is at least another surfer out there, so you can keep an eye on each other in case of an emergency. Always surf smart, and don't ever underestimate the power of the ocean.

Glassy conditions and a textbook takeoff at Ocean Beach.
Photo: Doug Acton

EQUIPMENT

Since you're going to have to make many equipment purchases for this great sport in a surf shop, let's address that first. A neophyte walking into a surf shop for the first time to buy equipment might expect a harrowing experience. You might be convinced that whatever your appearance and mannerisms were when you entered, you'll have bleached blonde hair and a few earrings in your lobes by the time you leave. You may think your simple clothing will be transformed into day-glo jams and sandals, and your vocabulary will become littered with words like "dude," "stoked" and "green room." Your car will be laden with fifteen bumper stickers advertising such products as "Sex Wax" and "Big Dogs." This perception probably keeps more people from surfing than anything else. It doesn't have to be that way. All types of people surf—all ages, sexes and body types. After getting into the surf scene, chances are you will end up like the shred grommets you see all around the surf breaks, but take it slow and don't be intimidated. Grab the owner of the shop and explain that you're a surfing virgin. If you act like you know what you're doing, you'll wind up buying a short, narrow surfboard that you'll never be able to ride, and surfing will not be a pleasant experience. Be straight on your ability so you can get the right board and surf equipment the first time. Today's beginner boards are easy to ride and will have you up surfing and shredding in no time.

The Surfboard:

Purchasing your first surfboard, or "stick," is one of life's great pleasures. It will feel good to hold and carry, and as soon as you pay for it you are a "surfer."

The size of a beginner's board depends on your size and weight. Get a big, fat, long and floaty board to start, so it will be easy to paddle and stable to ride. Also, to facilitate the learning curve, the board should have a rounded nose and be wide through its entire length. This will give it a lot of stability. The stability factor is key when you attempt to stand up on your takeoff. Without it, your feet placement and stance will have to be perfect, which doesn't happen very much in the beginning. You will wipe out constantly and the learning curve will become frustrating instead of fun. This added stability will result in a slower board, but it will give you a needed margin of error on the takeoff.

The length is not as important as the width and volume, but don't get a short, "sinker" board when starting out. A board that is seven feet six inches to nine feet in length, with a width of 19 to 23 inches in the middle should be fine. The surf industry calls these boards "hybrids," "mini tankers," or "fun boards." An actual "tanker" or long board is a lot longer (9 to 12 feet), which makes it heavier and harder to paddle out. You might want to get a long board after you have been surfing for awhile, because they are fun. But if you are just starting out, get yourself a hybrid that will be easy to paddle and fun to ride from the start.

The price of a used board ranges from $150 to $300; expect to pay about $450 for a new one.

You might have noticed we didn't go into the different aspects of what makes a surfboard click. That's because you will have enough on your mind learning to surf without worrying if your board has too much *rocker*, the *rails* are too tight, or whether you should be on a *swallow tail* or *fintail*. All that will come later. For now, all you need to know is that there are basically four types of boards:

1) **Fun Boards:** These are good beginner boards. They are seven to eight-and-a-half feet long, with a round nose. They are wide and very floaty, and are also called mini tankers or hybrid boards.

2) **Long Boards:** These are great fun. They come with a lot of length, thickness, and are easy to paddle. These boards allow you to get into the wave sooner and stand up quicker than a short or fun board. Also called tankers, long boards are great to learn on, although they can be very hard to paddle out.

3) **Performance Boards:** These are usually custom-shaped for the surf conditions at the breaks you mainly surf. Do not begin to surf on one of these because they are harder to ride than a fun or long board. The short boards in this category are usually six-foot four to seven feet in length, and will allow you to do hot-dog moves because they carry more speed in the wave and are easier to turn. Short boards do not have a lot of volume and do not float really well, so they are sometimes called "sinker boards." Longer performance boards range from seven to eight feet, and are more streamlined and faster (and not as stable) than fun boards of the same length. They offer greater surfing performance and speed. These longer boards allow you to paddle faster and are more stable than the short boards but do not execute turns as fast.

4) **Big Guns:** You need these boards when the wave faces are 12 feet and taller—as high as 20 feet. These boards are long (nine to 12 feet), thick, and narrow, so they can carry speed with stability. These big guns are designed for big-wave spots like Maverick's surf break in Half Moon Bay. You won't need one of these boards till you have become a very accomplished surfer and want to venture out in the really big stuff.

Leashes:

Leashes are the plastic ropes that connect the surfboard to your ankle with a Velcro strap. *The leash is the most important piece of equipment you'll own.* It will keep you from drowning when you wipe out in big surf and would otherwise lose your surfboard. It could be a long and dangerous swim back to shore without a board.

Leashes come in different lengths, strengths and prices. Longer leashes are for bigger surf; short leashes are for smaller waves and more crowed surf spots. Make sure to buy a good one, with a double Velcro ankle cuff, so you never lose your board. You don't want to be out in eight-foot or bigger surf without a leash—or with a cheap one that could break. The cost for a good leash is about $25.

Forget any fear that a leash will cause the board to boomerang back at your head. By the time you resurface after a wipe out, your board will be quietly waiting for you. Just jump back on and paddle back out for the next wave. Just so you know, regular footed surfers wear the leash on their right ankle, and goofy footers wear it on the left.

Wetsuits:
Wetsuits are a must in Northern California. *See the detailed explanation at the beginning of the Water Section.* The cost of a new wetsuit will range from $99 to $350, depending on the thickness of the neoprene. Used wetsuits can be purchased at surf shops that rent equipment; the price ranges from $80 to $150, depending on the condition of the suit. The simple rule of thumb is the better wetsuit you buy, the warmer you will be.

Hand Propulsion:
Fairly new to the surfing scene, these aquatic hand propulsion gloves make you look like the Creature from the Black Lagoon, but they do add power to your paddling stroke by making your hands webbed. You don't need them, but they could help you catch more waves by letting you paddle faster. They cost about $20.

THE LEARNING CURVE

Surfing looks pretty easy. Just paddle out, turn around and wait for the perfect wave to surf in. Appearances in this sport couldn't be farther from the truth. Just the paddle out can feel like a four-day affair if you don't know what you're doing, and riding the face of the wave takes uncanny balance, skill and ocean sense that is not learned in a day. The following breakdown will help explain the art of surfing, but a lot of practice in all types of surf conditions is the only way to really learn this awesome sport.

Reading the Waves:
There are a number of different breaks (places) where surf happens. Breaks are defined by the shape of the ocean floor or the type of obstruction that causes the waves to break. There are pier, reef, shore, point, and peak breaks. In the Bay Area, Ocean Beach is a peak beach break, where the waves are caused by moving sandbars under the water. Fort Point, a sweet left break under the Golden Gate Bridge (on the south side), is a point break that really cranks on a good northwest swell.

Each individual wave is then broken down into the face, shoulder, lip, trough and, if you're lucky, a tube. These parts can be easily identified on any wave that's breaking. Before you paddle out, spend some time watching the waves from shore to figure the different tendencies of that particular surf break. This studious approach will make your paddle out a lot easier by allowing you to avoid the impact zone, and your overall surf session will be a lot better.

Paddling Out:

The first important decision to make is where to begin your paddle out. Step back on the beach and find the channel—the deep water passage located left or right of the waves breaking in shallower water. Using this channel will make the paddle out a lot easier than trying to bang your head straight into the breaking waves.

Since at some point during the paddle out you will run into waves breaking, it is very important to learn to dunk your board, or you will be pushed back to where you started from. *This "duck dive" is the single most important aspect of surfing to learn right away, or you might never make it out to the breaking waves.*

The duck dive is like diving under a wave while bodysurfing or swimming. It's a lot easier to dive under the approaching wave than to swim through it. The only difference in surfing is that you have this big board, your friend, to get through with you. It's not that hard. As the wave approaches, paddle at full speed and push the nose of your board (with your weight a little forward) under the white water of the incoming wave. Quickly drop to the back of your board, keeping one knee on the tail and the other leg fully extended. This will force the nose of the board back up to the surface with forward momentum and stability. Resume paddling till you get past the break. You may have to execute as many as fifteen duck dives in a row to get out past the break on a big wave day.

Catching a Ride and Standing Up:

Once you've picked out the swell to ride, turn toward shore and start paddling hard. The biggest mistake new surfers make is not paddling hard enough. They stop paddling as soon as they think the wave has them, only to miss it. The first couple of times you catch a wave, don't even try to stand up. Just enjoy the ride laying down on your stomach. The speed will be fun enough. Get to know your board and the perfect "spot" to put your weight. If you are too far forward, you will drive straight down into the water and fly off the board. If you're back too much, you will never catch the wave.

Once you have catching the wave down, you are ready to stand up. The most important aspect is to find out whether you are goofy footed or regular footed. The best way to find out is to stand on a skateboard or put your surfboard on your bed and stand on it. If it feels more comfortable to stand with your left foot forward, you are regular footed. If you're most comfortable with your right foot forward, you're a goofy footer. Goofy footers will find going left a lot easier in the beginning and vice versa for regular-footed surfers.

The key to getting up on a surfboard is making one fluid motion from the paddle position to standing. As you're paddling and feel the wave start to take you, put both hands on the rails (edges), pushing down hard so the board stays in the wave. Use this motion to propel you to a crouched standing position as the board falls away. Make sure to keep your knees bent and your butt way down, to give you more stability. Keeping your feet well apart and knees bent will automatically put you in the right position. Your front foot should then push the board down the face of the wave. By now, your arms should be out in front of you to balance and correct. Put a smile on your face, because you are now a surfer.

Having Fun on the Ride:

Once you get the standing-up part wired, the real fun of surfing starts. In the beginning of the learning curve, you will stand up and ride the board straight down the wave toward the beach. This gets old real fast, because you will out run the wave, slow down, and the white water will then catch you and knock you over. Not cool. The key to successful wave riding is to develop a good "bottom turn" to get you back on the face of the wave and keep you riding. This bottom turn is executed after the takeoff, when you are out in front of the wave after shooting the face. This way your board has picked up some speed. These bottom turns are tricky in the beginning and you might fall a lot. Keep practicing, remembering to keep your knees bent and your butt down for stability. On a good long ride, you might execute four or five bottom turns while working up and down the face of the wave. After you master the bottom, you'll have to learn the off-the-lip moves, tail slides and floaters on your own. Just make sure you have the fundamentals down before you try these acrobatic moves. There is no better feeling in sport than when you are "on" and riding a surfboard in big, glassy surf.

Wipe Outs:

A wipe out is the fine art of falling off your board. You're going to have a lot of wipe outs, so don't get frustrated. They can take many forms, and can actually be a lot of fun. Just remember that there is a board attached to your foot, and there is a slight chance it may come back to hit you. The best thing to do when you fall is to stay under as long as the ocean wants to keep you there. Don't claw your way back to the top, because you'll only get tired. The waters here don't have the scary reefs like Hawaii, so there is nothing to fear in that regard. If you try to fight your way to the surface, there is a good chance you will run out of breath and possibly panic. Just relax, and when you do resurface, your board will be right there. Paddle back out quickly so as not to get stuck inside when the next set of waves comes through. Also, apply a lot of wax—or the newer track pads—for better traction on your board. The better the traction, the fewer the wipe outs.

Rules of the Road:

When the surf is good, there is usually some kind of crowd. This is true at the local Bay Area surf breaks, and at just about any break in the world. You have to know the rules to avoid accidents and bad etiquette, like dropping in on some other surfer.

Keep in mind this important rule: On a breaking wave, the inside surfer has the right of way. The inside person is defined as the one closest to the peak of the wave. On a right-breaking wave, this is anybody to your left. On a left-breaking wave, it is anybody to your right. If there is a surfer inside you, he/she has the right of way. Just back-paddle and pull out of the wave, making sure you hold on to your board. Do not drop in on other surfers, especially at new surf break. If you do, there is a good chance your fins will be broken off by some pissed-off locals.

The other very important rule of surfing etiquette is to always hold on to your board. This is especially important on the paddle out, when there could be other surfers behind you. Sometimes oncoming waves will try to rip the board from your hands as you execute a duck dive, so hold on tight. Runaway boards, even those on a leash, can hit surfers behind you in the head as the leash stretches. This move will not make you very popular out in the surf lineup.

WAVE RIDING ALTERNATIVES

Boogie Boards:
If the surfing learning curve seams a bit too steep in the beginning, riding boogie boards is a great alternative. You can be riding and understanding waves in an afternoon. Tom Morey, a Southern California inventor, came up with the Morey Boogie Board, which opened up wave-riding to the masses. You just slip on a pair of fins and lay on this two-foot-long Styrofoam board for some serious wave-riding thrills—without the long learning curve of surfing.

The costs of riding a boogie board are a bit more reasonable that those associated with surfing. A good boogie board and set of fins will cost about $120 to $160. Used boogie boards can be found for considerably less at some of the local surf shops.

Paddling out through the surf on a boogie board is a lot easier than paddling a surfboard, and you will be able to catch a lot more rides faster than if you were learning to ride a surfboard. For these reasons, it's no wonder why the sport has grown so fast. This great sport lets anyone experience the thrill of riding waves right away.

Also, keep in mind that even if you are an accomplished surfer, a boogie board has its uses. It's a safe, fun way to learn a new break.

Body Surfing:
Say you don't have the money to buy a surfboard or even a boogie board. You can still ride the local waves as a body surfer. You remember body surfing as a kid—why not do it now? Stinson Beach is a great place to start. The waves break a little farther out at Stinson and the other local surf spots (usually the water is deeper than standing depth), so make sure you wear a pair of swim fins. Without fins, you might get swept out in the rip current, which could have ugly consequences. The fins will give you the kick power to catch a lot of waves and you will feel totally safe in really deep water.

There is a school of thought among serious water men and women that body surfing is the ultimate and cleanest way to experience wave riding. And it's cheap. A pair of good wave riding fins (not scuba diving fins) will only cost you $30 to $50, and give you years of fun. Don't forget the wetsuit. Do not start body surfing at a radical place like Ocean Beach. Keep to the beaches with more manageable breaks and mellower rip tides, like Stinson or Rodeo Beach.

Wave Skis:
This addition to the sport of riding waves has been gaining popularity here in the United States after gaining popularity on the beaches of Australia and New Zealand over the last twenty years. Wave skis are sometimes hard to get out in big surf, but they offer a lot of speed and maneuverability on the wave face after you get the hang of paddling. The cost ranges from $200 to $400 for a boat and paddle. If that's too much money, rentals are available at **Outdoors Unlimited** (415-476-2078) for about $20 a day. The surf break at Bolinas Beach is the most popular for wave skiers due to the long swell, but they can be ridden at all of the local breaks if the conditions are right.

WHERE TO GO

There are some helpful surf report hotlines available locally, so you don't spend a lot time driving around looking for surf and getting skunked. Wasting time like that will get old real fast.

The **Wise Surf Shop** hotline is updated every day at 10 a.m., and can be reached at (415) 665-9473. The toll-charge surf-line phone number is (408) 844-SURF (charge is about $1.85 per report). This line offers a great report on the swell conditions all down the coast. Area-specific daily surf reports are available as well. The **Marin Surf Sports** surf-line can be reached at (415) 381-WAVE, and the **Stinson Beach** report has a phone number of (415) 868-1922. Both are normally updated at 8:30 a.m. Watch the weather patterns on the local television news and in the weather section of the newspaper for swells coming in.

The key to catching good surf is to keep your surfboard in the car with you from September till February. When you hear about good surf, sneak out of your job, forget yard work, do no errands, and get right to the beach to get wet. It will be well worth it.

The local surf spots include:
Ocean Beach: Located on the western edge of Golden Gate Park, along the Great Highway, Ocean Beach is the premier surf spot in the area. First ridden back in 1949, this awesome city beach offers more than two-and-a-half miles of peak break waves that come all sizes depending on what kind of swell is running. Usually, the waves are in the three- to seven-foot range, but there are many days when waves average eight to 15 feet. During a big winter storm, waves have been known to get even bigger than that. This

beach also seems to offer the best surf conditions on a receding tide with offshore winds.

The best months for surf are from late September till April, but Ocean Beach offers surfable waves all year round. *The fall and winter months are for more experienced surfers because this place can get pretty hairy.* Be aware of strong rip tides and big close-out waves. If you are not sure of your surfing ability, it might be best to boogie board here till you get the feel for the place.

Ocean Beach is a hard place to surf, but loved by the locals because it's never that crowded and offers some serious double-overhead surf. For the beginner, the summer months offer smaller surf that's fun on a long board. Go early in the day during the summer, because strong west winds will blow the place out by noon on most days.

The surf breaks along Ocean Beach are named for the streets that intersect the Great Highway at that point. The break at Sloat is usually the biggest, while VFW (corresponding to the Veterans of Foreign Wars Hall on the edge of Golden Gate Park) and Kelly's Cove (at the north end near the Cliff House) are the most popular breaks. You can usually find less-crowded waves at Taraval and Noriega because you have to park off the Great Highway making it a longer walk to the beach.

Wise Surf Shop is in the immediate area for wax and supplies. Wise is the local surf guru, and there are great pictures on the walls of his retail store showing some epic days at the beach (never call it "O.B."). He even formed a D.O.A. club, which stands for the Double Overhead Association, but on the really big wave days, that definition has been mistaken for the meaning used by the medical profession. **Wise Surf Shop** also sponsors a daily surf report at (415) 665-9485. The **SF Surf Shop** and the **End of the Line Surf Shop** are also in the area.

Be aware of the rip tides at this break. It is not uncommon to drift a half-mile down the beach during a surf session. The tide flows to the north on incoming tides, and to the south on outgoing tides. The surf is considered best on an outgoing tide, so consult your tide tables for the optimal time to go. Also, always know where you are in the water by picking out reference points on the land. If the tide, rip currents, or the size of the waves start to make you nervous, paddle back in and come back on a smaller surf day.

Pacifica: This area includes breaks like Rockaway, Pedro Point, and Linda Mar Beach. They are located just south of San Francisco along U.S. Route 1, near the small coastal town of Pacifica. The surf is usually a bit smaller than at Ocean Beach, and it is therefore a better spot for novice or intermediate surfers. However, it can get very big in winter swells. You'll see a lot of long boarders and surf clubs at these breaks, and some very good surfers.

Fort Point: Located at the base of the Golden Gate Bridge's south tower, this break offers one of the most picturesque surf spots anywhere in the world. When this place is going off, there is usually a gallery of tourists snapping pictures and shaking their heads in disbelief at the crazy locals. This break was formed with the construction of the fort in 1853, but was not surfed until 1963. The wave comes in to break left and can sometimes wrap around the whole point, offering an extra long ride. This break can be dangerous because of the many submerged rocks near the point, so make sure you are an experienced surfer before paddling out here. It might be a good idea to surf here first with a boogie board till you feel comfortable on a surfboard.

The conditions have to be just right to create surfable waves here. Usually, this happens on a nice-sized north to northwest swell and during medium to low tidal conditions. Fort Point doesn't go off that often, but when it does, drop everything and be there. You will love to surf here, especially if you are goofy-footed.

Cronkite Beach: This break is just north of the Golden Gate Bridge in the Marin Headlands. It is somewhat protected, which makes it a good place to surf in the summer, when other beaches are blown out by the local strong West winds. The waves at this break close out a lot quicker than at other local area because of a sudden drop in the water depth close to shore. Rides are usually short at Cronkite, but it is a great place to learn takeoffs. A fun spot with some really good surfers, this place also offers an easier paddle out than Ocean Beach or Pacifica. **Marin Surf Sports** is in nearby Tam Junction, offering rentals and other surf supplies.

Stinson Beach: *Stinson Beach is by far the best place for beginners to learn to surf in the Bay Area.* Located on U.S. Rt. 1 north of the city about 12 miles, Stinson is the best social beach in the Bay Area on sunny days, especially in the fall when tons of people are hanging out. You can surf for a few hours and then hang out on the nice beach for the rest of the day. The surf closes out quickly an awful lot here, but can be a lot of fun to surf or boogie board when the conditions are right. This is a great beach to learn to surf because you can practice the important takeoff maneuver over and over without an impossible paddle out each time. Most Bay Area surfers learned to surf at Stinson Beach. Surf equipment can be rented easily at **Live Water Surf Shop,** which is within walking distance of the waves.

Bolinas: Located just off U.S. Rt.1 a few miles north of Stinson, this break offers very good surf with not very crowded conditions. With more of a rolling swell, you will see a lot of kayakers and surf skis here, as well as surfers.

Secret Spots: Surf breaks and secret spots are located up and down the coast of California. If we listed them all, a lot of local surfers would want us hurt, so you have to find them on your own. Finding new surf breaks is part of the fun of surfing anyway. *Just remember to bring your surfboard whenever you travel up and down the coast.* Santa Cruz, or the new big-wave spot at Maverick's in Half Moon Bay, should be a definite stop— even if it's just to watch some really good surfers.

ADDITIONAL READING

Make sure you pick up a copy of Bank Wright's *Surfing California*, which describes the different surf breaks along the California coast. This book is available at any surf shop and has become every local surfer's traveling Bible. Call *Mountain & Sea Publications* at (213) 379-9321 if you can't find it. Additional fun surf reading can be found in *The Surfinary*, by Trevor Cralle (Ten-Speed Press, Berkeley), which explores the surf language phenomenon. Read this and you'll know the lingo to use when you're scratching for that wave with a twelve-year-old grommet. It might come in handy. Lastly, a great book on the sport is *The History of Surfing*, by Nat Young (The Body Press, Tuscon, AR).

SURF SHOPS IN THE BAY AREA

Wise Surf Shop: 149 Vincente, San Francisco; (415)665-7745; daily surf report (415) 665-9473. This is the oldest surf shop in town. It has been in business since 1968 and is located just a few blocks from the **Ocean Beach** surf break. It offers a large selection of new and used boards, along with a lot of wetsuits, great people and awesome pictures. The surf report is updated every morning. No rentals here. Wise is one of the legendary surf figures of the Bay Area and this shop is a must stop for every surfer.

End Of The Line Surf Shop: 3657 Taraval St., San Francisco; (415)566-7087; surf report (415) 566-5363. This shop is also very close to the Ocean Beach surf break. It also carries snowboards and in-line skating equipment to offer you thrills in the off-season.

SF Surf Shop: 3809 Noriega at 45th, San Francisco; (415) 661-7873, A welcome addition to the Ocean Beach surf shop scene, the shop carries all supplies, including wax and leashes, as well as custom surfboards and wetsuits. The owners usually stock a complete selection of surfboards, and specialize in shaping a custom board to your specifications. Demo boards are rented at about $20 a day, and the price of the rental will be deducted if you decide to purchase a board later.

Marin Surf Sports: 54 Shoreline Hwy., Mill Valley at Tam Junction; (415) 381-9283; surf report (415) 381-WAVE. Close to the Marin Headlands break and on the way to Stinson Beach and Bolinas, this shop is conveniently located just off U.S. Highway 101 at the Mill Valley/Stinson Beach exit. The surf report is updated at 9 a.m. every day. The store stocks a large selection of new and used surfboards, as well as wetsuits and boogie boards. This place also offers a huge selection of skateboards, so you can practice your surfing skills on land as well. The store is staffed by cool people who have helped a lot of beginning surfers get into the sport. The shop is the same building that housed Marin's original gas station and trading post in the early 1900s. They are still trading, but the fuel sold today is the adrenaline of being "tubed." Rental wetsuits, soft surfboards and boogie boards are available.

Live Water Surf Shop: 3450 Shoreline Highway, Stinson Beach; (415) 868-0333. Located in the center of town, this legendary surf shop offers complete rental equipment, along with new and used boards. This is the only surf shop located on the beach in this area. It has been in business since 1976 and has introduced many locals and tourists to surfing and boogie boarding.

Surf Berkeley: 1527 San Pablo Ave., Berkeley; (510)528-7873. This shop has been serving East Bay surfing equipment needs since 1986. The shop carries a good selection of surfboards and a fair amount of body-surfing fins. In addition, the store carries skateboards and gear. No rentals here.

Excelerate Board Sports: 655 Contra Costa Blvd., Pleasant Hill; (510) 798-4400. Also located in the East Bay, this shop also carries a lot of snowboard and skateboard equipment. The store usually has a complete inventory of surfboards on hand, some of them used. No rentals are available.

Sonlight Surf Shop: 575 Crespi Drive, Pacifica; (415) 359-5471). This surf and snowboard shop is very close the great surf breaks just along Rt. 1 just south of San Francisco like Rockaway, Linda Mar Beach, and Montara. The proprietor Danny Estrella also does the surf report for this area for the global publication *The Surf Report* out of Dana Point. Their daily surf report phone number is (415) 359-0353.

ADDITIONAL SURF SHOPS

There are many other surf shops located outside the Bay Area in some great Northern California surf towns. Many of these stores have a great selection of new and used boards—in case the local shops do not have what you are looking for. Call to see what is in stock, or better yet, stop by on one of your surf safari trips up or down U.S. Rt. 1. The drive south will take you through Half Moon Bay, which is the home of Maverick's, one of the classic big-wave breaks in the world. Sixty miles south of Half Moon Bay lies Santa Cruz, a truly epic surf town. A sampling of some of the surf shops follows:

Half Moon Bay

Cowboy Surf Shop: (415) 726-6968   **Aqua Culture Surf Shop:** (415) 726-1155

Santa Cruz

Arrow Surf Shop: (408) 475-8960
Freeline Design Surfboards: (408) 476-2950
Haut Surf & Surfboards: (408) 426-7874
Ocean Energy Surf & Sail: (408) 479-4814
O'neill Surf Shop: (408) 475-4151; **daily surf report:** (408) 475-2275
Santa Cruz Surf Shop: (408) 464-3233
Seabright Surf Shop: (408) 423-1451
Santa Cruz'n Surf Shop: (408) 458-5360 (longboards)
Full Speed Surf Shop: (408) 426-7873

Bodega Bay

North Surf Plus: (707) 576-1530

Bay Area Surf Breaks & Shops

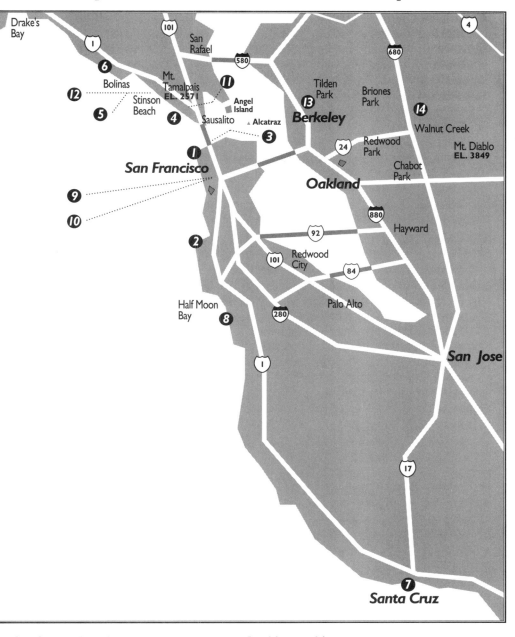

Between the San Francisco Bay Area and Santa Cruz, there ought to be enough good waves to keep you busy for awhile, but you should also look into some extended surf trips to Southern California and Mexico once you get into the sport. Southern California and the Baja Peninsula offer many phenomenal surf spots. For additional information on these spots, as well as the best surf sports worldwide, contact **The Surf Report**, P.O. Box 1028, Dana Point, CA, 92629; (714) 496-5922. This excellent monthly newsletter offers worldwide surf reports and other valuable information for any aspiring surfer. A subscription to this publication is very reasonably priced—only $35 a year. Detailed reports on almost any area in the world that has surf are available for only $6 a copy. Worldwide surf trips are also advertised in the back pages of national surfer magazines. Once you get good at surfing, these trips offer awesome fun.

COST OVERVIEW FOR SURFING

Cheap Budget:
You can pick up used surfboards from $50 to $125 at garage sales, from friends that surf, or in the garbage heaps in the back rooms of surf shops. Make sure to check the ding repairs on the board closely to make sure there is no water leakage into the foam core of the board. If there is potential for leakage, the board will hardly float after thirty minutes in the water. It is no fun surfing on a water-logged board, so make sure to repair all dings. You also will give up some wave-riding performance on older, well-worn boards in this price range, but if you're just starting out, you won't notice the difference. You will also need a wetsuit. Used wetsuits can be found at some of the local surf shops for $80 to $100. A new suit will cost $150 or more.

Moderate Budget:
Boards in this budget bracket are in the $150 to $250 range. There might be a ding or two on the rails of these slightly used boards, but otherwise they are in good shape. Sometimes, you can find surfboards that were only ridden a few times and traded back in. The surfboards in this price range will work great for any beginner or intermediate surfer. They will also save a little money over the price of a new one.

High-End Budget:
Save the big bucks for when you step up to your first new board. You can either pick it off the rack or have it shaped for you by an accomplished local surfboard shaper. The advantage of getting it shaped is that you can explain to the shaper the breaks you will mainly be surfing. The board will then be shaped for those conditions and your ability level. You also get to pick the color scheme and input any ideas you might have into the design. The only negative to ordering a custom board is that it takes up to eight weeks for delivery. A new board on display at the surf shop can be ridden the same afternoon you buy it. The price of a new surfboard will range from $300 to $450.

Bay Swim

Season: All year, but best April through October,
when the water is warmer.
Learning Curve: Very fast if you are an
intermediate-level pool swimmer.

If your definition of adventure sports does not include swimming in the San Francisco Bay, try competing in an open-water swim race from Alcatraz to Aquatic Park. With choppy seas and a strong current, you'll have more than a thrill trying to get inside the mouth of Aquatic Park before the tide sweeps you toward the Golden Gate Bridge and Hawaii.

It takes courage and training to compete in a rough water swim around here. The bay offers some classic swims. Group swims and races are usually held in the early morning, offering spectacular sunrises, glassy water and, presumably, a slack tide, although predicting the local tides is no exact science. A mixture of ripping cross currents, fog and choppy seas can materialize for some races, making for interesting results. All races offer great support for the swimmers, with surfboard and kayak spotters to help anyone who gets in trouble.

Most daily open-water swimming is done in **Aquatic Park**, located directly in front of Ghirardelli Square near Fisherman's Wharf. This area offers a protected cove with relatively flat water and protection from strong winds. This is a great place to train for open-water swims in safety, even if you swim alone. Stay close to shore till you are confident in your ability.

It's amazing to talk to people about swimming the bay, because most local residents have never even gone in the water. But take one swim on a twilight summer evening, with the lights of Ghirardelli Square reflecting on the water, and you will be a bay swimmer for life. Open-water swimming in the Bay Area is great fun and a challenging workout. The perception is that you have to be a great swimmer to get involved in open-water swims. This is simply not the case. There are a lot of very average swimmers who have completed the organized Alcatraz and Golden Gate swims.

The hardest thing about bay swimming is getting accustomed to the water temperature. Sure, swimming fast helps, but the real key is to get your body and mind acclimated to the cold by swimming in it. Once you are used to the water temperature, you can easily make any of these swims. Start with a fifteen-minute session and build from there. Grab a cap and some goggles and start practicing.

You should note that anytime you venture into open water outside Aquatic Park, the sea conditions can get tough. Do not ever swim alone far from shore. Also make sure never to underestimate San Francisco Bay. Swim safely at all times; know exactly what the tide is doing and how it affects you. It's a good idea to swim at slack tide when you start out.

Swimmers sprinting into Aquatic Park to start a race.
Photo: Kenneth Lee

EQUIPMENT

There is no cheaper sport than open-water swimming. The basic equipment includes a pair of swim goggles ($8 to $30) and an orange swim cap made of thick wetsuit neoprene for warmth ($20). The color should be bright for safety; it offers easy visibility to boats that might be in the area. You can get by with a cheap rubber swim cap ($3), but you won't keep as warm. Most experienced bay swimmers wear the neoprene swim cap and one rubber cap for optimal heat loss protection.

The major equipment debate in this town is whether to wear a wetsuit to stay warm or to swim bareback. A wetsuit will be cumbersome at first, and might slow you down a bit, but will keep you warmer in these chilly waters. With the increased popularity of open-water swims as part of triathlons, wetsuit manufacturers have started making specialized suits just for swimming. These open-water swim suits add buoyancy and are very streamlined; you will swim faster. The cost of these specialized suits ranges from $180 to $300. If you don't want to add that expense to your sports budget, but you want to wear a wetsuit, use your surfing/wind-surfing suit. It will keep you warm, but may slow you down a little. Better to swim a little slower and stay warm than to get hypothermia.

Bareback, of course, means it's just you and your bathing suit (which is optional on full-moon swims). This will feel ultra fast, but you're going to feel the cold in a big way. Hypothermia is a very real danger given the water temperature range of 60° F in the summer to the 40° F in winter.

In spite of these cold temperatures, a lot of the older, serious swimmers detest wetsuits and feel the swimmers who wear them are a bit less macho. Our feeling is swimming should be fun, with no macho stigmas attached, so do whatever you want. Most people start out with a wetsuit, and as they get used to the water temperature, they begin to go without. Make sure you wear a good neoprene swim cap if you decide to go bareback, because most of your body heat escapes through your head. Always be aware of the signs of hypothermia (see the detailed explanation at the beginning of the water section).

Lastly, know the tides, because the bay can throw up some four- and five-knot tides at times that no swimmer, even an expert, would be able to swim against. Not knowing the tide situation only leads to trouble, so get a tide book or follow the tides in the daily weather section of the newspaper.

LOCAL SWIMMING CLUBS & RACES

There are two local clubs that make outdoor swimming in the Bay very easy, offer a great way to get in shape, and even meet interesting new people. **The Dolphin Club** (415-441-9329) and the **South End Rowing Club** (415-776-7372) are located next to each other on Jefferson Street, near Fisherman's Wharf and Ghirardelli Square. Both clubs rest on the waters edge of Aquatic Park. Members and out-of-town or drop-in guests (for a $7 charge) get full use of a piping hot sauna and showers that will warm a swimmer after a chilly dip in the bay. Both clubs also offer an active social and swim calendar, free weights and rowboat usage for members. Tide and water temperature information is also available on the blackboard, which is updated daily. Some elder members offer a tremendous amount of bay swimming history and nostalgia to anyone that asks.

Annual membership dues to these clubs run about from $350-$400, which translates into $30 to $35 a month for unlimited hot showers, a nice beach and a health club. Both clubs are more than 100 years old and offer a rich tradition of swimming the Bay. These clubs also sponsor the majority of open-water swim races in the Bay. And there are a lot of races. These include Alcatraz swims, as well as races at Gashouse Cove, Pier 39, the Golden Gate Bridge, Crissy Field and more. A yearly schedule is published, so you can plan and train accordingly. Don't miss the annual New Year's Day swim from the Alcatraz "rock" to Aquatic Park. In most cases you have to have been a member for about six months to participate in club-sponsored races.

If you don't want to spend the money to join a swim club, you can swim for free in Aquatic Park whenever you get the urge. Other swim races are open to the general public—that is, anyone who is crazy enough to want to swim in the bay. People just like you. These races sell out quickly. To get a schedule of open swims, it is best to consult the local publication of *CitySports,* the *Schedule*, or even the local sports papers for race announcements. They change every year according to race permit availability.

An open Alcatraz swim is usually put on every summer by **EnviroSports** (415-868-1829) for race director Dave Horning), and has more than 400 entrants, many of them first-timers. Other open swims are put on by the **Alcatraz Challenge Group** (415-903-0341) for race director Joe Oaks), including some Aquatic Park cove races, an Alcatraz swim and biathlon, and a demanding Bridge to Bridge swim that goes from the Golden Gate to the Bay Bridge. You will meet interesting people at these open-water swim events, and get in great shape as well.

If you are not confident in your swimming ability, or you are just starting out, call your local YMCA or health club for basic swimming lessons. After a few lessons in the pool, you will be able to open-water swim in no time. Don't let this thrill pass you by.

SWIM STROKES & LEARNING CURVE

The most popular swim stroke by far for open-water swimming is the crawl (freestyle). This stroke is the most efficient for covering long distances over time. In this stroke, most of the power comes from the arms pulling through the water. The kick is used mainly to stabilize the body. It is assumed that you can crawl before you ever attempt open-water swimming. If you do not feel comfortable executing this stroke, it would be advisable to practice in an indoor swimming pool till you feel more confident.

Swimming a straight line in open water is not nearly as easy as swimming a lane in an indoor pool. There is no black line down the middle of the bay to keep you on course—no flip turns either. On your first few swims, it would be a good idea to look up frequently so you don't veer too far off course. This technique is called "spotting." After you adjust to the initial cold and the straight-line directional thing, open-water swimming will really begin to get fun. Your stroke will change from survival swimming to enjoyment swimming, and the sport will get into your soul, becoming very addicting. You'll find yourself looking forward to that afternoon dip at Aquatic Park.

WHERE TO GO

Most bay swimming is done in the calm, protected waters of Aquatic Park. The park is located just off Ghirardelli Square and close to Fisherman's Wharf. Both the local swim clubs, Dolphin and South End, are located here as well. There are public bathroom facilities under the grandstands at Aquatic Park that can be used by swimmers, with hot showers available spring through fall, but you might want to spend the money for the day fee to use the swim clubs, which are a lot cleaner and offer a warm sauna and lockers in which to leave your valuables.

The cove in Aquatic Park offers a number of swim course alternatives by either using the buoys or taking a long lap around the whole thing, called doing a "cove." *It is strongly advisable not to go outside the cove entrance of Aquatic Park into the open bay.* The bay tides are very strong and can easily take the best of swimmers out into the dangerous middle of the bay. That's oil tanker country out there as well. Stay in Aquatic Park for your training swims and do the longer swims with supervised groups only.

Because of a number of dangers, do not attempt any of the longer swims detailed below on your own. These swims should only be attempted in qualified, organized group swim races supervised by an experienced swim-race director. The race should include support boats and emergency medical teams, in case the dreaded hypothermia monster grabs anyone. The best pre-race strategy is to get in good shape in a lap pool, then train as often as you can in Aquatic Park to get used to the water temperature. With enough practice, all of these beautiful swims can be accomplished with ease. If you get into any trouble, there will be support boats close by to help. Be sure to listen to the pilots of these support boats. They have your best interest at heart.

Classic Swims of the Bay

Alcatraz to Aquatic Park: This is a demanding adventure of 1.5 miles across the open channel into the mouth of Aquatic Park to finish at the beach. Your stomach will be in knots as the boat drops you off at "the rock," at a place called "Sharks Cove" (it's just a name—don't read into it). Really proficient swimmers will complete this course in 20 to 25 minutes. Slower swimmers will take up to an hour. The longer you are in the water, the colder you will get. With every extra minute, you run the risk of the tide changing, which can cause you to miss the opening at the Aquatic Pier. Because of these factors, never attempt this swim without a support boat.

Golden Gate Swim: Usually starting at Fort Point and finishing past the North Tower of the Golden Gate at Fort Baker, this is a demanding 1-mile swim with awesome views of the bridge. Timing the tides is the key to successfully completing this swim. Halfway across, you will start to wonder whether you will make it, or whether you'll soon be on your way to the Farallon Islands and Japan. This swim should only be done at slack tide, and should never be attempted without a support boat. This is a gorgeous swim that allows you to use the bridge above as a lane marker. Throw in a little backstroke for a view most people will never see of one of the world's most famous bridges.

Gashouse Cove to Aquatic Park: This course starts at Gashouse Cove Marina, located in front of the Marina Safeway, and takes you out into open water before coming into the mouth of Aquatic Park. This swim is best done on a flood tide. Never attempt this unless in a group swim with support boats. Be very careful to watch for boat traffic. Check out incredulous looks on the diners' faces in the Greens Restaurant in Fort Mason as you swim by. This course also can offer big waves, which give you a body-surfing feel as you get pushed down the city front.

Pier 39 to Aquatic Park: This course starts at Pier 39 and heads through open water before coming in at Aquatic Park. This swim should only be attempted on an ebb tide, and should only be done in groups with a support boat as well. This swim takes you into the seal territory at Pier 39. These crazy seals are very friendly and will love to play with you as you swim past them.

Additional Swimming Beaches: There are many nice swimming beaches all over the Bay Area. Make sure the area you want to swim at is somewhat protected from the strong tides and big seas that occur in the open bay. Some of the best spots include *Schoonmaker Beach* in Sausalito, *Olympic Circle* in the Berkeley Marina and *Hospital Cove* off Angel Island. North Bay swim beaches include sweet *Paradise Beach* in Tiburon, off Paradise Drive. The East Bay comes in with *Crown Beach* in Alameda. And lastly, for the South Bay, there is some classic swimming in the waters off *Coyote Point Beach* near San Mateo.

Bay Area Open Water Swim Clubs & Courses

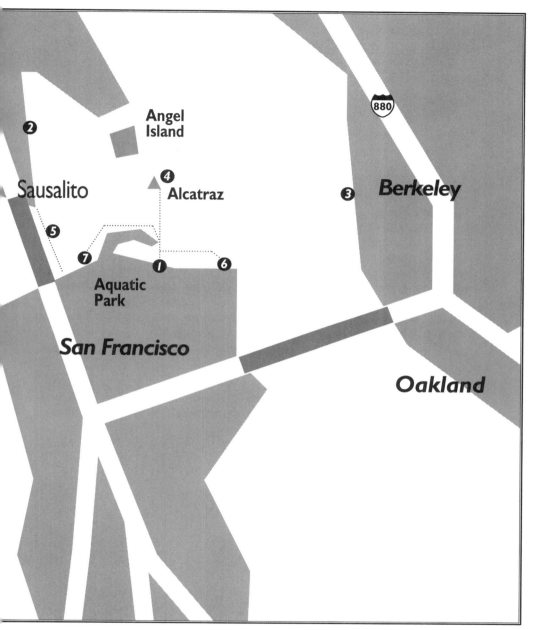

❶ **Aquatic Park**–Dolphin & South
   End Swimming Clubs
❷ Schoonmaker Beach, Sausalito
❸ Olympic Circle, Berkeley
❹ Alcatraz Swim Course
❺ Golden Gate Swim Course
❻ Pier 39 Swim Course
❼ Gashouse Cove Swim Course

COST OVERVIEW OPEN-WATER SWIMMING

Cheap Budget:
Find the cheapest set of swim goggles (that don't leak), put on your bathing suit and a rubber cap, and jump in. Total cost will be a one-time purchase of about $11 for goggles and cap.

Moderate Budget:
In this price range, you can get swim goggles that are more comfortable to wear, and more expensive swim caps made from neoprene that will keep your head warmer. If you want to wear a wetsuit (we would), you can pick up a basic 3/2 thickness at any of the bigger sports stores, or go to a surf shop for one that you can use for other water sports as well. The cost will be $99 to $300 for the wetsuit, and about $45 for the goggles and swim cap.

High-End Budget:
This is strictly about whether you want to buy a really nice, specially designed swimmers wetsuit, or use that money to join one of the local swim clubs at Aquatic Park. The cost of joining a swim club is from $350-$400 a year. Wetsuit prices range from $199 to $450. If you want a specialized swimmers wetsuit, pick up a copy of the national magazine *Triathlete* and go through the advertisements in the back for ideas and information. There are some really nice specialized triathlete retail stores around the Bay Area that offer a great selection of these wetsuits as well.

CHAPTER THREE

Sea Kayak

Season: All year round.
Learning Curve: A seven-hour course completed in
one day for the basics, and fun for a lifetime.

Sea kayaking in the Bay Area is not only beautiful and surreal, it's a really good workout and the conditions can get pretty wild if you want. You can go early in the morning to get flat, glassy water for a calm paddle, or you can wait till the afternoon and be greeted by 20-mph winds and swells up to four feet. In short, the Bay offers everything a sea kayaker could want.

Sea kayakers prepare to head out of Aquatic Park at dawn.
Photo: R. Blick

For those who demand even more wild times, lots of adventure and tougher sea kayaking await you up and down the beautiful California coastline just outside the Golden Gate. This beautiful coast offers waves to ride, rock gardens to navigate and sea caves to explore.

The joys of this adventure sport are that it can be picked up very quickly and can be done all year long. Another great feature is that the set-up time is only about five minutes. Just take the kayak off the car, change clothes, check the gear and safety equipment, and you're gone. And you're in for a big treat. One clear full-moon paddle on the bay and you will be an avid sea kayaker for life.

What follows is an explanation of the equipment, local schools, the best places to paddle and the costs involved. If you have taken an introductory sea kayak course in another city, just explain this to the local kayak shop owners and you will probably be able to rent a boat right away—after correctly answering a few questions about paddling technique and safety.

EQUIPMENT

The Boat:
Deciding what kayak to use is quite a challenge, because at first look, there are many different models designed for different types of paddling. Kayaks on the whole are broken into two main groups—river kayaks and sea kayaks. The river boats don't work very well on the bay. They are not long enough to track (go in a straight line) very well and don't have enough surface area to really get moving, no matter how hard you paddle. They are also a lot less stable than sea kayaks, which means these river kayaks go over fairly easily. *We would definitely advise against using a river kayak in the bay.* These river boats can be a blast in the world-class rivers a few hours' drive from here, but not on San Francisco Bay.

To paddle in this area, you will want instruction in and follow-up rental or purchase of a legitimate sea kayak. These boats are easy to recognize with their long lines, dugout seat and razor-tip bow and stern. The length of a sea kayak is usually between 16 and 19 feet, and the weight depends on the material the boat is made from. Stable sea kayaks come in plastic, wood and fiberglass, and can weigh as little as 35 pounds or as much as 70. The lighter the boat, the easier it is to paddle, and the faster it will go on the water.

Sea kayaks are then further divided into boats that have rudders and boats that are rudderless. The rudder set-up usually costs a bit more (about $150 extra), but will enable you to track in a straight line much better, which gets you to your destination a lot faster and with less energy wasted.

The last choice you have to make is whether to go with a washdeck or spray-skirt sea kayak. The washdeck has an open deck and a self-bailing cockpit that drains the water that continually comes in as you work your way through the choppy seas. Paddling a washdeck kayak will make you feel like you're part of the water, as you're cruising along just inches off the surface. An open cockpit boat will not fill up with water if, and when, you get turned over. But remember, you will definitely get a whole lot wetter in a washdeck kayak.

The spray-skirt sea kayak, which is the more traditional kayak, will tuck you into the boat and make you feel more protected from the elements. This spray skirt acts as barrier between you and the water so you stay warm and dry. To make an analogy between these boats and sailboats, the spray-skirt kayak feels like a yacht, whereas the washdeck feels like a dinghy. The price you pay for this protection is that a kayak with a spray skirt can fill with water when you tip over. It is easy to drain the boat and climb back in, but will take a little time. The good news is that once you become a proficient sea kayaker, you hardly ever flip over (unless you paddle in extreme conditions).

Your choice of boat will depend on the type of sea kayaking you envision yourself mainly doing. If you want to play in the bigger surf, or any other wild conditions where you have a good chance of flipping over often, you will want the easy on and off access of a washdeck sea kayak. If you primarily see yourself kayaking in the calmer waters inside the bay, the spray skirt will keep you dryer and a lot warmer. The spray skirt models are by far the most popular and have a historic tradition in the area. Spray-skirt kayaks are used by almost all the local sea kayak centers for classes and rentals.

When you decide to purchase your own sea kayak, you'll find the cost of different boats depends on the construction material. The lightweight fiberglass, and even better Kevlar, boats are very sweet but can get costly. Plastic boats are very reasonably priced, but weigh more than fiberglass or Kevlar kayaks, so they are slower in the water. There is even a portable kayak that fits into small bags for traveling. It's a good idea to rent different boats for awhile till you find the kind that's best for you. A new kayak will cost between $600 to $2500, which usually includes the paddle and all the safety equipment. New boats paddle beautifully if you can afford them.

There are many places to find these boats, at the outdoor retail stores like REI and Marmot, as well as the many specialty kayak stores and schools in the area. Check the local kayak centers listed later in this chapter or in your local *Yellow Pages* under Canoe & Kayak. If a new boat is too expensive for your budget, used sea kayaks are available from $300 to $800, and will work fine for most recreational paddlers. Local kayak schools usually sell rental boat fleets at the end of the fall, offering some really good deals. Ask at your local kayak center next time you go paddling. Also, make sure to check the bulletin boards at these paddling centers for a good selection of private owners looking to sell their boats.

The Paddle:
This piece of equipment is not as simple as you would think. Paddles come in all types of materials, ranging from wood to carbon fiber, as manufacturers search for the strongest but lightest paddle. Usually, the less expensive paddles will weigh the most, with the more expensive ones nice and light to give you more performance. Paddles range in price from $50 to $350. Most recreational paddlers need not spend a great deal of money on the paddle. Used ones are readily available, especially if you can find a good used boat with the paddle included. This will work fine until you want to upgrade.

Flotation Bags:
These inflatable bags fit snugly into the hull in front and behind you to give the boat excellent flotation. The flotation will help lift the boat higher in the water, which translates into more speed and easier paddling for you. Each bag costs about $20, and two are needed for each boat, unless wooden bulkheads are built into the boat.

Safety Equipment

Paddle Float: This is a necessary piece of equipment. This float allows you to rescue yourself in case the boat flips over, which it will at some point in your paddling career. You just inflate this float, attach it to your paddle, and use your paddle like an outrigger to steady the boat while you crawl back in. Cost is $25 to $30. This nifty invention was developed by Bob Licht, a local sea kayaker and owner of *Seatrek*, about eight years ago. These float bags have made sea kayaking safer and are exported worldwide.

Bilge Pump: Another necessity. This will allow you to rid the boat of the water that somehow always get in without having to go back to the shore to bale it out. Cost is $15 to $20.

Spray Skirt: This attractive skirt goes around your midsection and covers the open cockpit to prevent sea water from getting in. Many colors are available, and the cost runs from $30 to $60.

Wetsuit: At some point, you are going tip over and wind up wet, so you need to wear your wetsuit (or drysuit). Experiencing hypothermia after you fall in the water is not a fun way to spend an afternoon, especially when you're just learning the sport. You can use the same wetsuit you use for windsurfing, swimming and surfing. See the detailed explanation of the wetsuit at the beginning of the water section for more information.

Life-jacket: Pure necessity, and it is law that you have to wear one. Don't go out in the bay without one. Conditions can change quickly from a beautiful sunny day to 25-knot winds and white-capping seas that can easily flip you over. Cost is $10 to $70.

THE LEARNING CURVE

The Bay Area has a lot of experienced sea kayak centers where you can learn this fun sport. Definitely take the introductory course, even if you have your own kayak. You will learn more in the seven hours with instruction than you can learn in months on your own. All the places that rent kayaks require that you take the introductory course before you can rent a boat. Plus, you'll be confident you can handle the boat in all types of sea and weather conditions, especially when it gets hairy. All paddling centers offer rentals, so getting into this sport can be cheap and fun. The cost to rent kayaks can be as high as $45 a day but you can bring that cost down to about $5 an hour by purchasing blocks of time

SeaTrek: (415) 488-1000 weekdays & (415) 332-4465 weekends. These sea kayak experts have been in the area for over 12 years. The center was founded by local waterman Bob Licht in 1982. The center offers all levels of instruction, as well as rentals for local paddling. The introductory course is $80 and takes seven hours (one full day).

This place offers a wealth of knowledge about sea kayaking in this area, with organized trips to nearby paddling hot spots like Tomales Bay and Point Reyes, as well as guided full-moon paddles that are a blast. Call Seatrek, and they will send out a full class and trip schedule so you can plan accordingly. **SeaTrek** also organizes group paddling trips to the Pacific Northwest, including the San Juan Islands. Try to get in good paddling shape for the annual SeaTrek Regatta in the middle of October, which attracts sea kayakers from all over the country.

In the late November, **SeaTrek** sells its rental fleet, offering some good deals on used boats. The center also has monthly storage facilities if you want to leave your boat right next to the water at Schoonmaker Point in Sausalito. Special three-month paddle passes offer unlimited rentals for only around $70. The mailing address is P.O. Box 561, Woodacre, CA 94973.

Cal Adventurers: (510) 642-4000. Located in the Berkeley Marina and associated with the University of California at Berkeley, Cal Adventurers offers a marina full of fun for sailing, windsurfing, and especially sea kayaking. You do not have to be associated with UC Berkeley to join up, and the organization welcomes new members. The introductory course will take one full day. After completion of this course, the group offers a great rental deal in a three-month pass that offers unlimited boat use. They also sponsor low-key, well-organized trips to Mono Lake, Tomales Bay and Bolinas for some great sea kayaking adventures. Call for a brochure.

Outdoors Unlimited: (415) 476-2078. Located at the University of California, San Francisco, O.U. is affiliated with UCSF but welcomes everyone from the community and outside. The group offers great rates on rentals. and the introductory course costs about $50. Call for an up-to-date catalogue. The address is 633 Parnassus (near 4th Ave.), San Francisco.

California Canoe and Kayak: (510) 893-7833. These paddlers are located at 409 Water St., on Jack London Square in Oakland. This is a well-stocked retail store for both sea kayaking and out-of-town river kayaking. Great, knowledgeable, friendly people put on basic and advanced classes, and provide rentals. The store also sponsors a few sea kayak races each year, as well as overnight trips to Mendocino and Angel Island. In the last year CCK has also opened a new facility under the same name in Half Moon Bay, near the Half Moon Bay Yacht Club at 214 Princeton Ave. Call (415) 728-1803 for information.

Off The Beach Boats: (415) 868-9445. This center offers sea kayaks and wave ski rentals right on the beach at Stinson Beach. The address is 15 Calle Del Mar, Stinson Beach. The shop is closed on Wednesdays.

Blue Water Ocean Kayak Tours: This place is run out of the North Bay area town of Fairfax. The paddlers can be reached at (415) 456-8956, and offer sea kayak tours throughout the Bay Area.

Ocean Kayak Inc.: Based out of Stinson Beach, professional instruction is offered by local water adventurer Scott Tye. Call (415) 868-9603 for information, or write P.O. Box 885, Stinson Beach.

Tamal Saka Inc.: (415) 663-1743. Based out of Marshall in the North Bay, this company offers scheduled sea kayak trips on beautiful Tomales Bay Thursdays through Sundays. The office is located near the Marshall Boat Works.

WHEN YOU FLIP OVER

At some point you will tip over in your sea kayak, especially if you're having fun and pushing the boat. It happens to everyone and is no big deal. The water will actually feel good. The key is not to panic. You have two choices as you go upside down. You can wait till you have rolled over, then slip out of the boat. When you resurface the unsinkable kayak will be waiting for you, probably upside down. Don't worry that the spray skirt will lock you in the boat, because it is designed to slip off as you come out of the boat. After you resurface, have a nearby paddler stabilize the boat while you drain any water that might have gotten into the vessel. If you are alone, inflate the self-rescue float and slip it on your paddle. This will stabilize the kayak and allow you to climb back in after you drain the excess water. If you are in a washdeck sea kayak, this process is even easier because the boat can't fill with water. You just jump back in after the boat has steadied.

The other choice is learn the Eskimo Roll. This super-cool move allows you to roll all the way around and resurface without ever leaving your seat inside the boat. It really is not as hard as you would think, and offers you a quick way to keep going without having to stop and get back in the boat. It also keeps you a lot dryer. Practice in a pool if possible, because it's easier and warmer than learning this skill in the bay. There are "roll clinics" put on by such groups as **Cal Adventurers** (510-642-4000). For about $10, the center will supply the pool and the boats, along with some instruction.

The Eskimo Roll is well worth learning and fun as well. Once you get it down, you can move on to tackle the sport of river kayaking as well. Oh boy, yet another sport.

WHERE TO GO

Once you're set up, confident, and ready to go, the San Francisco Bay and surrounding areas offer some classic paddles. *Make sure to carry safety equipment with you at all times, and be very aware of the tidal conditions before you leave the beach.* You should be an experienced sea kayaker before attempting any of the paddles listed below. It would be a good idea to limit your paddling to either Richardson Bay in Sausalito or Olympic Circle in the Berkeley Marina till you feel comfortable taking your paddling game into the open bay and beyond.

The classic paddles of the area are:

Richardson Bay to Angel Island or Alcatraz: This is the same route taken by the SeaTrek Regatta every October. The Angel Island loop is about 10 miles, while the Alcatraz loop is about 15 miles. It's a great workout with beautiful scenery. Make sure to check the tide tables before you go, as well as weather conditions. Remember, anytime you paddle against the tide you are probably doubling your work effort. Try to paddle with the tide whenever possible.

The Golden Gate Bridge Towers: Hang out near the north and south towers of the Golden Gate Bridge. You can start in Sausalito, Crissy Field or Fort Baker. It's great to paddle around under the bridge, especially when there is a decent north swell that takes you up on an elevator ride at the south tower. Again, always make sure to time the tides and weather conditions right. You do not want to be there on a big ebb tide or during bad weather. The sea conditions can get unsafe pretty quickly in this area, so only go here on calm days.

Tomales Bay: A favorite trip spot, Tomales Bay is located up U.S. Route 1 about 60 miles north of the city. It offers a spectacular paddle and scenery. In August and September, you can actually see the meteor showers during night paddles. In addition, you can hit some of the famous oyster bars that are located on Tomales Bay on your way home. A great paddle spot.

A Member of the Tsunami Rangers paddles in extreme conditions off Franklin Point near Ano Nuevo.
Photo: Michael Powers

OTHER GREAT PADDLES

Full-Moon Paddles: Paddle from anywhere on the bay—just get out there—on a clear evening with a full moon. The local schools all sponsor full-moon paddles, or you can just go with a friend, if you have access to a sea kayak. It's one of the special local events to do. Make sure to wear a beacon light on your arm so you can be seen by any passing ships. It's a good idea—and the law—to carry a horn with you as well. The best places to leave from are Sausalito and Berkeley Marina. Again, make sure to check the tides before you go.

The Coast: There is some wild and adventuresome sea kayaking at many different spots along the California sea coast, including some beautiful areas with sea caves, rock gardens and big surf. Always be aware when you venture offshore that the sea and weather can change very quickly. An easy and mellow sea kayak can turn into a nightmare pretty fast, with big seas and 25 mile-per-hour winds. Make sure you are an experienced enough kayaker to handle the conditions the sea presents, and carry all the necessary safety equipment. Your first trip on the coast will probably be the epic paddle south from Muir Beach to San Francisco, going through Pirates Cove and Rodeo Cove, past Point Bonita and into the Golden Gate. After that awesome paddling experience, the rest of the coast will find a way into your life.

Half Moon Bay: This quiet little seaside town is about 30 miles south of the city down U.S. Route 1, and has become a serious sea kayak hot spot for beginner and expert paddlers. A wide range of sea conditions offered here from calm seas to the mega swells of Maverick's. Marimar Beach is the home of the famous extreme sea kayakers called the Tsunami Rangers. There are also rentals and lessons available from **California Canoe & Kayak's** new facility; call (415) 728-1803 for information, or stop by the shop at 214 Princeton Ave., HMB, CA 94018. You also can join **Half Moon Bay's Marimar Sea Kayak Club**. For a one time fee, you have unlimited lifetime access to the club's kayak fleet, along with some expert instruction from Tsunami Ranger Mike Powers. Call (415) 726-2748 for information.

Elk and The Lost Coast: About a two-and-a-half hour drive north of the Bay Area, you'll find unbelievable sea kayaking with sea caves and good swells. Elk is the home of the Force 10 extreme sea kayakers, who will go as far as seven miles out to sea in 35 knot winds. For more moderate tours of the area write **Force 10 Ocean White Water Tours**, P.O. Box 167, Elk, CA 95432, or call (707) 877-3505. Tours are run by Steve Sinclair, a legendary extreme sea kayaker who has done it all.

Monterey & Santa Cruz: Both towns have become popular areas for sea kayaking in the past few years, with schools and rental fleets available. Both are great places to go seal watching, ride some swells, or explore some sea caves. Call **Monterey Bay Kayaks** (408-373-5357), or the **Kayak Connection** (408-724-5692) for information on the Monterey and the Moss Beach area. For Santa Cruz, call **Adventure Sports Kayaking** (408-458-3648), **Venture Quest Kayaking** (408-427-2267), or the **Kayak Connection** (408-479-1121).

Surf Ride Paddles: Sea kayaks are not very good in surf of any size because of their length and lack of maneuverability side-to-side, but they can be fun in small rolling surf. To kayak in bigger surf, you need a river kayak.

You can also have a great time riding waves on a wave ski. The best places to take both of these wave-riding machines are Bolinas, Pacifica, or Santa Cruz. There's an open contest every November at Stinson Beach, and in late February at Steamer's Lane in Santa Cruz. Check the monthly publication *CitySports* for information.

You should be able to Eskimo Roll the river kayak before you venture out into the waves. Wave skis techniques can picked up in a weekend. They are easier to paddle than kayaks because the cockpit is open, so if you go over, you just right the boat and jump back in. Wave skis can be rented from places like **Outdoors Unlimited;** call (415) 476-2078 or visit the shop at 633 Parnassus on the UC San Francisco Campus.

Races: With the increased popularity of sea kayaking, a number of big-time paddling races have flourished throughout the Bay Area. They are usually put on by the local retail paddling centers or clubs, and can draw up to 400 entrants. These are great fun to participate in, and will make you a better all-around sea kayaker very quickly. Some of the best races include the SeaTrek Annual Regatta in mid-October, the Race for Treasure in July, and the "Get Yer Boat Salty" Kayak Surf Contest sponsored by **California Canoe & Kayak**. Check at any local sea kayak center for a complete year-round schedule of events.

Bay Area Sea Kayak Centers

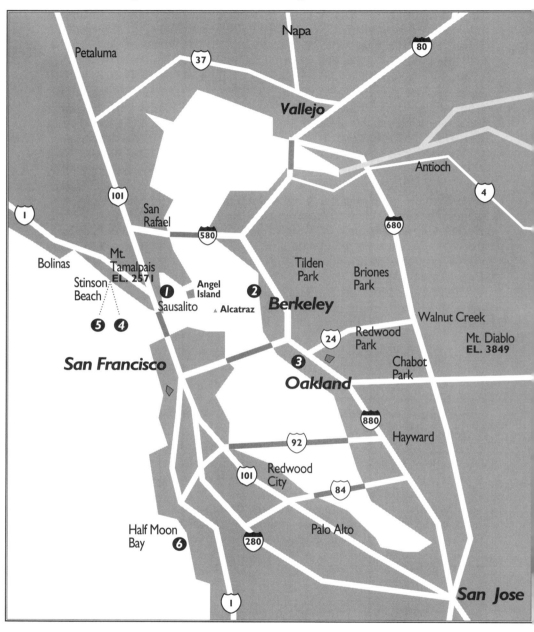

❶ *Seatrek Kayak Center*
❷ *Cal Adventurers Kayak Center*
❸ *California Canoe & Kayak*
❹ *Off the Beach Kayaks*
❺ *Ocean Kayak, Inc.*
❻ *California Canoe & Kayak– Half Moon Bay*

LOCAL SEA KAYAK CLUBS

The most popular and active local paddling club is the **San Francisco Bay Area Sea Kayakers,** or **BASK** for short. This non-profit club is affiliated with Outdoors Unlimited and has a very active membership of over 400 sea kayakers. BASK is a very friendly organization dedicated to making sea kayaking fun, safe and available to everyone. The club organizes weekend trips to beautiful sea kayaking destinations like Mendocino and Monterey, as well as longer trips to places like Baja, the Channel Islands and the Pacific Northwest. The club also sponsors clinics to improve your sea kayaking abilities, including clinics on surf paddling, sea cave explorations and safety. The annual dues are a cheap $25 a year. You get a monthly newsletter (called *Bay Currents*) to keep you up-to-date on trips and clinics, as well as the chance to make friends that share the same love of the ocean and sea kayaking you do. BASK holds monthly meetings the last Wednesday of each month, which are open to the general public. Many of these meetings feature guest lecturers with beautiful sea kayak slide shows from destinations all over the world. For information on **BASK**, contact Penny Wells, the editor of the monthly newsletter and a pillar of the club. The contact phone number is (415) 457-6094; the mailing address is 229 Courtright Road, San Rafael, CA, 94901. This club has no rental equipment, but sea kayaks can be rented from **Outdoors Unlimited** (415-476-2078) for the club paddles.

The other local sea kayak club is the **Marimar Beach Kayak Club**. This club operates out of Half Moon Bay and is run by local waterman legend Michael Powers. For a one-time fee of $300, members are given full privileges to use the sea kayaks and gear of the club. The club also sponsors various sea kayak races and festivals. To get information, call (415) 726-2748; the address is #1 Mirada Road, Half Moon Bay, CA, 94019.

Kayaks await the start of the annual SeaTrek Regatta.
Photo: Will Nordby

This club is also home of the famous Tsunami Rangers. Formed in 1984, this ocean-adventure kayaking team gets its kicks by sea kayaking the isolated surf zones, complex rock gardens and mysterious sea caves around Half Moon Bay and beyond. The kayakers are well-known for their "extreme condition" exploits. They have been featured in *National Geographic* magazine, as well as many other publications, and do a tremendous job promoting both the sport and safety in sea kayaking.

ADDITIONAL READING

The following monthly magazines offer a wealth of knowledge about sea kayaking and more. They are available at most newsstands and sea kayak retail shops in the area. The best include *Canoe & Kayak, Paddler*, and *Sea Kayaker*. They will keep you up-to-date on new equipment technology, paddling techniques, exotic kayak vacations and some great stories. The pictures are pretty sweet in these magazines as well. As far as books on sea kayaking, one of the best is *The Essential Sea Kayaker*, by David Seidman, published by Ragged Mountain Press, Camden, Maine (1992). Additionally, for the history of the Tsunami Rangers, pick up a copy of The *Tsunami Ranger Anthology*, available from Eric Soars, P.O. Box 339, Moss Beach, CA.

COST OVERVIEW FOR SEA KAYAKING

Cheap Budget:
Find the least-expensive beginner kayak course offered in this area by calling the schools listed above, then buy blocks of rental time from a kayak paddling center, instead of paying the more expensive hourly rate. Some of the sea kayak centers also offer season passes. You can get into sea kayaking this way for a total cost of about $125 to $150.

Moderate Budget:
Within this budget, you can own your own boat. Used sea kayaks, along with a paddle, cost $300 to $700. And just think, by buying a boat you will never have to pay a rental fee again to paddle. Most of the Bay Area sea kayak centers sell off some of their rental fleets in the Fall, offering some good deals. Also, check the bulletin boards at the local paddling centers for a listing of private owner sales.

High-End Budget:
In this budget bracket, you can buy a brand-spanking new and lightweight sea kayak. You will be convinced on your first paddle that your boat flies on the water. New sea kayaks range in price from $900 to $2,500, depending on the construction materials. Plastic boats are more durable but heavier, so they are cheaper. Fiberglass kayaks are more expensive because they weigh less; they are also a bit more fragile. On the high end are Kevlar boats, which are even lighter. Accessory items like the paddle, life-jacket, spray skirt and safety equipment are necessary, and will add another couple of hundred dollars to the overall cost.

CHAPTER FOUR

Sail

Season: Best from March through November, but can be done all year.
Learning Curve: Five lessons about four hours each
for the basics. Lifetime to master.

Sailboats racing towards Blackhaller Buoy.
Photo: Latitude 38 Archives

Sailing the Bay:

These three words conjure up a vivid picture of beautiful weather, strong winds, great scenery and awesome sailing. It's all true. *The Bay Area is one of the premier sailing spots in the world.*

Every international class of racing sailboats looks forward to its stop on San Francisco Bay, to the frantic thrills and challenging sailing. Driving a majestic sailboat in heavy winds and big seas while waves are crashing over the deck is an adventure tough to beat. The racing fleet here is one of the most competitive in the country. Going into the last mark in a race with five or six boats relatively even can really get your juices flowing. To live here, or visit, and not at least try sailing is a travesty, especially when the well over 5,000 sailboat owners at local marinas are usually looking for crew.

The sailing is best from March to November. The early and late season offers flat seas, clear skies and moderate winds from 10 to 20 knots. June through August offers afternoon winds up to 30 knots and choppy seas with swells up to five feet. There is also, of course, some fog to contend with during the summer. You can sail in the winter months as well, but the wind is not consistent. Without going into a chapter-long explanation of the summer weather pattern, this is basically what happens: the inland valleys heat up to temperatures of 90° to 100° by the afternoon. These hot inland temperatures pull cooler air through the Golden Gate, creating a wind funnel that pushes the west winds to more than 20 knots. The bay can be flat and still at ten in the morning, and blowing a consistent 20 knots by 1 p.m.

Sailing here is very easy to learn, with more than 25 licensed schools located in the Bay Area. Classes can be scheduled to suit, with a minimum of hassles and cost. After just a few weekend classes, you'll be cleared to rent boats on your own. You can then take your friends out sailing and open a new world to them as well. If you are just visiting and have sailing experience, or your own boat back home, you can easily rent a boat for a great day of local sailing. Just call one of the rental boat marinas and explain your wishes. You will get a verbal dockside checkout just to make sure you know what you're doing, then you'll get the keys, along with some good insight on where to go.

At first, sailing appears very hard, extremely expensive and an exclusive world with its own vocabulary and rules. Nothing could be further from the truth. Each year hundreds of local people, with no previous experience, pick up sailing and stay with it. Some get into racing, living aboard, chartering, worldwide cruising, or just local weekend escapes. First, break down the alien sailing language to make asking questions easier. Here is a short list of the sailing vocabulary and definitions:

Regular English	Sailing term
Left	Port
Right	Starboard (the starboard boat has right of way)
Rope to bring sails in	Sheet
Rope to raise sails	Halyard
Wire supporting mast	Rigging
Front	Stern
Back	Aft
Forward sail	Jib
Big sail	Mainsail
One-mast boat	Sloop or cutter
Two-mast boat	Ketch or yawl
Turn into the wind	Tacking the boat
Turning downwind	Jibing the boat

Regular English	Sailing term
Incoming tide	Flood tide
Outgoing tide	Ebb tide
Sailing into the wind	Beating
Sailing downwind	Running
Sailing off the wind	Broad reaching

Well, that's a start. Next time someone tells you to "bring in the mainsheet, mate, we are preparing to jibe the boat to catch the flood tide and run before the wind," you might know what they mean.

The adventure sport of sailing has been mistakenly described by some neophytes as "the fine art of going very short distances uncomfortably, at slow speeds and at great expense." This chapter will show you how to do it cheaply. The distance is up to you, and the "going slowly" part sure doesn't feel that way when you find yourself screaming along the water with the ocean spray in your face. The comfort level depends on what kind of conditions you go out in, as well the type of boat.

One of the best features of sailing is that one does not need to be a great athlete to learn. Let's face it, famous sailor Dennis Conner doesn't quite have the athlete's body, and he's considered the best sailor in the world. He is so good other skippers say he can spot wind shifts and puffs of wind over the racing course before they even happen. Sailing is a great adventure sport that is available to everyone no matter what their athletic ability. Just get out there and give it a try. You will be hooked and challenged by a sport that can give you a lifetime of enjoyment and thrills.

THE LEARNING CURVE & COST

Getting Started:
The first thing to do is hit the local library or bookstore and get a basic book on sailing. Pick the most basic of the lot, and read it prior to getting on a boat. It will give you the sailing vocabulary, describe different boat types, and offer a mental feel for the wind direction and its effect on the boat. You will be way ahead of the game.

Now that you can sail in your living room, it's time to get on the water. *We strongly suggest you learn from a qualified sailing school.* Be smart and learn from the experts. The option of learning from friends, if you're fortunate to have friends with boats, looks good in theory (and is cheaper), but a lot of friendships and relationships have ended because something breaks on the boat or one person lost his/her temper. After you learn the basics, there will be plenty of time to go sailing with your friends on their boats.

Most schools offer a two-hour introductory sail for $30 to $50, so you can see if you want to sign up for the full basic course. It's a good idea to sign up for one of these. The full basic sailing course usually consists of on-the-water sail time once a week for six weeks. The cost can be as low as $95 or as high as $400, depending on the size of the boat and the student-to-teacher ratio. The courses tend to be more expensive on bigger boats. When you learn on small "dinghy" boats, it can get pretty wet, since dinghies can tip over due to a small mistake in steering. Large boats offer you a lot more comfort, but you won't get the same feel for steering as you will in a dinghy that is planing right on the water.

Before you choose a class, consider what type of sailing you envision yourself doing after the basic class has ended. If you want to get into sailing dinghies, then you should learn on a dinghy. Just know it is going to be a cold and wet experience.

Small boats are great, and the old adage that if you can sail a dinghy, you can sail anything, still holds true. All the big-time sail-racing "rock stars" like local Paul Cayard and Dennis Conner started in dinghies. On small boats, every adjustment you make has a big effect on boat handling, so you really learn sail trim and weather helm. It's okay if you get wet—that's what your wetsuit is for. The cheapest way to learn to sail is on a dinghy. For example, **Cal Adventurers'** basic sailing course given on smaller boats is only $95.

If you want to be less frustrated and can afford it, you might want to learn on a bigger boat. The learning experience will be more enjoyable, and you can learn to sail a dinghy after you understand the basics. Instruction on bigger sailboats is drier and more hands-on, because the instructor is right on the boat with you, not shouting instructions at you through a bullhorn from the shore, as is the case in dinghy sailing classes. Crews on bigger boats usually consist of one instructor and three to four students.

Classes taught on the bigger sailboats are usually full-keel boats, about 24 to 36 feet in length. Most local sailing schools have really nice modern boats, which makes the learning curve even easier. The first time you grab the wheel or tiller to steer in high winds, you will be convinced the boat will tip over, leaving you and the crew in the drink. This move would not make you very popular. Don't fret. Full-keel boats have so much weight in the bottom of the hull and keel that it's really hard to for it to capsize. *You have to convince yourself that the boat is not going to go over.*

Once you get in your head that the boat will not tip over, it's easy to progress in the sport of sailing. Then the steering gets fun. After a few lessons, you will start to feel more comfortable behind the wheel or tiller. Students take turns being the designated skipper, then trim the sheets as part of the crew. After four or five more sailing classes on topics that include right of way rules, sail trim, docking, reefing, anchoring and boat handling, you will be ready for the final test of the class. You take this "final exam" with either just your instructor aboard, or in some schools with just the crew and no instructor. This test is to show that you are proficient in all the basic aspects of sailing a boat. When you arrive safely back at the dock without any mishaps, you pass. It's the most fun you've ever had in a final exam in your life.

After completion of the basic sailing course, you are eligible to rent boats on your own. Local sailing schools also offer classes in spinnaker sailing, coastal navigation, overnights, racing and celestial navigation, if you want to continue your studies. A complete list of sailing schools is included in this chapter. Call for a brochure that explains costs and scheduling.

Getting Addicted:

Once you are qualified to take a boat out, the world of sailing is open to you. Be careful though, because this sport can be addicting. When the wind is up, you will cancel any other plans you had to go sailing. Don't worry— your good friends will understand, because they will probably be on the boat with you.

After you get into this sport, sailing magazines will find their way on your coffee table at home. You will find yourself walking the docks at local marinas to see the different kinds of sailboats. You might even cancel vacations to visit your in-laws in the Midwest, instead heading for the Channel Islands, the Caribbean, Fiji, or even Greece on a beautiful chartered sailboat vacation. (Hopefully, your in-laws will be with you to keep the family together.)

Everyone on the high side.
Photo: Dan Nelson

Sailing is one of those sports than can, and will, get into your soul. Just being on the water is a large part of it, and in the sport of sailing you have the time to sit back, relax, and really enjoy it. Once you have the sailboat trimmed properly and you're steering the right course, there is nothing left to do. In most other sports, you can't totally relax. Sports like windsurfing and hang gliding require total concentration—a total relaxation/spaceout could cause a major wipe out in those sports.

Getting On A Boat:
The great part of living, or visiting, the Bay Area is that sailing is so accessible, even if you don't have friends who own sailboats. *Everyone can afford to sail here.* It can be done real cheap. For example, renting a full-sized sailboat costs as little as $80 to $100 for the day. Divide that price between a crew of three or four, and a day of sailing costs only $20 to $25 apiece.

If that's too expensive, some of the local sailing schools offer passes for unlimited sailing on their boats for only about $75 for a three-month pass. Go just once a week over the twelve weeks, and sailing is cheaper than buying yourself lunch—and a lot less fattening.

If that's still even too much to spend on this great sport, you can sail for free on someone else's boat. After you pass the basic sailing course, any boat owner would welcome you as crew, and probably buy you lunch as well. Put a notice up at some of the local clubs and yacht harbors, or a classified ad in the local monthly sailing magazine *Latitude 38* (available at any marine store for free). All you have to do then is wait by the phone, and soon you'll be sailing every weekend for free. This method is also a great way to gain a lot of sailing knowledge by listening to more experienced sailors on the boat.

WHERE TO GO

Sailing The Bay:
Where to sail is sometimes a tough choice, because the bay offers so many great alternatives, all with different weather conditions. You can go directly for the Golden Gate Bridge on any summer afternoon for howling winds and wet sailing, or dip behind Angel Island for flat, calm water and sunny conditions that allow you to swim off the boat at anchor.

Just never forget that this is a tough place to sail. The weather and wind conditions can change quickly. You can leave the dock in 90° heat wearing shorts, and twenty minutes later be on your ear in 25-knot winds and a cold 55° air temperature. Use your head at all times and be careful not to carry too much sail. Have the right clothing, in case conditions get rough. *Foul weather gear is a must if you sail here.* These clothes enable you to stay dry and warm no matter what hits you. Being cold and wet on a sailboat is one of the most miserable feelings in the world, and it's dangerous. Hypothermia can set in fast when you are soaking wet.

Also make sure you know the tides, especially if you want to go out the Golden Gate into the open ocean. It is best to schedule that trip so you catch an ebb tide out the gate and a flood tide on your way back in.

Lastly, always check to make sure you have all the necessary safety equipment on the boat. The short list includes life-jackets, flares, compass, running lights, charts, man-overboard pole and reefing lines. *Never overcrowd the boat.* Always be a safe sailor. The local Coast Guard has enough to worry about without having to rescue your boat.

A partial list follows of some of the Bay's different sailing spots and their characteristics:

City front: This great sailing area spreads from the South Tower of the Golden Gate Bridge, and all along the waterfront to the Bay Bridge. This usually high wind area offers the bay's wildest sailing with strong gusts, fog in the summer and big choppy seas. Throw in the tanker traffic, fishing boats and windsurfers to create more havoc and things can get pretty wild here. This is a real test for any sailor. Most of the big sailboat races start and finish along this beautiful city front. Try docking overnight at Pier 39 or South Beach Harbor, so you can hit the city night life without having to worry about driving home.

East Bay: This includes the waters around Alameda, Berkeley, and Emeryville. There is a lot of wind around the Berkeley Pier and Olympic Circle. Most dinghy races are staged here because conditions are a little more protected than on the open bay. The Oakland Estuary offers a great overnight sail trip, with nautical restaurants and guest slips available for docking the night. There are also many sailing schools located in this area, making the sailing learning process very convenient.

Peninsula: Big winds whip the waters off Candlestick Park and Coyote Point near the San Mateo Bridge. This area is less crowded and usually less choppy than other parts of the bay. Know the tide tables so you can run down on a flood tide and beat your way back on an ebb.

North Bay: This includes the waters around Sausalito, Tiburon, Angel Island, and San Pablo Bay up to Richmond. You usually will find warmer weather without the fog of the city, along with consistent, calmer winds and flatter seas. In other words, the Marin County area offers beautiful sailing. Try anchoring overnight off Angel Island, or cruise into Sam's Anchor Cafe in Tiburon for brunch. Sausalito offers a lot of sailing schools, with rentals as well.

Weekend Escapes:
We are fortunate here to have some great weekend getaways close by. Head out the Golden Gate for some challenging open ocean sailing, or cruise up the Sacramento River Delta to escape the fog that usually engulfs the city in July and August. Try to take advantage of these great spots.

On any offshore sail, even just for the afternoon, make sure the boat is seaworthy and all the necessary safety gear is aboard and in good working condition. Do not sail a dinghy in the open ocean; the conditions are too dangerous. Only go offshore in a full-keel boat.

Some of the best weekend escapes include:

Half Moon Bay and Santa Cruz : These two weekend getaways offer a classic downwind sailing, surfing swells in the open ocean. Spend the night in the seaport town of Half Moon Bay or Santa Cruz before the beat to windward on the way home.

The trip down to Half Moon Bay is about 28 miles. With good wind, this will take about four hours, depending on boat size and speed. The trip home usually takes about twice as long because you are usually heading into the wind. While in HMB, take a quick trip to the Moss Beach Distillery Bar & Restaurant, and watch the sunset from the lawn.

The Santa Cruz adventure will take quite a bit longer; it's about sixty miles down the coast past HMB. This trip will take you further offshore to experience more ocean-like conditions. If possible, plan your trip with a full moon, and as with any trip of this nature, make sure to check weather conditions, boat safety gear and navigational charts. If sailing at night, make sure every crew member wears a safety harness attached to a jackline on the boat, and that all the navigation lights work so other boats can see you. Also, make sure to bring your surfing and windsurfing gear to Santa Cruz, so you can have fun while you're tied up in the harbor there.

If you don't want to do these trips on your own (such a trip can be kind of scary, especially the first time), you can opt to join the annual fun races to Half Moon Bay in October, and to Santa Cruz over the Labor Day weekend. You will be in a pack of boats, if that makes you feel more comfortable. Look for notices of these races in *Latitude 38* sailing magazine, or call the *Yacht Racing Association* at (415) 777-9500 for information.

The Delta: This trip offers escape from the summer fog for many local boaters, who can spend weeks exploring the miles and miles of the Delta from Vallejo to Sacramento. This place offers the whole gamut of weather, from wild winds with choppy seas, to zero wind areas that bake in the sun, so you can work on that summer tan. There are many marina bars and restaurants scattered all over the Delta waterfront to quench your thirst and appetite.

Farallon Islands: You can sail the 30 miles of open ocean to this nature conservatory and back again in one day. Leave early for a slow beat to windward on the way out to the islands. A screaming downwind blows you home to the Golden Gate. The annual double-handed race is in April, and the single-handed race is usually in March, if you and your boat are looking for some challenging adventure racing.

Drake's Bay: Another fine open ocean trip. This trips heads Northwest past **Stinson Beach** and **Bolinas** to Drake's Bay, the spot where Sir Frances Drake supposedly put in for repairs on his famous exploration. There is no marina here so you'll have to practice your anchoring skills. The trip is usually a tough beat upwind on the way there, but your reward is a classic downwind run for the way home, turning the corner for the Golden Gate. This is a great rugged trip that will bring you back a more experienced sailor.

Bay Area Sailing Centers

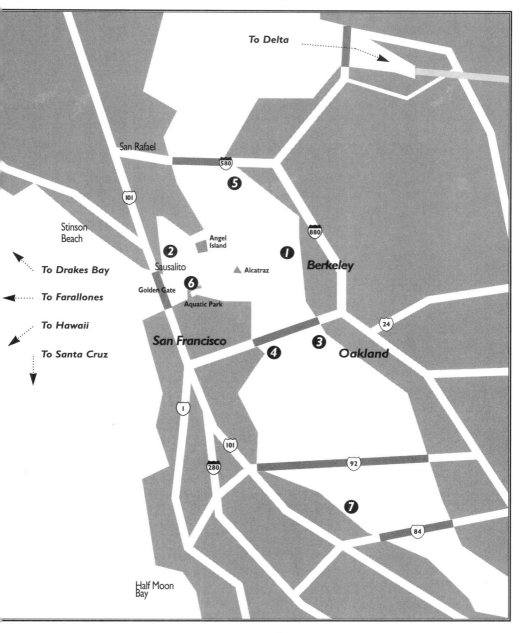

① **Berkeley Marina** –*Cal Adventurers, Cal Sailing Club & Olympic Sailing School*

② **Sausalito** – *Cass Sailing School, Modern Sailing Academy, Club Nautique & Hawaiian Chieftain*

③ **Alameda** – *Club Nautique*

④ **South Beach Harbor** – *Spinnaker Sailing School, Adventure Cat*

⑤ **Richmond Marina** – *Tradewinds Sailing School*

⑥ **Fort Mason** – *Sailing Educational Adventures*

⑦ **Redwood City** – *Spinnaker Sailing School*

RACING

Sailboat racing on San Francisco Bay can be traced all the way back to the mid-1800s, when the clipper ships used San Francisco as the finish line in races to get supplies and miners to the gold fields. In 1849 alone, more than 700 ships set sail from the East Coast with San Francisco as their destination. These early speedsters raced around Cape Horn and up the West Coast in less than 100 days as they tried to beat the gold seekers who traveled across America by land to the California gold fields. A lot of these gold-miner transport boats were then left to rot as the crew headed inland in search of fortune. The rotten ships eventually became part of the landfill that makes up downtown San Francisco's financial district.

Today, most local racing is sponsored by the **Yacht Racing Association**, commonly known as the **YRA**. This group stages up to 250 races a year for all classes of boats. In conjunction with the monthly publication of *Latitude 38*, a master schedule is published to make planning even easier. Call the **YRA** at (415) 771-9500 for information and scheduling.

Some of the classic races include the Double-handed Farallons Race in April, the fully crewed Vallejo Race, and the Master Mariner Race in May. There are so many races put on during the year that it is easy find ones that fit your needs. They range from the ultra-serious, like the Big Boat Series put on by the St. Francis Yacht Club over five days in the month of September, to any of the casual "beer can" races put on by the different yacht clubs on Tuesday, Wednesday or Friday nights. These informal sailboat races are great fun and will teach you a lot. A friendly barbecue is usually held after the race at the sponsoring club, so you can meet some other sailors.

ADDITIONAL READING

We are fortunate to have a great sailing magazine available locally called *Latitude 38* . This monthly publication has become the Bible for all Bay Area sailors. It is available free at all marine stores on the first of the month. The magazine has a great classified section listing used boats for sale; ads for sailing schools; great sailing articles; boat merchants ads; and the racing scene information. Call (415) 383-8200 if you have any trouble locating a copy. It's a good idea to browse through the latest issue before your first sailing lesson or boat ride, because you will pick up just enough sailing knowledge to help you not look like a total novice on your first day.

In addition, a very good local book on sailing this area was published a few years back by Kimball Livingston, entitled *Sailing The Bay* (Chronicle Books, San Francisco). It's hard to find because it is out of print, so you might have better luck at the local libraries.

On the national front, there are some great sailing magazines like, *Sail, Sailing and Cruising World*. These insightful publications are available at any newsstand. Jump to the back for some great out-of-town chartering ideas.

There also are two very good local sources for sailing books. The *Armchair Sailor* (42 Caledonia St., Sausalito, ph. 415-332-7505) and the **Maritime Bookstore** (Historic Hyde St. Pier, San Francisco, ph. 415-775-2665) offer a large selection of all types of maritime books.

Hiked out on some Aussie 18 sailboats on a peaceful San Francisco Bay.
Photo: Shaw Hazen

LOCAL SAILING SCHOOLS & COSTS

It is estimated there are as many as 25 sailing schools located in and around the Bay Area. All the schools also offer day trips on the bay for those who just want an introduction to sailing. The trips cost $25 to $40 per person, which usually includes free beverages; call for information.

Listed below is just a sample of the local sailing schools. Each will send a free brochure explaining actual costs and schedule of classes, so call a few to compare.

Full-keel boat classes offer more hands-on instruction, with the instructor-captain on the boat with you and three or four other students. The basic course of this type will range from $250 to $450.

Dinghy sailing classes are a little rougher, with the instructor on the dock yelling directions through a bullhorn. The dinghy course will be tougher, especially in the beginning, because the boat will tip over a lot. Because the boats are smaller and less expensive, dinghy sailing classes are way cheaper. For example, **Cal Adventurers'** basic dinghy sailing class is only about $95.

The choice of which sailing school to attend depends on the type of sailing you ultimately want to do, and on your budget. A number of local sailing schools offer free introductory sailing days to prospective new students to give them a feel for what sailing is all about. These open-houses give you a chance to sample a few sailing schools before you decide which one to attend. Call for details at the various schools listed below.

Make sure you don't base your decision solely on price. If you are the type of person who has no interest in getting wet, you should take lessons on the biggest boat you can find, no matter the cost. Don't try to save $50 or $100 by signing up at a sailing school that may not be right for you. If you love getting wet, then definitely look into the dinghy courses. These boats are quite thrilling.

Local sailing schools include:

Cal Adventurers: Berkeley Marina, (510) 642-4000. After completion of the very reasonably priced, but wet, basic sailing course, you're eligible for a full-season pass for unlimited rentals for about $80. The fleet consists mostly of dinghies, and the sailing is mostly conducted in the high-wind Olympic Circle area in Berkeley.

Cass Sailing School: Sausalito, (415) 332-6789. Learn on full-keel boats out of beautiful and usually windy Sausalito. Rentals are available and a few chartered sailing trips are organized each year, so that members can sail in exotic locations around the world.

Cal Sailing Club: Berkeley Marina, (510) 287-5905. This club is open to all and teaches basic sailing and higher-level sailing courses in small day-sailor boats. The courses are reasonably priced. After completion of the basic course, three-month boat use passes are available for a reasonable fee.

Club Nautique: Alameda at (510) 865-4700, and **Sausalito** at (415) 332-8001: The club offers a modern fleet of nice full-keel sailing boats. Rentals are available and rates very reasonable.

Olympic Sailing School: Berkeley Marina, (510) 843-4200 or 1(800) 223-2984. The school offers a basic course on full-keel modern sailboats. Rentals are available, as is additional instruction.

Spinnaker Sailing School: Redwood City (415) 363-1390, and **San Francisco** at (415) 543-7333: This school and rental fleet is conveniently located both on the Peninsula and in downtown San Francisco at Pier 40. The basic course is on full-keel boats, and rentals are available.

Sailing Education Adventures: Fort Mason, San Francisco, (415) 775-8779. S.E.A. is a non-profit community sailing program that starts its students off in dinghies and works up to full-keel boats. Basic sailing courses are offered, along with additional courses in piloting, intermediate sailing, spinnaker handling and piloting.

Tradewinds Sailing Club: Brickyard Cove, Richmond, (510) 232-7999. Basic sailing instruction is offered, with a nice fleet of sailboats available for charter. This school also is affiliated with Moorings Tropical Charters, which offers out-of-town charter trips to exotic locations.

DAY SAIL COMPANIES

Adventure Cat: This company offers four-hour day sails for about $20 per person. This is a great alternative for out-of-towners in need of a day of sailing who don't want to rent a boat themselves. The boat is docked at the South Beach marina in downtown San Francisco to make it very convenient to all. The phone number is (415) 777-1630, or call toll free at 1(800) 498-4228.

Hawaiian Chieftain: Another Bay Area day-sailing charter company, the ship is an 18th century-style square rigger operating out of Sausalito. Three-hour sunset sails are offered for $25. Call (415)331-3214.

Apache Sailing Adventures: A beautiful 60-year-old sailing schooner offers day sails out of Pelican Harbor in Sausalito. This area usually offers better weather than the city in the summer. Call (415) 331-8153.

Let's Go Sailing: This company offers day sails out of easy-to-reach Pier 39 on a 50-foot sailboat. Call (415) 788-4920. Three-hour sails cost $20.

EQUIPMENT

Buying a Sailboat

It is commonly said that buying a first boat is one of the happiest times in a sailor's life. Having your own boat means no more begging to get on someone else's boat, or renting different boats each time you want to go sailing. You will hear negative people tell you that owning your own boat will be a nightmare of costs and long days at the dock doing boat upkeep and repair projects. This definitely does not have to be the case, if you buy the right boat.

Make sure the boat you're looking to buy is in good shape and of the modern, low-maintenance fiberglass variety, unless you want a work-project wooden boat. Today's fiberglass boats are almost maintenance-free, and with recent design improvements, the sailing is simply exhilarating.

There is a large selection of used sailboats on the market in the Bay Area, so getting a good deal on a boat is easy. The only regular cost after the initial purchase is the monthly slip rental at a local marina. In the Bay Area, the cost of docking a full-keel boat will range from $4 a foot in the highly competitive East Bay marinas to $7.50 a foot in places like Sausalito. Pier 39 and South Beach Harbor offer monthly slips right in the city for about $6 a foot. Of course, dinghies can be stored on a trailer in the backyard for no charge. The pivotal ingredient in the boat-buying recipe is to figure out exactly what kind of boat would best serve your sailing needs. Make sure it is a boat that you can use a lot, because there is no sadder sight in sailing than a beautiful sailboat that hasn't been used. To simplify this process, it is best to examine the broad categories of sailboats and the advantages of each one.

The different classes of boats are:

Dinghy Sailboats: These small boats offer the wild ride of sailing. They range from 8 to 24 feet in length, and can usually be transported to the water on a trailer behind your car. Many of these great small sailing machines will even fit on car racks.

These boats offer a world of sailing knowledge to you. All of the big-name sailors dominating the latest America's Cup races started out in dinghies.

It is up to you how much performance you want on the boat. You can get a very simple boat, with only a mainsail, like the popular El Toro or Laser, or a more-complicated and faster boat with the mainsail, jib and spinnaker sail, like a 505 or International 14. Remember, the more sail you can put up, the wilder the ride and therefore the more unstable the boat.

The advantages of dinghies are numerous. These boats are real low in maintenance cost and time, and you have the option of sailing any water you can drive to. This opens up all the lakes and rivers around here, as well as sailing in regattas in Southern California, or all over the West Coast.

The sailing thrills offered by dinghies are phenomenal. You are almost right on the water, so you'll get wet as the sea chop comes flying over the bow. The old adage of sailing is worth repeating: "If you can sail a dinghy boat well, you can sail any boat." Once you learn to sail a dinghy, it is easy to step up to any larger boat. Dinghies are so tippy that you really have to learn the correct sail trim and body position, or else you are going over. This can be a downer for a novice sailor, so get some good instruction.

Other than the lack of stability, the only downside to dinghies is that sailing conditions on the Bay are fairly treacherous on spring and summer afternoons. Only experienced dinghy sailors are able to sail in the middle of the bay in choppy seas and high winds. Less-experienced sailors will have to sail in the calmer spots, like Richardson Bay in Sausalito and Olympic Circle in Berkeley.

The price of a dinghy varies based on what class of boat you decide to buy, and the shape of the boat. Generally, you'll spend about $1,000 for a used mainsail dinghy (like a Laser) in average condition, on up to $3,000 for a new one. For a faster, high-tech boat like a 505 or an International 14, the price will range from $1,500 for a used one to $10,000 or more for a top-of-the-line new racer.

If you want high-performance multi-hull sailing, a good option is a day sailing catamaran, like a Hobie 16, which can be found for around $1,500 used, and about twice that new. These multi-hulls are less tippy than mono-hulls, and offer some serious speed in any kind of wind. On the downside, catamarans cannot go to windward as well as mono-hauls, and when they do tip over, they are a bit harder to right.

In a nutshell, dinghies offer a low-cost alternative to buying a more expensive, bigger, full-keel boat. They also offer high-performance sailing that will ultimately make you a better sailor.

Day Sailors: Just like the name suggests, these boats are made without much accommodation for overnight stays, or for heavy ocean sailing. The boats are designed for sailors on a budget who want more comfort and stability than they'll find in a dinghy. Some of these boats can be hauled on a trailer, but this is not the norm, so factor in some monthly slip costs into the budget.

These boats offer some excellent sailing and will range in length from about 20 to 29 feet. They cost more than the dinghies, with used ones ranging from about $2,000 (for a Cal 20 type), on up to about $7,500 for a used Catalina 27. There are a number of great racing classes in this niche, with large fleets on the Bay. An example is the J-24 boat class, one of which can be purchased for $8,000 to $10,000 used. New ones cost considerably more, and you probably don't need to consider one unless you want to get into some serious racing. Boats that fall into the day-sailing class are great fun on the bay and won't break your pocketbook too badly. Be aware that these boats are not designed, nor built, for extensive off-shore cruising.

Small Racer-Cruisers: These boats are a large step-up from the day sailors and range from 30 to 36 feet in length. They are designed with functional sleeping quarters, so you can cruise overnight around the bay, or to Santa Cruz or Half Moon Bay. This type of boat ranges in price from $10,000 to $50,000 for a used one, and a fair bit more for a new one. The advantages of small cruisers are that they are dry and comfortable even when the wind conditions pick up.

Off-Shore Sailboats: The next class up, these serious sailing machines are 37 feet or longer. They are designed and built for off-shore conditions and long-distance cruising, where the sailing conditions can get pretty wild. Twenty-knot winds and five-foot seas are normal spring and summer sailing conditions off-shore in these parts, so the boat has to be strong. These boats can also make great live-aboards, offering some of the least expensive waterfront living in this area. The cost of these boats ranges from about $35,000 to hundreds of thousands, depending on the size, design and condition.

The best place to begin a search for your perfect boat is in *Latitude 38*. Every boat broker in the area will have ads showing their inventory listings, and an extensive classified section lists a large number of individuals selling boats as well.

COST OVERVIEW FOR SAILING

Cheap Budget:

The least expensive way to get into sailing is offered by **Cal Adventurers** and the **Cal Sailing Club**. For a very reasonable price, you can take a basic sailing course, and then qualify for a season pass deal of around $80 to $100 for unlimited boat use over a three-month period. The sailing is done primarily in dinghies, and you are limited to sailing only in the Olympic Circle area. Total cost will be $125 to $150 for the instruction and a season pass, and you're a sailor.

As far as buying a boat, the best deal in this price range will be to pick up a used dinghy for $750 to $1,500. These boats can be found for sale in the local daily newspaper classifieds, and also on the bulletin boards of the small boat sailing centers.

Moderate Budget:

With this budget, you can take your basic sailing course on a full-keel modern boat. You are then eligible to rent all types of sailboats from almost any sailing center around the Bay Area. The basic sailing course costs about $300, and daily rental rates range from $100 to $300, depending on the size of the sailboat.

To buy a boat on a moderate budget, you'll have to spend anywhere from $4,000 to $15,000. Then, figure on about $100 to $200 a month to dock it. It makes a lot of sense is to go into partnership on a boat with a friend or two. This way, all the costs are divided by two or three, and you will have no trouble finding people to sail with.

High-End Budget:

If you have the money to spend, you can hook yourself up with a fleet of beautiful boats by joining one of the really nice sailing clubs around town. You must pay an initiation fee ranging from $500 to several thousand dollars, depending on the club. If you think of it as a lifetime of fun, the costs of the initial fee are mentally easier to take. Once you've joined, you can rent boats of between 24 and 45 feet for very reasonable rates. The daily rental fee is kept down to encourage you to sail often.

These clubs are a great alternative for those who don't want to own a boat. The fleet of sailboats at these clubs are modern, clean and very well kept. Examples of these clubs are **Club Nautique, Tradewinds Sailing Club** and **Olympic Sailing Club** to name a few.

As far as owning a sailboat on this budget, the price can range from $15,000 for a 30-foot sailboat, to $150,000 or more (with many choices in the middle) for a blue-water racing or cruising machine. Actually, you could easily spend even more than that for a really beautiful boat capable of sailing anywhere in the world—with you on it.

CHAPTER FIVE

Windsurf

Season: Best March through September.
Learning Curve: One full season to get proficient. Fun after two
weekends of basic instruction. A lifetime of fun to master.

Windsurfing the Bay.
Photo: Doug Acton

Windsurfing is a relatively new sport, having been invented only
20-odd years ago in Southern California by Hoyle Schweitzer and
Jim Drake. They successfully attached a sail to a large surfboard to harness
the wind and the rest is history. The sport's popularity has grown in
America and in Europe to where now it's one of the world's most popular
water sports. It's now being practiced on inland lakes and rivers, as well as
on bays and oceans all over the world—anywhere with good wind.

The technological advances in windsurfing equipment have kept pace
with the growth of the sport. Today, the early pioneer's sails and boards, or
for that matter, any equipment older than five years, is totally obsolete.
Modern windsurfing equipment is that good. Equipment advances have
pushed the envelope of windsurfing speed, wave riding, and jumping to
levels never thought possible ten years ago, and the envelope is being
expanded daily on high-wind days in places like Maui, the Columbia River
Gorge and the San Francisco Bay Area.

From the waves of Waddell Beach to the chop of Crissy Field, the Bay Area is one hot place for windsurfing. The season starts in late March, just when the winter surf season winds down (perfect timing), and runs till about the end of September. The beauty of windsurfing here is that during the spring-to-fall season, there is always wind somewhere. The key is to know where, and that depends on the local weather conditions. The development of the phone line "wind talkers" has taken a lot of the guesswork out of knowing where to be. Use these phone hot lines, because there is nothing worse than driving for an hour to a windsurf spot and being greeted by no wind.

A friendly word of warning up-front: this sport can be totally addicting. Keep your other plans light during the windsurf season. The feeling of being locked into your footstraps and seat harness as you scream along the top of the water at 20 or 25 knots is hard to match, even by the other adventure sports in this book. You're going to love it. Try to learn windsurfing with your spouse or significant other; if you don't, it might create problems when you blow off other commitments because the wind is howling. Also, don't schedule too many afternoon meetings during the summer months. Go to work early so you can sneak out for a few afternoons of windsurfing. They will be some of the best afternoons you have ever had.

THE LEARNING CURVE

Getting Started:

Let's face it, windsurfing is not an easy sport to learn. The best sports never are. *The key is to get good instruction right away.*

Pick up a basic windsurfing book at the local library or bookstore before you have your first lesson. This will make the classes much easier. Resist the temptation to teach yourself on borrowed equipment because you will be so frustrated after three sessions you will never want to go again. The hard part of learning this sport is there are no fun stages in the beginning. You can't feel the sensation of windsurfing and then go learn it, as you can sports like sailing, parachuting, or even hang gliding. In all of these other sports you are able to go on tandem flights, jumps, or sails where a novice can experience the thrill of the sport alongside, or attached to, an expert instructor. Even with the best instruction, windsurfing will always be you, the board and the sail alone. Every movement you make has a dramatic effect on the rig. This can be a bit frustrating when things don't go as planned, especially since in the beginning you spend more time in the water than on the board.

The good news is that in the Bay Area, there are some great schools with up-to-date equipment to make this task a little easier. The beginning lesson usually is a weekend affair, with an on-land session to teach theory and rigging followed by an on-land simulation to give you the sensation of windsurfing. Then, you hit the water on the school's windsurfers, which are usually giant boards with small sails to give you more stability. You'll learn uphauling (heaving the sail out of the water), getting going, tacking, jibing, and overall sailing sense. The key is to learn at a place that has good wind of between 10 and 15 knots. There is no sense learning lake in light winds if you want to sail the bay, because most of what you learn will not be applicable in heavy winds and choppy seas. You'd have to learn everything again, so you might as well learn on the bay to start.

There are professional schools with rentals available in the Berkeley Marina, Candlestick Park area, Alameda Beach, and Larkspur Landing. We strongly suggest you learn at these spots (a listing of schools is included in this chapter) so you will progress faster and get the real thrill of windsurfing sooner. Don't buy a board till after you have taken the beginning class and rented equipment from the school a few times after that. This will save you money, since you won't have to buy a beginner's board that you will outgrow quickly and have a hard time selling. Renting for a few months also gives you time to find the right first board for you. Make sure to rent as many different models as you can, so you get to know different boards.

A Learning Alternative:
In recent years, the sport's growth has led to vacation getaways just for windsurfing. These windsurf camps are in exotic locations with warm water and consistently high winds such as Maui and the Columbia River Gorge in the summer, and Baja, Aruba and the Grenadines during winter. It's possible to go on a one-week vacation to one of these windy destinations, with no prior windsurfing experience at all, and come home with the ability to waterstart, use a harness and footstraps, and have the sailing knowledge to go right to a local high-wind center like Crissy Field. These trips are not cheap (about $1,000 with lodging and car rental), but if you can afford it, it's a nice alternative to learning locally at the slower pace.

Destination windsurf companies advertise in the national windsurf magazines available at any news and magazine store. Just take a look in the back of one of those magazines for a complete listing of available trips and costs, or call the **Vela High Wind Center** located at 125 University Ave. in Palo Alto (1-800-223-5443). The company will send you a free brochure detailing good deals on trips to beautiful destinations. These trips are even better once you become an experienced windsurfer, because the sailing conditions are usually so great you will want to stay an extra week after you get there.

Real Windsurf Sailing:
Windsurfing is actually two sports. The first involves going to a resort that gets only light winds, climbing on a big, heavy, beginner board and fumbling around in winds of 10 knots or less. The real sport of windsurfing doesn't kick in till the winds reach 18 to 20 knots, and you get into some serious action at 25 knots or more.

The good news is that the Bay Area offers many places that fit the real windsurfing criteria. From April to September, this is a great place to do some cranking windsurfing. Although light-wind windsurfing can be fun at times, it is the high wind windsurfing that this area offers so magnificently. For that reason, this guide will concentrate on high-wind areas.

The key step in progressing from beginning windsurfing to real sailing is the waterstart. Once you start nailing the waterstarts you can essentially windsurf anywhere. Try to learn this waterstart in your first month of windsurfing. It will make the sport so much more fun, and less frustrating than the uphauling method.

The Waterstart:

As you progress on the learning curve of windsurfing, nothing is more important than learning the waterstart. This nifty maneuver lets you forget uphauling (which saves your back muscles), because you let the wind do the work of lifting you out of the water to a standing sailing position. The waterstart will allow you to sail anywhere, and in any heavy wind, with confidence. Without the waterstart, you are stuck uphauling for the rest of your life, thereby limiting your sailing to light wind areas. You'll miss the real fun and thrills of windsurfing.

At first, waterstarts appear very hard to master, but with some good instruction and practice they can be learned in two weekends. The key is to practice them in enough wind to get yourself up. Don't waste your time trying to learn in winds less than 12 to 14 knots, because you will have to rig up too big a sail (6.0 or bigger), which will be way too cumbersome to position in the water.

To learn the waterstart, find a shallow spot close to shore on a day it's blowing 14 to 17 knots. The important part to a successful waterstart is in the set-up. If your rig waterstart preparation is set up wrong, cool waterstart maneuver will be impossible to execute. To summarize the easiest method, begin by resting the boom on the tail of the board. Position the board almost directly into the wind, with your body on the windward side. Grab the boom with both hands and pull the mast and boom off the board toward you. Extend your arms up into the wind. Get one foot (whichever one feels more comfortable) on the board and tread water with the other to keep the board off the wind and in the correct position. Now, just lay back with arms fully extended, and push the board slightly more off the wind. You will feel the sail fill with wind and start to pick you up. As you are getting pulled up, lift your other foot onto the board, get your feet properly positioned on the deck, and you're sailing.

The biggest mistakes beginners make are trying to learn waterstarts in too light of winds, and trying to pick themselves up instead of letting the wind do the work. Another common mistake is not bringing the mast a little forward to fill the sail with wind after you get up. If you mistakenly point the board directly into the wind, it will kill your speed and you will fall down. There are two helpful hints to make waterstarts easier to learn. First, practice with a life vest on for buoyancy. This will keep you from sinking while you try to raise the sail. Secondly, lower the position of the boom on the mast a little bit to improve leverage and stability as you move the rig around.

The best places to practice waterstarts are Olympic Circle in the Berkeley Marina, the Delta near Sherman Island, inside Harding Rock at Crissy Field, Larkspur Landing and Alameda. Remember the wind has to be blowing at least 15 knots, and preferably 16 to 19, to really practice or you will go crazy laying there waiting for the wind to pick you up. Don't get frustrated when waterstarts don't come to you right away. The key is to keep practicing. Most local windsurfing schools also give waterstart lessons and it is a good idea to take one. There are many video cassettes available on waterstart instruction for home use. Just stay with waterstarts till you can do them both ways in your sleep. The fun world of high-performance windsurfing will be open to you as soon as you get it.

High Performance Sailing:

Once you're able to get up and go with a waterstart, the beauty of this sport is you never stop learning. As you progress to higher winds, the learning curve gets much more fun. You get to learn all kinds of jibes, jumps, wave sailing, and even loops if you're crazy enough, all while screaming along at up to 30 knots. The sport starts to get in your blood at this point. You'll find yourself dialing the wind talkers daily, and waiting anxiously for the afternoon wind to pick up. Keep your windsurf equipment on the car so it's always with you during the season. Go to work extra early so you can sneak out when it's blowing. It will be worth it, because windsurfing will bring you some of the best sport thrills you will ever experience.

EQUIPMENT & COSTS

Your First Board:

Once you can uphaul and ride a beginner's board out from and back to the beach with some degree of comfort, it might be time to get serious and invest in your own equipment. The questions at this point are: how big a board do you get, and should you buy new or used equipment. The size of the board at this point depends on your honest assessment of your ability. You can, if you feel up to it, go for an 8-foot 6-inch to 9-foot 4-inch slalom board that you will be able to ride for the next few years. Just be aware that a slalom board will be a bit more difficult to ride than a transition board. A transition board is usually 10 to 11 feet long, with a lot more volume (floats easier) and will allow you to uphaul easier than the shorter slalom boards. A transition board will make the learning curve of waterstarting and riding in higher winds of 15 to 20 mph a lot easier, thereby saving you a lot of frustration. The choice is up to you, but we would suggest the transition board unless you got awfully good very quickly. Another option is to continue renting transition boards till you have progressed on the learning curve enough to then buy a slalom board.

As to the question of investing in a new or used rig, it's a matter of budget and your decision on purchasing the transition board. If you decided to go with the transition board, go for a used one because you will probably outgrow the board after one sailing season. Then you can keep this transition board for your friends to use while you get your own slalom board.

We are fortunate here in the Bay Area to have a lot of windsurf shops that sponsor swap meets a few times a year, offering an excellent selection of used boards, sails, booms and other equipment at a fraction of the new cost. You can usually negotiate the purchase of a whole rig, with the board and a quiver of sails. Check with the local retail stores mentioned later in this chapter for swap meet schedules. The big swap meets are usually held in the spring, just as the windsurf season starts, so you will have all season to play on your new board and gear.

If you decide to go for a high-performance slalom board right away, it's up to your budget whether to go with a new or used one. From experience, we can tell you your first board will get pretty beat up as you get bounced around on the learning curve, so a used one makes more sense till you know exactly what you want in a board. The price range of a used slalom set-up (board with rig and sails) will be anywhere from $500 to $950, depending on its condition.

We suggest you attend swap meets with a knowledgeable windsurfer who can steer you away from outdated junk and into some good, previously owned equipment. Chances are you will have to piece together your complete set-up over time, visiting a few swap meets and meshing in some new equipment as well. A new board can range from $800 to $1,200, but most stores will package a whole set-up (board, sail, mast, boom and base plate) for $850 to $1,600, depending on the model. You still will need to get a few extra sails in different sizes to round out your quiver, so you can sail in all types of wind.

Sails:
The sails represent the horsepower for your board so don't waste time and money on junky, blown-out sails. Whether you decide to go with brand new windsurf sails or quality used ones is a matter of personal preference and budget. Just realize you are going to need at least three of them, and preferably four or five, for the different wind conditions you will encounter here.

The sail size is determined by measuring the square meters. A 4.0 sail translates into four square meters of sail to power you on your board. The wind conditions, along with your weight and sailing ability, will determine which sail you'll use on any given day. If the wind is blowing 20 knots, a windsurfer weighing 130 pounds will probably be on a 4.7 sail, while a person weighing 175 will be on a 5.1. For your personal quiver, as a general guide, you'll need a 4.4 for when the wind is honking, a 4.9 or 5.0 for use on decent wind days, and a 5.6 for days the wind is not as consistent, or averaging 15 to 17 knots. Also, you'll want a small 4.0 when it's really screaming nuclear so you're not overpowered having to use your 4.4 in those conditions. Rigging the right sail for the wind conditions will become quite an art.

As for light-wind windsurfing, after you have been into this sport awhile and are nailing your waterstarts, it's not going to be a lot of fun when you have to uphaul the rig. If it's blowing less than 13 or 14 knots, you probably won't go. Higher wind sailing is so much fun that it makes the light wind sailing kind of boring. There is not a lot of need for the 6.0, 6.5 or bigger sails used for lake or light-wind sailing; you'll only need big sails if you get into racing. Save your money—if the wind is that light, go play in another local sport. The cost of quality used sails will run from $100 to $250, and sweet new sails will range from $250 to $500 each.

The Mast and Boom:
It is imperative if you plan to do any high-wind sailing that you don't skimp on a mast or boom. Remember that if they break, you somehow have to get back to the beach, and swimming in while pushing your board and broken rig is not a lot of fun. These situations are also not very safe. This does not mean you have to go out and purchase the most expensive, top-of-the-line set-up, but whether you buy new or used, just make sure they are strong, brand name products. Ask lots of questions at your local windsurf shop before you purchase.

All the windsurf booms now are of the clip-on style, which makes rigging very easy. If you see a tie-on boom for sale, resist the urge to buy it, because it would be too old and a pain to rig. A good used boom at a swap meet will range from $50 to $110. New ones are nice if you can afford them, and will range from $200 to $300.

Windsurf masts have gone through a lot of changes in the past few years. Gone are the heavy fiberglass one-piece masts that could break out of nowhere. These have been replaced by carbon fiber two-piece masts that are lighter and stronger. You can usually find a good used one for $75 to $120. Make sure there are no stress points that could cause it to break in a good gust or wipe out. You might want to invest in a new one just to be safe, which can range from $150 to $300.

Additional Equipment:
When you buy a complete rig, either new or used, sometimes the necessary additional equipment is included. In case it's not, you are going to need a harness and harness lines. These great inventions let your body weight do most of the work instead of your arms. Harness lines, along with footstraps (now standard equipment on all boards), changed windsurfing from a light-wind sport to a nuclear high-wind riding experience. You also will need a base plate and mast base. Together, these amazing inventions connect your mast to the board. Lastly, you will need some good rigging lines to rig the sail's outhaul and downhaul. Make sure to replace any frayed lines so they don't break while you're out sailing.

It is also a good idea to carry a fanny pack filled with an emergency kit in case of rig failure. This kit should include one long line in case you have to get towed , and one line to tie up your sail. Also, carry some flares in case of a real emergency, so you can be spotted. Always carry these items

A windsurfer screams off Crissy Field.
Photo: Doug Acton

with you because the one time you need them, you'll be awfully happy to have them. Also on the safety front, it is not Coast Guard required that you wear a life-jacket when windsurfing, but it is sure a good idea.

The only other piece of equipment needed to windsurf these waters is the ubiquitous wetsuit. See the detailed explanation on wetsuits in the beginning of the water section.

WHERE TO GO

A list of the local windsurfing spots follows. On any day during windsurfing season, one sailing spot can be throwing off 25 knots of wind while a spot 15 miles away can be dead calm. For that reason, it pays to watch the weather patterns closely. Also you can call the **Bay Area's wind talker** at 1 (900) 844-WIND. For about $2 a call, you will get the current wind speed at all of the most popular sites. This will save you driving time and get you to the windiest spot that day with no hassles.

In addition, a new wind locator service called **Wind Sight** now serves the **Bay Area**. This innovative company has developed wind reports from all the local launch sites, along with an on-site live report on the current sailing conditions. The average cost of this service works out to be only $.35 per sensor report. Call for a free demonstration at 1(800) 695-9703.

The launch sites listed below are by no means all of the windsurfing locations in this area but a selection of the best. For a more detailed explanation of each site, pick up a copy of the locally published reference book, *Windsurfer: A Complete Guide to the SF Bay Area and Beyond*, by M. Godsey, M. Kast, and E. Hughney. This excellent book acts as every local windsurfer's Bible for windsurfing around this area. The local windsurf retail shops listed below should have copies available. There is also a very informative map of Bay Area launch sites put out by *WindTracks* magazine, published out of Hood River, Oregon. For about $5, you can get a great wall map detailing every sailing spot in the area. Call direct at (503) 247-4153 for ordering information.

The Bay Area's best windsurf spots include:

Crissy Field: Located inside the Presidio near the Golden Gate Bridge, this place offers it all—big wind, classic views and choppy seas for lift off. Don't be intimidated by the place, but you should be proficient at water-starts to sail here. *This is not a beginner launch site.* Also, be aware of the tide conditions when sailing here, because a big flood tide here can mean drifting all the way down the city front to Fort Mason or Alcatraz. A strong ebb tide can send you floating out the gate, so don't be the last one out there as the wind is falling off at sunset.

While we're addressing the risks, be careful as well of the oil tankers, ferry boats, cruise ships, pleasure boats and other windsurfers. This place can get crowded when the conditions are good and requires constant visual checks while sailing. This is especially true when you are preparing to execute jibes. The right-of-way rules regarding collision avoidance with other windsurfers are the same as in sailing. This means the starboard tack (the sail in to the beach on a typical summer day with west winds) has the right of way over the sailor on a port tack (the sail out from the beach in west winds).

Other than the potential obstacles, this is a great place to windsurf. The wind and chop conditions usually increase on your way out toward the north tower of the Golden Gate Bridge. This paves the way for some serious air jumping off the swells. The area closer to the north tower offers a flat-water speed zone with big wind. You can also head out past the bridge to ride the big, slow rolling swells before broad reaching back to the beach.

Your first Bay crossing will be one of the highlights of your life. The summer winds will usually pick up sometime after 2 p.m., which leaves the morning for surfing, in-line skating, or other great sports.

Olympic Circle: Located at the Berkeley Marina just over the Bay Bridge, this area gets some good wind that comes through the "slot" wind funnel that runs from the Golden Gate Bridge, gains power as it threads between Angel Island and Alcatraz, and winds up screaming at Olympic Circle. Windsurf rentals are available here from **Cal Adventurers** (the company also offers a rental season pass for about $75), as well as daily rentals and instruction. This is an excellent beginner launch site because you can stay close to shore while learning.

Alameda Beach: Located just over the Bay Bridge in the city of Alameda, this is another good beginner spot, with shallow water to learn waterstarts. Rentals and classes are also readily available here. This area offers a nice beach to picnic on while you take breaks from the learning curve of windsurfing.

Candlestick Park & Flying Tigers: This area is great for flat water and good winds to practice waterstarts, jibing and sailing in your footstraps. Rentals are readily available right from the launch site. This spot can be great when Crissy is fogged in.

Windsurfing Waddell Creek.
Photo: Shaw Hazen

Coyote Point: This high-wind place is located a bit further south of Candlestick near the San Mateo Bridge. This launch site offers some of the longest tacks anywhere in the Bay. Classes and rentals are available close by. This is definitely one of the best of the local windsurfing spots, especially when the July fog engulfs the local city spots. Coyote is a great sailing area for all board sailors of all abilities because you can stay close to the shore till you get good enough to head all the way out where conditions can get good and crazy. Check the tide tables and be careful of drifting on a flood tide. As with most of the local windsurf sailing areas, conditions are best on an ebb tide or slack tide. The flood tide goes the same way as the usual summer West wind, which tends to push you far down the beach.

Larkspur Landing: Marin County's high-wind spot is located right next to San Quentin Prison. This launch site offers consistent windy conditions and usually avoids the summer fog that can kill the wind at Crissy Field. Larkspur also offers the opportunity to jump the wake trailing the commuter ferry as it steams toward the landing dock. Rentals and classes are usually available on site.

The Delta: Located in the Rio Vista area, hold on to your hats at this windy place. The best spot in this big area lies about fifty miles due east of downtown San Francisco (take U.S. Rt. 80 east out of town to U.S. Rt. 4). Rio offers great winds, especially during the summer, when the Bay Area can be fogged in. It's a great spot to camp out for the weekend, so you will be rigged and ready for early-morning sailing sessions that can bring 25-knot winds. This area of the American River delta offers consistent high-powered winds all summer long. Rio is California's answer to Oregon's high-wind Columbia Gorge area. This area is actually called the "California Gorge." Summer lessons are available from a few local sailing schools in the area. The best sailing spots are Sherman Island, Powerlines, and Brannan Island. For information, call **Windcraft Windsurfing**, a retail outlet located in Rio at (916) 777-7063; or dial the wind talker at (916) 777-7007 for the current wind speed at Sherman Island.

Waddell Creek & Santa Cruz: This is located on U.S. Route 1 roughly 75 miles south of San Francisco. Some say Waddell is the premier wave sailing spot in California, offering high winds, big waves and great ocean-sailing conditions. Make sure you are an experienced sailor who is comfortable in waves, with waterstarts, and with jibing before venturing out here. Call the wind talker for this area at (408) 423-0610 for up-to-the-minute conditions. No rentals or classes are offered here. *This is definitely not a beginner launch site.* Located further down the coast, Santa Cruz offers some great ocean sailing from Natural Bridges State Park.

Stinson Beach: Located about 13 miles north of the Golden Gate Bridge along U.S. Rt. 1, Stinson doesn't go off that much because it needs a north wind, which doesn't occur with regularity. But when the conditions are right, you should be there. This beach offers great ocean windsurfing, with wave jumping and long tacks. There are no rentals or classes here. Be experienced in waterstarts and jibing to sail here.

Tomales Bay & Bodega Bay: Both these launch sites are located a bit further north of Stinson Beach along U.S. Route 1. These two spots offer some of the best spring sailing in the Bay Area. Speed-sailing windsurfing regattas are held here in March and April to take advantage of the flat water and honking spring winds, which bring on speeds of more than 30 knots a lot of days. No rentals or classes are offered, here so bring your own equipment.

LOCAL WINDSURF SCHOOLS, RENTALS, & RETAIL STORES

What follows is by no means a complete list of all the windsurfing schools and retail stores located here. New stores and schools open every year, but this is a start. The windsurf shops around the Bay Area include:

Cal Adventurers: Olympic Circle, Berkeley Marina (510) 642-4000. The basic course is about $75, with about six hours of instruction. These guys also offer a great deal with a season pass for unlimited rentals for only about $75. All sailing is done in the good wind of the Olympic Circle area.

Outdoors Unlimited: Associated with UC San Francisco (415) 476-2078. The basic windsurfing course costs about $75. These sports-oriented people also sponsor the Bay Area Boardsailors Group, to help keep you going in the sport long after your introductory class ends.

Sausalito Sailboards: Located at 4000 Bridgeway, Sausalito (415) 331-WIND. Classes are taught close to the shop at Schoonmaker Marina Beach on Richardson Bay. These windsurf retail entrepreneurs also own **CityFront Sailboards** near Crissy Field and Berkeley Sailboards as well. The basic windsurf course is about $80. The course is followed by a good price deal on any equipment you might want to buy from the shop.

Cal Sailing Club: P.O. Box 819, Berkeley (510) 287-5905. All lessons and rentals are given in the Olympic Circle sailing area in the Berkeley Marina. A very reasonably priced school that also offers a $75, three-month pass for unlimited use of rental equipment after completion of the basic windsurf class.

San Francisco School of Windsurfing: This school gives lessons at the Candlestick Park windsurf sailing site. Instructors can be reached at (415) 750-0412.

Berkeley Sailboards: Located at 843 Gilman St., Berkeley (510) 527-7873. This is close to the high-wind Olympic Circle area at the Berkeley Marina.

CityFront Sailboards: Located at 2936 Lyon St., San Francisco (415) 929-7873. This retail and short-board rental store is just minutes from Crissy Field and staffed by some of the best windsurfers in the area.

You also can get up-to-the-minute local conditions for Crissy Field on the wind talker that is available to windsurfers upon joining the San Francisco Boardsailing Association. This worthwhile organization does a lot for the sport in this area. An application to the SFBA is available at **CityFront Sailboards**. Dues are about $15 a year, which includes a monthly newsletter of Bay Area windsurfing news.

ASD-Advanced Surf Designs: Located at 324 Lang Rd., Burlingame (415) 348-8485. This place is on the bay at the Coyote Point launch spot, and offers excellent rentals and a retail shop.

Windsurf Warehouse: Located at 428 S. Airport Blvd., South San Francisco (415) 244-4830. This large-selection retail store is close to the high-wind Candlestick Park sailing area.

Windsports: Located at 1595 Francisco Blvd., San Rafael (415) 459-1171. This innovative store is close to the Larkspur Landing sailing area. The shop sets up a large van for on-site rentals at this spot all summer.

Vela San Francisco High Wind Center: Located at 351-C Foster City Blvd., Foster City (415) 525-2070. This retail shop is only a short distance away from the Third Ave. launch site in Foster City. It sells quality used equipment from the demo fleets of the Baja and Cancun Highwind Centers. Rentals are also available at the Third Ave. launch site.

Spinnaker Sailing At Shoreline: Located on the water in Shoreline Park, Mountain View (415) 965-7474. The group offers lessons and rentals in the lighter winds of Shoreline Park.

Windsurfing Lake Del Valle: Located on the shores of Lake Del Valle in Livermore (510) 455-4008. This place offers some good flat-water lake sailing with some nice hot weather. The windsurfing is usually not as hairy as on the bay.

Windsurf Diablo: 401 Sunset Drive, Antioch (510) 778-6350. Located close to the Rio Vista sailing area, these guys give lessons and offer rentals.

Bay Area Windsurf Launch Sites

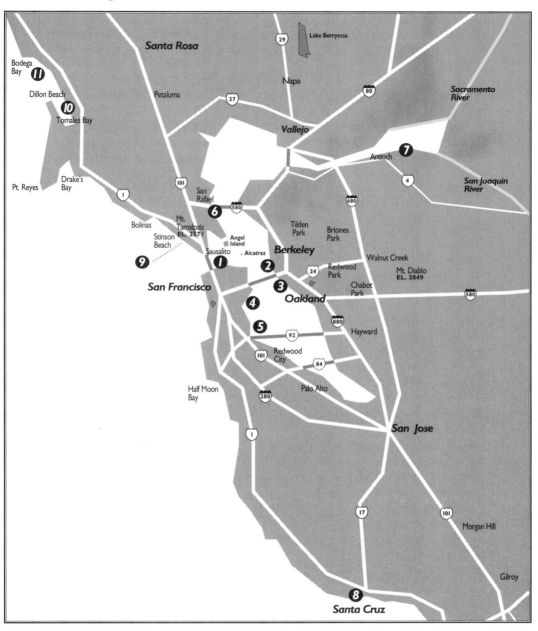

❶ Crissy Field
❷ Olympic Circle
❸ Alameda
❹ Candlestick
❺ Coyote Point
❻ Larkspur Landing
❼ The Delta

❽ Waddell Creek/Santa Cruz
❾ Stinson Beach
❿ Tomales Bay
⓫ Bodega Bay

Windcraft Windsurfing: 17124 E. Sherman Is. Levy Rd., Rio Vista (916) 777-7067. This high wind area is fondly known as the "California Gorge," and gets the howling summer winds, especially when the fog blankets the Bay Area in July. Rentals are available, along with a complete retail shop.

Delta Windsurf Co.: 3729 W. Sherman Island Rd., Rio Vista (916) 777-2299. This shop offers rentals and retail equipment close to all the high-wind sailing spots of the Delta.

With all these options you should have no trouble finding a local school for lessons, and the right equipment to get you set up in the sport of windsurfing. You'll be shredding on the water in no time. Don't let this great adventure sport pass you by.

COST OVERVIEW FOR WINDSURFING

Cheap Budget:
By far the least expensive way to get into this great sport is to start dating a person that happens to windsurf already. They will want to take you sailing all the time. All you will need is your own wetsuit and you can get them to teach you all the basics on their equipment.

If this is not an option, it is cheapest to attend one of the lesser-priced windsurf schools. After completion of the basic lessons, you can rent windsurf equipment each time you go. Some of these schools even offer season passes for as little as $95 for three-months unlimited rental.

To buy your own equipment on a cheap budget, look for equipment that is two to three years old at the swap meets around town. Most used equipment can be found at very reasonable prices. Just be very careful that the equipment can last out in the 20-knot winds we regularly experience here.

Moderate Budget:
This budget can range from $500 to $1,600. On the lower end is all used equipment that can be easily found in very good condition at local swap meets. A lot of windsurfers put together equipment by purchasing some new pieces like the mast and boom, then buying a used board and sails. Do whatever is best for your pocketbook. This budget could also get you into a new equipment package. These will range in price from $900 to $1,600. Just get the basics to start, then build up with additional sails down the line.

High-End Budget:
If you want to spend the money, the top-end windsurf equipment available today is just phenomenal. A quiver (four sails of different sizes) of brand new sails can go for as high as $2,000. They are worth every cent if you can afford them. A complete set-up of the high-end windsurf equipment will run about $3,500. This would include a very sweet board, four top-of-the-line sails, and a high-end mast and boom. Considering the price of cars, sailboats and computers in today's world, this isn't that much for the complete thrills the sport of windsurfing will give. You will definitely get your money's worth.

CHAPTER SIX

Row

Season: All year long, but it can get cold on some days in winter.
Learning Curve: One four-hour course for the basics. Lifetime to master.

Open-water rowing at dawn in the fog.
Photo: R. Blick

R owing is a generic term that includes sweeping and sculling, two different kinds of rowing. Both represent an adventure sport that can be taught in an afternoon, but takes then a lifetime to master. The good news is that along the way, from the first time you step into the boat to your first open-water regatta, rowing offers a whole lot of fun. Eventually, it may become a part of your life. Rowing also is one of the best aerobic workouts around, so you'll get in great shape.

The San Francisco Bay Area offers an early-morning rower flat water, unsurpassed beauty, and a support network of local rowing schools conveniently located to help you achieve maximum results. There is something special about being on the bay alone at sunrise cranking stroke after stroke as the scull picks up speed. Sweat drips from your every pore, cleaning out any of life's mundane problems from your head.

OPEN WATER vs. FLAT WATER

This distinction between open-water rowing and flat-water rowing has to do with the water conditions found on different bodies of water and the design differences of the boats made to handle each most efficiently. The boats are very different, even though they look similar.

Flat-water shells belong on the calm water of protected lakes and slow-flowing inland rivers. These conditions allow for light, extremely narrow shells geared for one purpose: straight-line speed. Ocean swells or choppy seas would knock these boats over in a minute. Because flat-water shells are light, long, very narrow and extremely unstable, you have to be a pretty good rower to use one. The boat can be as narrow as 12 inches across the beam (widest part) and can be as long as 27 feet. In the Bay Area, there are a few excellent places to practice this art. The two big lakes in the area are Lake Merritt in Oakland and Lake Merced in San Francisco. Both are local flat-water rowing Meccas. These sleek rowing shells are often used by those who might have rowed in college or clubs, and are continuing in the sport.

Open-water boats, on the other hand, are designed for the choppy water conditions you will sometimes face rowing on San Francisco Bay. Open-water shells come in many forms and designs, from sleek, light and ultra-fast to heavy and wide for more stability. Novice training boats can weigh up to 75 pounds, and are wider across (in the beam), so they are very stable even in choppy seas.

As your rowing ability improves, beginner boats will seem slow to you. At this point, you can move up to a faster intermediate boat like the Maas Aero, which at 40 pounds and 21 feet in length will fill your need for speed for awhile. Alas, you eventually will want still more speed. At the high end there are very light, skinny machines—like the Maas 24, which is three feet longer than the Aero and only 14 inches wide—that will take you to warp speed if you so desire. Once your power and technique are in perfect sync, rowing one of these shells is like nothing you've ever experienced. You will love this sport.

The key to any of these boats, or shells as they are called, is the sliding seat. These seats allow the rower the ability to incorporate the power of the leg muscles into the stroke. This is way more efficient than depending on the weaker arm muscles for every stroke. Originally invented in the 1870s, the sliding seat changed rowing forever. No more greasy pants and sore butts, the sliding seats of today's rowing machines are actually comfortable on the tush. The sliding seat's design evolution has also come pretty far. Today, the majority of the power generated from the rowing stroke comes from the leg muscles. This means more speed and longer rows.

SWEEP vs. SCULL

Now that you know a little about the two different types of shells, you should also know about the two different types of rowing—sculling and sweep rowing. Sculling means the rower has two oars to propel the boat. This is normally done in shells with one rower, called singles, or two rowers in doubles. Sweep rowing is where each rower has only one oar. Sweep rowing can't be done in singles, of course, because going in a straight line is impossible with only one oar; sweep rowing is practiced in pairs, fours and eights. The eights are about 60 feet in length. The shells that you see on San Francisco Bay are sculls, primarily singles (some doubles are used as well). For that reason, this guide will concentrate on single sculling.

BASIC SCULLING TECHNIQUE

The stroke is broken down into four main parts. It starts with the *catch*, where the oar blade is dropped into the water. The *drive* is accomplished by pushing the legs against the foot stretcher while pulling the oar though the water. The sliding seat rolls in the direction of the bow. The third part is the *finish*, when the drive ends and the oars are released from the water to get them ready for the *recovery*. In this last phase, the oars are brought back to the catch position, parallel to the water's surface and only a few inches off it. This basic rowing technique can be taught in a few hours, but will then take the rest of your life to master. Some days you will go out there and feel like your stroke is textbook, while the shell just flies over the water. On another day, your stroke can be horrible, you'll feel like the boat is crawling. The good thing is even a bad day of rowing will beat a good day of most other things you can do.

THE LEARNING CURVE & COSTS

Getting Started:
Sculling requires some lessons, because the shells are very unstable and the necessary rowing stroke can only, in reality, be taught by an expert rower. The technique may look simple, but there's a lot more to it than you think—a subtle marriage of power and dexterity.

It is definitely a good idea to skim through a basic rowing book from the library or bookstore before your first class. You will pick up the instruction that much faster. The introductory course begins with about an hour of dry-land instruction on rowing technique and safety. This is immediately followed by on-the-water time in a novice shell. These boats are heavier and beamier (wider) than the racing shells you eventually will be rowing. They usually weigh about 70 pounds, and are about 18 to 20 feet in length. The beam of the boat can be as wide as 25 inches, so the novice shell is fairly stable. The boat is very forgiving, so a rowing stroke mistake or two will not send you into the drink. You can relax, stop thinking about getting dunked in the chilly water and just concentrate on your rowing stroke.

Your instructor in this class usually will row right next to you to point out any technique problems you might be experiencing. This way, you learn the correct form from the start and won't develop bad habits. You will also be instructed on boat preparation and break down, maneuvering and all safety precautions in the event of a capsize. Upon successful completion of this course, you can use club shells to your heart's desire and really get into this great sport. This basic intro course will take two to four hours and the cost will range from $65 to $95. The cost of the lesson includes equipment rental.

Stage II Class:
The intermediate class is more of a coaching clinic than a class. The expert rowing instructors at the local schools and clubs will pick apart your stroke to make it more efficient and also refine other boat-handling skills. Upon completion of this class, you are cleared to use intermediate shells. These boats are up to 30 pounds lighter than novice boats. The speed and lack of stability of these shells may surprise you at first. After a few sessions, you will get used to the better performance of these shells and the idea of going back to one of those heavy, slow beginner boats would be unfathomable. You are now starting to become a sculler. This coaching session will cost $25 to $45.

Advanced Class:
At this stage, you will have spent so much time on that sliding seat that the intermediate boats will feel sluggish to you. The "need for speed" will have reared its head in your mind; it's time to move up to the warp-speed machines. Additional coaching will prepare you for the beautiful, lightweight sculls that move so fast you feel like you're flying on the water. You will also go through a real live capsize in this class, just to make sure you feel comfortable if the boat ever does go over. Completion of this class allows you to use these shells on your own and will solidify your love of rowing forever. These coaching sessions cost from $25 to $45, which includes the boat use cost.

The rowing learning curve also dictates where on San Francisco Bay you can row. Novice rowers are usually restricted to the calmer water areas of the bay. This means you stay close to the schools, so someone can keep on eye on you. As you progress and go through the special rough water training, the rowing center will let you expand your rowing out into the middle of the bay.

LOCAL ROWING SCHOOLS, RENTALS & CLUBS

There are many great open-water and flat-water rowing clubs throughout the Bay Area. All of the rowing schools have shells available to any rower who has successfully completed the basic introductory course. The boat fleets of these local rowing centers are really spectacular, with modern pristine shells. Shells are available every day with enough time slots to fit any schedule. An early row will start your day off right.

The cost of using shells is either by the hourly rate or by a monthly membership rate. The hourly rates range from $8 to $16 at the various clubs. Monthly-use rates can bring that hourly charge down to a very reasonable $5-$7 an hour. That is pretty cheap when you consider everything is provided for you—the shell, oars, a life jacket and the launch dock. All you provide is the horsepower to move the boat.

The rowing clubs in this area are plentiful, friendly and welcome new members. The private clubs do tend to attract more sweep rowers, whereas open-water rowing centers specialize in scullers at every level. To join a club, you usually pay an initiation fee of $150 to $300, and a flat membership fee of between $200 and $350 a year, depending on the club. This gives you the ability to row the club shells as much as you want at no additional cost. You can also experience both sculling and sweep rowing in the four and eights as most clubs have all types of shells in their fleets. The clubs also offer a complete racing schedule if you want to get active in the sport. Call the clubs directly for additional information from the listing below:

OPEN WATER

Open Water Rowing Center: Located in Sausalito on Richardson Bay in the Schoonmaker Point marina complex. "OWR" was started by Shirwin Smith, one of the sport's great female rowers, and no expense was spared to offer the public a great rowing center with a lot of instructional courses. The club shells are excellent as well. Classes and shell use are open to everyone from recreational users to those who are aiming at competition. They also put out a bi-monthly newsletter that lists all the West Coast open-water regattas and results. Call (415) 332-1091 for information, or visit at 85 Liberty Ship Way, Sausalito.

Cal Adventurers: Located in the Berkeley Marina at Olympic Circle, "C.A." is affiliated with U.C. Berkeley, but offers classes to everyone in a low-key learning atmosphere. The center has plenty of boats available. The basic rowing course costs about $75. The phone number is (510) 642-4000.

Dolphin Club & South End Rowing Club: The headquarters for both clubs are located at the end of Jefferson St., at Aquatic Park. Call (415) 441-9329 for the **Dolphin Club**, and (415) 441-9523 for **South End**. These clubs are famous as the city's open-water swim clubs, but they offer great rowing facilities. There also is a healthy competition between the clubs. The club boats are available to all members after they have completed a basic rowing course given by the club boat commodore.

FLAT WATER

Los Gatos Rowing Club: Although this club recently lost its boat house and equipment in a fire, give it a year or two and it will be active again. This place served South Bay and Peninsula rowers, offering lessons, boat rentals, shell storage and an active rowing club. The club is located at Lexington Reservoir in Los Gatos, and can be reached at (408) 354-9754 or (408) 354-9795.

Marin Rowing Association: These rowers ply their trade out of Greenbrae in Marin County. They offer beginning and intermediate lessons open to all. They also have a very active rowing club, if you want to get into some racing. Call (415) 461-1431 for more information. The address is 50 Drakes Landing Road, Greenbrae. This association also offers sculling, but the emphasis is on sweep rowing.

Lake Merritt Rowing Club: The boathouse for these rowers is located right on Lake Merritt in Oakland. Lessons in sweep rowing and sculling are offered and memberships for shell use are available. Call (510) 273-9041 for information.

UCSF Rowing Club: This club has its boathouse at Lake Merced in San Francisco. The club is open to all, although it is affiliated with UC San Francisco. The club provides lessons and has shells available, as well as boat storage facilities. This is all offered at very reasonable prices. The club can be reached at (415) 661-9307, 661-8011, or 586-6558. The annual membership fee runs about $200 a year.

North Bay Rowing Club: Located at the Foundry Wharf in Petaluma (707-769-2003), this club offers the great weather of northern Marin and the many miles of spectacular rowing on the usually flat surface of the Petaluma River.

Dolphin & South End Rowing Clubs: Both the downtown San Francisco clubs also offer a fully stocked boathouse at Lake Merced. After completion of the basic course, you are permitted to use the club shells stored on the lake. For information, call the clubs at their downtown headquarters—(415) 441-9329 for the **Dolphin**, and (415) 441-9523 for the **South End**.

For information on rowing clubs outside the Bay Area, contact the **American Rowing Association**, 201 S. Capital Ave., Suite 400, Indianapolis, IN 46225, or call 1(800) 314-4769.

Bay Area Rowing Centers

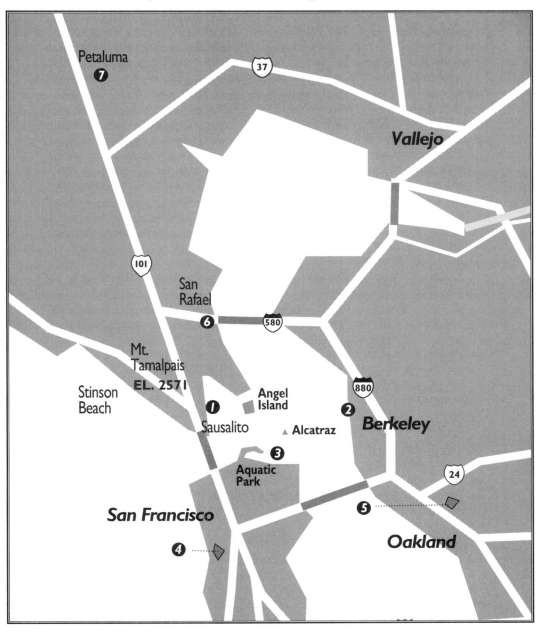

- ❶ Open Water Rowing Center
- ❷ Cal Adventurers Rowing Center
- ❸ Dolphin & South End Rowing Clubs
- ❹ Lake Merced–UCSF Rowing Club, Dolphin Rowing Club, South End Rowing Club
- ❺ Lake Merritt–Lake Merritt Rowing Club
- ❻ Marin Rowing Association
- ❼ North Bay Rowing Club

EQUIPMENT & COSTS

Buying a Boat:
As you journey into the world of rowing, there will come a time when you will think about buying your own shell. You will row a lot more if you own one, which will make you a very good rower in a short period of time. Be forewarned, however, that rowing shells are not cheap, even used ones. It will be easier if you look at this as an investment that will give you the freedom to row where and when you want, and with little cost after the initial cash outlay of buying the boat. This might make it easier to write a check for at least $900 (and probably $1,800) for a used shell.

The nice thing about modern shells is they are almost maintenance free. In the 1970s, when fiberglass was introduced to the marine boat market, rowing shells were changed forever. The boats of today can weigh as little as 30 pounds. The big question you have to ask yourself when buying a boat is whether you want a more stable open-water shell that you can row on all types of water, or a flat-water shell that can only be rowed when the water is very calm.

The advantage of buying an open-water shell is that you will be able to go out in all types of weather and surface water conditions and feel comfortable. The disadvantage is that you will lose some speed, because these boats are wider than flat-water shells. If you choose a flat-water shell, it will be very sweet when you get to use it, but the water has to be pretty flat for you to really enjoy it and be safe.

The key is to figure out before you buy how far you want to take this rowing thing. If you have no interest in racing on a serious level, then novice shells are fine. The cost will be $500 to $1,000. For $1,200 to $2,000, you can get a good intermediate open-water rowing shell. This price usually includes oars. The most advanced new shells, open-water or flat-water, cost roughly $3,000 and up. We suggest buying your first boat used, till you know exactly what you want. You won't know this until you have rowed many strokes.

The more advanced open-water shells you learned to row in the advanced instructional course range from $1,800 up to $2,400 on the used market, including the oars. A new one will cost a fair bit more. If you're rowing on flat water, you might find older wooden shells that may not be in pristine condition for a lot less money. This is a good alternative if you are into woodworking because the maintenance cost and time will drive you crazy unless you are skilled, patient and have a wood shop. You might wind up spending equal time repairing and rowing. For those into woodworking, these are sure beautiful boats with a history.

To find a good listing of rowing shells for sale, just check the bulletin boards and monthly newsletters at the rowing centers mentioned above. (These centers will also store your boat at their dockside facilities for a monthly fee.) It's advisable no matter what type of boat you want to buy that an experienced rower check out the boat with you. A member of the local rowing center will be happy to do this if you bring the shell by. Be aware that some of the used boats on the market have not been rowed for years, and this lack of use can be a huge negative because it usually means no maintenance has been done for awhile.

You'll also need to buy oars. Modern technology has been hard at work here and there are many choices, ranging in price from $200 a pair to $425. The price depends on the weight of the oars. The most expensive oars are those made out of high-tech carbon fiber.

Additional equipment includes a life-jacket. Although you can't wear one when you row because they are cumbersome, you are required by the Coast Guard to carry one in your shell. The full-sized vests cost only about $10, but to fit in the shell, you may need one of the inflating vests that cost between $60 and $70. Although expensive, they fit neatly behind the foot rest and won't impede your stroke. Don't ever row without one. You can also upgrade your boat with electronic instruments that will give speed, stroke count and distance traveled information. These will help your rowing progress. There will be some costs involved with these electronics (up to $500 for the top-end stuff), but they are really nice to have if you start rowing a lot. If you don't want to spend the money, don't worry about them. Rowing was around a long time before boat electronics ever came on the scene.

ADDITIONAL READING

There are many books about rowing available in your local library or bookstore. For the open-water rowing in this area, two of the best are:

Open Water Rowing Handbook, by Bruce C. Brown, International Marine Publishing, Camden Maine, 1991.

The Complete Recreational Rower & Racer, by Stephen Kiesling, Crown Publishers Inc., NY, NY, 1990.

American Rower Magazine, published bi-monthly by the United States Rowing Association, is also a useful tool. A subscription to this great rowing magazine is included in the yearly dues to the **U.S. Rowing Association**, which will cost about $40 a year. The **USRA** can be contacted at 1(800) 314-4769, or by writing 201 S. Capital Ave., Suite 400, Indianapolis, IN 46225.

RACING

With the increase in popularity of open-water rowing over the last couple of years, the racing schedule has increased dramatically. Below is the short list* of the local rowing races that you can train for once you get into rowing. These fun, competitive races usually are set up with short course and long course options, so anyone can enter. Awards are usually given for different shell classes (intermediate/advanced, etc.) as well as different age groups. This keeps all the races as competitive and as fair as possible. Contact your local rowing center for a complete updated list. The major rowing races of the year are:

Early April. . . . . . . **Coyote Point Regatta** ....(415) 342-5130.
Mid April. . . . . **Open Ocean Regatta** ....(415) 332-1091.
Mid June . . . . **Petaluma Race** ....(707) 762-1832.
Late June. . . . . **Lake Tahoe Rowing Classic** ....(916) 546-7248.
Late July . . . . **Lake Merritt Sprints** ....(415) 873-7326.
Early August . . . . . **Monterey Bay Crossing** ....(408) 425-0638.
Mid September . . . . **Santa Cruz Lobster Row** ....(408) 425-0638.
Late September . . . . **SF Bridge to Bridge** ....(415) 398-1221.
Early October . . . . . **Catalina to Marina Del Ray** ....(415) 332-1091.
Late October- . . . . . **Head of the Estuary Regatta** ....(415) 332-1091.
*List courtesy of Open Water Rowing Center Association Newsletter.

COST OVERVIEW FOR OPEN-WATER ROWING

Cheap Budget:
The cheapest way to get into rowing is to take a basic course. Some of the schools then offer season passes for unlimited rowing for around $95 for three months. Other rowing centers offer blocks of time that will get the price down to about $4.50 an hour—about the cost of a lunch sandwich, and a lot better for you.

Moderate Budget:
Learning to row on this budget will put you in one of the beautiful local rowing centers with the newest shells. Also in this bracket, you can purchase your own used shell for $950 to $2,300 (probably including the oars). Cheaper boats will be heavier, probably slower, and be a bit more beat up than new ones, but will work fine for any recreational rower.

High-End Budget:
If you can afford a new shell, you will have bought yourself some great rowing experiences. The cost ranges from $3,000 to $7,000, including the oars. It is a good idea to rent as many different kind of shells as you can before making a purchase of this magnitude. That way you will know exactly what kind of shell you want.

Part 2
LAND

The San Francisco Bay Area offers its residents and visitors the most diverse city playground in America. Within a 60-mile radius of the famous Transamerica Pyramid in downtown San Francisco, there are more than 600,000 acres of public park lands set aside for recreational use. That's a big play area and the possibilities are endless. Beautiful trail runs out to the beach, in-line skating down Mount Diablo's enticing paved summit road, rock climbing in Berkeley, and of course, more miles of mountain bike trails and road bike asphalt than you could ever consume.

The only problem is that getting involved in most of these great land sports will cost you a little money. A decent mountain or road bike goes for at least $399, and in-line skates run $150 and up. Seeing as how your life depends on your ropes, harness, and climbing shoes in rock climbing, you don't want to skimp on the gear, which will run you at least $200 bucks for the basic gear.

But when you really stop to think about the initial cash outlay, the thrills and pleasures of these adventure sports will more than merit the cost. As a matter of fact, it will seem cheap, since these sports are free after you invest in the equipment. So be crazy. Treat yourself to a bicycle and some skates. You deserve it.

Trail Maps:
There are over 40 state and regional parks located within the boundaries of the San Francisco Bay Area. Inside these wonderlands are hundreds and hundreds of trails and fire access roads. It's very easy to get lost. *Always carry a trail map with you when venturing into these parks.*

Area maps fit very easily into a fanny or bike pack, and only cost about $6 each. That will seem really cheap if you ever get lost as darkness sets in. Some of the best trail maps are published by **The Olmsted & Brothers Map Co.**, P.O. Box 5351, Berkeley, CA 94705 (510) 658-6535. These detailed maps include elevations so you know how bad the uphills will be.

They also show, in complete detail, every paved and unpaved road, single track trail and fire road in the park. *Trails of the East Bay Hills, and Trails of Mt. Tamalpais & the Marin Headlands* are a must for every outdoor athlete of this area. These maps are available in all local bicycle shops, or call the **Olmsted & Bros. Map Company** for mail order information.

Another great map alternative is offered by the **Bandanna Map Company.** For about $10, you can get a bandanna with a trail map silk-screened on it. You can sweat on it at the same time you are figuring out where you are. These useful maps are available at most bicycle shops as well. The company can be reached at P.O. Box 2638, Mill Valley, CA 84842, if you have any trouble finding one.

CHAPTER SEVEN

In-Line Skate

Season: All year long, except when it is raining or wet roads persist.
Learning Curve: A few weekends for the basics and fun right away.

In-Line skating on the hills of the Presidio.
Photo: R. Blick

The history of in-line skating goes back almost 300 years to the Netherlands, where wooden spools were attached to shoes to simulate winter ice skating. Conventional roller skates were invented here in America in the 1860s and have been the craze of society more than once. In the mid-1980s, some ice hockey players from the Midwest rediscovered and refined the in-line skate as we know it today.

These sport pioneers redesigned a roller skate, placing four skinny wheels in a row so the skate would be more maneuverable and perform similar to an ice skate. The original intent was to use them as a way to train for hockey in the off-season. What started as an experiment has grown into the modern-day Rollerblade In-line Skate Company. First, other hockey players took notice. Then a recreational skate was brought out in 1986, and the sport took off.

In-line skating could become the sport of the '90s. Today, in-line skating is the fastest growing sport in America with more than 14 million happy participants of all ages, abilities, and sexes. Locals in the Bay Area use skates to race, cross train, play hockey and even commute to work. For a visitor, in-line skates enable you to cover the whole city without paying for taxis or worrying about parking a car. Bring your skates with you when visiting the Bay Area. Better yet, buy a pair here and then bring them home with you.

If you're lucky enough to live here, in-line skating has got to find a way into your life. Take the enjoyment you had roller-skating and ice-skating as a kid, throw in the workout you get cross-country skiing, and add in the thrills of downhill skiing to finish it off. You can begin to imagine the allure of in-line skating. The more than 40 steep hills (and many other smaller hills) that make San Francisco the hilliest city in the world allow you to skate up and cruise down for some great thrills—in case skating the flats ever gets boring. The beauty of in-line skating is that it is a non-impact sport (assuming you don't fall on hard pavement), so it will not beat you up like long-distance running can.

Strapping on your first pair of in-line skates will be a fun and challenging workout. It will also be a bit scary. Taking spills on a pair of in-line skates is not recommended. Almost all in-line skating accidents and injuries happen to beginning skaters. After about 8 to 10 skating sessions, chances are you will not fall again (well, maybe once more), thereby minimizing any chance of injuries. The secret to not falling down is understanding the importance of body positioning and where to focus your weight. So many people just strap on the blades and start skating without understanding this, and the results are not pretty. This ill-advised method can easily result in a trip to the emergency room of your local hospital with a broken wrist, or at best, a lot of road rash. These asphalt pavement burns cause a lot of pain when showering and wearing clothes for the next week or so. Needless to say, this will not be a pleasant experience, so make sure you grasp the importance of the correct body position and form while in-line skating. Also, learn how to control your brake so you can stop in any situation. Good form and the ability to stop, along with some common sense, will prevent you from ever getting hurt while you push the envelope of this great sport.

EQUIPMENT

In-Line Skates:
The crucial equipment—skates—can be rented from a lot of shops and roaming vans all over town for $8 to $10 an hour. You can also get committed right away by purchasing your own pair of skates at almost any sports store or the new specialty in-line skate retail stores in the city.

If you opt to buy, make sure you go to a store that is well-versed in the sport, because you are going to have some questions. The cost of new skates ranges from $99 to $300, and they come in all styles and colors. Today's skates are much more specialized than they were only 2 years ago. The skate boot has been refined so it fits better, is lighter and comes in nylon/leather or polyurethane versions. The key is finding a skate boot that's comfortable, so you'll be able to stay in them for hours at a time.

The skate frame can be made of aluminum, fiberglass woven with carbon, magnesium-compounds, or a host of other materials. This frame creates a strong yet lightweight wheel base for strong ankle support, and enables you skate over almost any road surface easily. The big names in the in-line skates manufacturing business are Rollerblade, Bauer, K2, Roller Derby, Koho, CCM, and Ultra-Wheels. With the growth of the sport over the last few years, each skate manufacturer has developed up to 15 different models. There are racing skates (usually with five wheels), recreational skates, and hockey models—each with different features. Make sure you explain to the salesperson what type of skating you expect to be doing. That way you will get the right skate for you. As for price, we recommend you put your hard-earned cash into a good component skate. Forget about getting those cheapos for $69, because they won't last very long, or worse, some important component will explode on you when it's needed most; and you'll come screeching to a stop while cruising at 25 miles per hour. The initial cash outlay might hurt a bit, but the better skates will be worth every cent. Step up and get a skate for $175 or more if you plan to do any hard skating.

A new skate comes complete. An explanation of wheels and bearings follows, so you'll know what to expect when you have to replace them.

Wheels & Bearings:
The performance of your urethane wheels and bearings will be of major importance to you when you hit higher speeds, so buy some good ones. Simply put, better wheels roll better. When purchasing wheels, it's best to go to a shop that knows something about in-line skating so the salesperson can answer all your questions. There are different types of wheels for hockey, stunt skating, distance racing, half-pipe skating, steep-hill skating, and regular recreational cruising. A lot of big-chain sporting goods stores sell in-line skates, but they don't have a sales force that knows very much about them. We strongly recommend that any in-line equipment be purchased from a knowledgeable skate store or department.

We could write a whole chapter on the many wheels available to the in-line skating community, but that would take too much space. Basically, the wheels are made from different types of urethane with specialized cores. They are rated in durommeters, which translate into the density of the wheel, or hardness. The wheels are rated on an "A" scale, where a higher number reflects a harder, and therefore faster, wheel. A 72A rated wheel is softer and used for rougher paved roads and bike paths. Those rated 78A and 82A are for smoother surfaces, like new asphalt roads and sidewalks. An 85A is for tennis courts, and on the high-end, 90A and up are for indoor surfaces.

The prices of wheels vary as well. Some top-of-the-line wheels can run from $45 to $75 for eight. The major wheel manufacturers are Hyper Wheels, Labeda Wheels, UFO and BrakerWheel, to name a few. The less-expensive wheels you'll find at big sporting goods stores run $25 to $30, but may not last as long or be as responsive as the better wheels.

The wheel bearings and spacers are an important part of the whole skating process. They rest between the spinning wheels and the rigid wheel bolts, so are subject to a lot of friction. Bearings are usually made of heat-hardened chrome steel, so they roll smoothly. The spacers can be plastic or metal. Make sure to clean these bearings often because a tremendous amount of dirt and goop seems to wind up here. And you don't want anything to slow you down.

In today's world of in-line skating, the boots, wheels, bearings and brakes are a lot more specialized than they were just a few years ago, so there are different types for different uses. Always remember to rotate the wheels often to ensure even wearing. Be careful not to lose the skate wrench that comes with newly purchased skates. (See the skate maintenance explanation that follows for the details of wheel rotation.)

Accessory Pads & Helmet:
Before you strap on your in-line skates for the first time, make sure you cover yourself in padding. A helmet is a necessity in the beginning and should be worn every time you skate. There are specialty in-line skating helmets if you want to spend the money, but your bicycle helmet will work just fine. Never skate without your helmet, because it only takes one minor screw-up to cause a major injury.

Wrist guards are a requirement as well, because you will fall down. Because of this certainty, we also strongly advise that you outfit yourself with the plastic-covered arm and knee pads as well. These pads fit very comfortably and don't slow your skating down at all, so it's worth it to wear them no matter how experienced a skater you become.

It only takes one silly fall without pads and you could be wearing a cast for the six weeks. That means no windsurfing, mountain biking or rowing for a few months, and that's just not worth it.

Usually all of these items are included for a small additional charge when you rent. To purchase the whole package, you'll spend roughly $50 to $90.

Brake Pads:
The skate's brake pads will have to be replaced fairly often if you do a good amount of skating. This is especially true if you want to spend any time on the hills.

Be aware that brake pads are not universal. They are specialty fitted for each skate model. The best place to find replacement brake pads is the shop where you bought the skates. Buy a few at a time so you build a backlog at home—that way, you will never lose a day of skating because you are out of brake pads and don't have time to go to the store. The pads cost $3 to $5 each.

Remember to make sure to keep a hold of the skate wrench that comes with the brand new skates. It's a good idea to carry a spare brake pad and wrench when you go on longer skates, just in case they are needed.

THE LEARNING CURVE

Your First Skate:

Now that you're covered from head to toe with padding, you can strap on your ski boots with the skinny wheels on them. The first time out, we strongly recommend you stay near something you can hold on to. Even better—have a friend in street shoes to spot you while you get used to skating on a small strip of smooth blacktop. Also, make sure there are not a lot of people around, because you will make a fool out of yourself learning this sport, and you also don't want to hit anyone.

Most injuries that occur in this sport (broken wrists are the #1 injury) happen during the first few days of the learning curve, so take it slow. You'll have very few injuries after you become an accomplished skater. The first mistake you will make is standing too straight up, with no bend in the knees. This will quickly throw your weight back, sending the wheels under your feet swooping forward—and you are history . . . airborne central . . . and landing hard. It's a good thing you have the pads on! A few more of these and you will be guaranteed not to derive pleasure from this magnificent sport.

Think about your form before you ever put the skates on. Your knees have to remain bent and you should position your head, arms and chest forward, so your weight always remains forward. The body position is very similar to that of downhill skiing, where a lot of weight is placed on the balls of your feet. Practice this stance. If you can retain this form, you will very rarely fall down, and in-line skating will be a blast from the start.

Never, under any circumstance, lean back on your heels while skating. You will quickly discover that leaning back too far will result suddenly in a nasty fall.

The other problem that props up as you begin to cascade forward on these skinny wheels is the inevitable attempt at stopping. This is where correct body position is of major importance. If your weight is properly placed over your skates, you simply have to follow the steps listed below, and you will grind to a safe and controlled stop.

Stopping:

1) Put the skate with the stopper (usually the right skate) out in front of you by straightening your leg, putting most of your weight on the other skate. You will have to put your chest forward for balance, and drop your butt down by bending at the left knee.

2) Put your arms out to the sides to help balance while keeping your chest forward and head up.

3) Apply the brake, allowing friction to stop you. Start applying pressure slowly, and gradually increase the pressure till you stop.

It does take some space to execute this maneuver, so don't get near moving cars till you are experienced. Also, replace the break pad as soon as it is worn down.

Practice stopping over and over till you feel you can stop at any speed. Then you can think of attempting some downhill skating.

Recently, some skate manufacturers have developed easier braking systems for some of the newer skate models. One new brake method is called ABS (Advanced Braking System by Rollerblade Inc.). This system enables the skater to simply straighten out the brake skate leg, which tightens your calf muscle and puts pressure on the brake pad. A number of Rollerblade's new in-line skate models offer this brake method.

Another braking system uses the same principles as the brakes on a bicycle. The skater holds a grip in each hand, which controls the braking process. Simple hand pressure activates the brake attached to each skate through a cord that runs up your leg from the wheels of the skate. The manufacturer of this new product is **GRIP** (5375 Western Ave., Boulder, CO 80301, 1(800) 510-GRIP). These new systems are nice options for anyone who has trouble stopping with the conventional brake method.

Once you get the correct form down, the sport of in-line skating is easy. Just push off and roll, making sure your arms are out in front of you and your weight is forward. Push off on each leg one at a time, alternatively putting all weight and pressure on one skate while the other one rolls.

As your speed starts to exceed 15 miles an hour, the skates can start to wobble. This can be alarming, but is easily corrected by using your momentum to turn back and forth as in slalom skiing. Always shift your weight to the downhill skate, and you will stay in control. As you begin to feel comfortable with this technique, you will notice the similarities to downhill skiing. When this occurs, you will be hooked on this great sport for life.

Skiing down Mount Tamalpais.
Photo: Scott Tucker

Taking a Fall:

Falls happen—the key is to keep them to a minimum. The best way to avoid falling is to know your skating ability and not overstep it. Don't attempt a cruise down Mount Tam your third time out. Keep on the flats till you get your form and braking mechanics down pat.

When you do fall, don't fight it. Do the "tuck and roll" you learned as a kid. Be especially careful not to break your fall with your arm. This could easily result in a broken wrist. *Always wear your wrist guards and helmet, no matter how good and confident a skater you become.* When you are relaxed and wearing all your pads, a fall can actually be kind of fun. This may seem unbelievable when you are just starting out, but it is true.

Intermediate Skating:

The beauty of in-line skating is that you progress very quickly if you skate often. By the end of your first weekend on skates, you will feel very comfortable picking up speed and stopping at will.

Quite simply, the more time spent on your skates, the better you will become. After a short while, you will begin to feel the road under your wheels and will control your speed by just turning, not even using your back brake. Still, always keep the brake on the skate and in good working order, even if you don't use it much, just in case some car jumps out in front of you while you're cruising.

Once you are comfortable on your skates, you can begin taking your game to the rolling hills of San Francisco's Golden Gate Park, an in-line skating wonderland. Here you will see some of the city's best skaters. Watch them closely and learn from them, but don't get frustrated— remember, the goods ones have been skating for some time.

Advanced Skating & Steep Hills:

Once you are really comfortable on your skates, it's time for the real fun and adventure. Speeds of up to 25 miles an hour can easily be attained on the flats once you know what you're doing, and even higher speeds in the many hills of this area. By now, you'll have been skating the flats for so long it might have become a little boring.

We are, of course, blessed with an abundance of hills in the Bay Area. These hills are thrilling to skate. Be most careful to not get too much speed going though, because it is easy to lose control. Falls tend to be pretty ugly at this skating level, so know how to use your brake. If you skate smart you won't have any falls.

Make sure to skate where you know there are not many cars or obstructions. In addition, only skate on nicely paved roads with no potholes, cable car tracks, or gravel. Never skate in the rain or on wet roads, because you won't be able stop, and stopping is important when skating the hills. Know your ability. Don't get in over your head and always skate in control.

Going up and down hills is a great workout and a lot of fun. *Using a pair of ski poles can help tremendously while skating in the hills because they will help your balance and let you pivot on each turn as you descend.*

That way you will never get out of control. Skate up like you're a cross-country skier and descend like an alpine skier (except there is no lift ticket to buy). This is local and free of charge fun. Ski poles also will be of monumental help on the uphills by forcing your arms to do some of the work. This way, you can skate uphill at a pretty good clip. It's a good idea to put old tennis balls or rubber stoppers on the bottoms of your ski poles so they grip the pavement and don't cause sparks. There are specialized rubber stoppers available on the market that are made to protect the ski pole tip. For a pair of these Skislide Tips ($9.95), contact **Marika Fitness** at (415) 388-6786. Without ski poles, the way up will be a bit harder but an awesome and satisfying leg workout.

When you stand perched on top of your first hill preparing to descend your knees might be shaking. The only way to stay in control is to traverse back and forth, using the ski poles to plant before each turn and to keep your speed in check. If you don't want to use ski poles, bend at your knees, waist, and butt to keep your center of gravity low, and make many short turns to keep your speed down. Never lean back. Never, never, never lean back on in-line skates. If you do, you are guaranteed to over.

If you feel like you are losing control, simply use your brake to slow down or turn up into the hill to stop from gaining too much speed. Never go straight down the hill. You will gain speed so quickly it will be impossible to slow down. This sets up an ugly fall potential, where you can get hurt. Stay in control by putting turns together with good forward form, like you did last winter at the Lake Tahoe ski resorts on your alpine skis. The steeper the slope, the more crouched you must be and the deeper bends in your knees.

At a certain angle on some of the local downhills, in-line skates just spin out because the wheels can't hold the pavement anymore. Make sure the hill you're tempted to skate is, in fact, able to be skated. As the hill begins to run out after the steepest part, you can open up your turns and gain some serious speed—be careful to still have time to come to a safe stop.

Make sure you know your skating ability before venturing into the hills, and don't get hurt doing speeds over your head. Always be on the lookout for freshly paved roads when driving or biking around town, so you can come back on your skates.

There are probably some great hills right outside your front door or hotel. The city of San Francisco has some 43 hills inside its boundaries, some as steep as 31 degrees. We have found some classic downhill skating runs (mostly legal) in the Presidio, Twin Peaks, city streets, Fort Baker, Sausalito, Mount Tam (just the top section from the summit to the Pantoll parking lot), Mount Diablo (an 11-mile downhill), and the Berkeley hills (good steeps).

To reiterate the important points for city skating, be careful of cars, pedestrians and bicycle traffic. Be able to stop quickly. When venturing onto the steeper hills, make sure you are wearing all protective pads, including a helmet. Install a new brake pad before skating any steep hills, just to make sure it will last the duration of your workout.

Your first descent from one of the local mountain summits will be a memorable one and a whole lot of fun. Always skate in control and you won't pick up too much speed unless you want it. If you are going to skate in the hills a lot, it would be smart to add a brake pad and casing to the left skate as well as the right. This way if one of them ever fails, you will have a backup. Stop by any skate shop to get set up with another brake and casing for about $12. It also can help to wear a leather coat on the real steep stuff in the beginning, just in case you do fall. Skate safe and in control, but rip it.

WHERE TO GO

There are so many miles of pristine asphalt around the Bay Area that we could be here for pages upon pages. The most important decision with regard to where to go skating should be based on safety. Make sure you pick roads with few or no automobiles, buses, bikes, pedestrians, cable car tracks and potholes. Any and all of these obstacles can cause major accidents and lead to serious injuries. Always skate defensively, leaving yourself an "out" at all times, in case someone drives into you. Assume the person driving that car or bus does not see you. That way you won't be surprised when they cut you off.

The most popular roads to roll in-line skates on are the many miles of bicycle lanes and paths that weave through the Bay Area. You also can skate on almost all blacktop roads and smooth sidewalks around town. You can also jump the curbs on city blocks or cruise down the steep hills of your own neighborhood.

A word of caution when skating on sidewalks; be careful of the center stringer down the middle of the sidewalk. It is very easy for your wheels to get caught in this stringer. This can send you into a fall. Always keep your skate at an angle to this center stringer, and you will be fine.

Other great places to skate are local retail mall parking lots (when they are empty of cars), and school playgrounds. The urethane wheels on in-line skates can glide over almost every kind of hard surface imaginable, so you're able to skate almost anywhere.

Remember that it's a lot easier on your elbows, knees and overall body to skate on the nice blacktop surfaces instead of the old, weather-beaten streets that are strewn with potholes and gravel. Skate anywhere that is fun and always skate safe. A sampling of some of the best skating spots include:

San Francisco: *Golden Gate Park* is a paradise for in-line skating. Most of the city's best skaters congregate here every weekend for some of the best free-styling you'll ever see on blades. The *Marina Green sidewalks* and the *Presidio* area also offer great skating roads. Try to attend some of the skate nights sponsored by local retail shops, and cruise the city with a group of fun skaters (detailed later in this section). There is also some great skating in the hills of some of the less-crowded neighborhoods, like Noe Valley, Portrero Hill and Twin Peaks.

Marin County: *The Sausalito-Mill Valley bike path* and *Tiburon bike path* are home to many Marin skaters. Both offer some nice, flat-out asphalt speed skating. The *Fort Baker* and *Sausalito* area come in with some steep hills and nice blacktop as well. The top section of *Mount Tamalpais* offers a challenging uphill skate. as well as a kamikaze downhill. Be sure to make a lot of turns on this downhill so you don't gain too much speed.

Any Mount Tam assaults should be planned early in the morning, before the automobile traffic picks up. Park your car in the Pantoll ranger station parking lot, located off Panoramic Highway, but do not skate on Panoramic Highway as there is no shoulder and too much automobile traffic. From Pantoll, start the long, challenging skate up to the East Peak summit of Mount Tam. Your reward will be awesome views of the entire Bay Area. Then you'll get to skate one of the more memorable downhills on the planet.

East Bay: The *Walnut Creek* area has become a popular skating area. The *Iron Horse bike path* and the *Livorna Avenue hill* offer a really great skate. The *Berkeley* area has become a popular in-line skating area as well. The fact is, there are so many miles of bike paths throughout the East Bay that you should have no trouble finding some great spots to skate. For some challenging hills, check out *Tilden Park* in Berkeley. You could even plan a cruise down *Mount Diablo*, if you are confident enough on your skates.

Other fun spots to skate are any of the huge shopping-mall parking lots after the stores close and the cars are gone. Malls are scattered all through the East Bay, so there is probably one close by your house, work, or hotel.

Peninsula: *The Palo Alto* area has become a big hangout for skaters because of the many miles of nice asphalt bicycle paths that weave through the area. The Peninsula also offers a ton of empty mall parking lots (after the stores have closed) that allow great, well-lighted skating at night. The asphalt is usually in pristine condition at the malls, so you can get some serious speed built up. For those of you looking for a challenge, there also are some steep hills in this area.

Since all bike paths can be used for in-line skating, please refer to the road bike chapter for additional places to skate.

Bay Area In-Line Skate

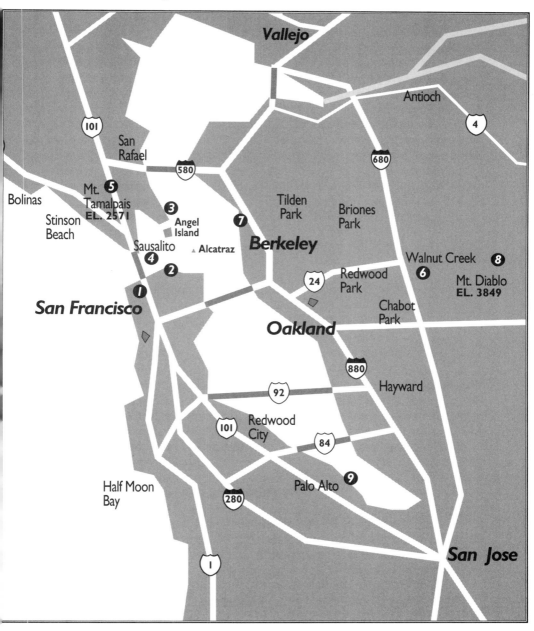

① Golden Gate Park
② Marina Green & Presidio
③ Sausalito-Mill Valley-Tiburon
   Bicycle Path
④ Fort Baker
⑤ Mt. Tamalpais Descent
⑥ Walnut Creek Area
⑦ Berkeley Area
⑧ Mt. Diablo Descent
⑨ Palo Alto Area

RACING

In-line skate racing is gaining popularity both in the Bay Area and nation-wide. Organized races are helping the sport grow. There are now in-line skating races all over the country that are usually sponsored by different skate manufacturers.

A lot of local races are put on in the Bay Area during the year. A list of upcoming local events can usually be found in the complimentary magazines *Skate Express or CitySports*. A listing of races all throughout the country is available—in case you are going to be out of San Francisco—in *Inline*, the national skaters magazine published in Boulder, Colorado (815-734-1116 or 303-440-5111). Other races and skate tours are put on by the **California Outdoor Rollerblading Association** (write for a schedule at 2549 Irving Ave., San Francisco, CA 94122).

More proof that in-line skating is awfully good here comes from some of the country's best racers; most notably legendary skater Eddie Metzger, chose to live in the Bay Area, and can be seen cruising the streets all over town.

Most of the local races are held at Golden Gate Park, and we should thank City Hall for some really nice skating pavement out there. Races can really be fun, and your skating will improve rapidly by participating in any of them. All the races have different classes and course lengths (from 10 to 100 miles), so never fear—there will be a race class group for you.

HOCKEY

In-line hockey is beginning to boom for both men and women in this area and nationwide. There is even a professional league, with a team representing the Bay Area, the Oakland Skates, doing well. The sport is drawing fans to see great hockey without the ice in the middle of summer.

You can get involved. Leagues and pickup games occur in the city's playgrounds most nights of the week and on weekends. You can get information on these open leagues by asking at any of the specialized in-line skating stores around the area (the phone numbers of these shops are listed later in this chapter).

Better yet, stop and ask about joining up when you drive by a playgrounds where crazy in-line hockey players are having fun. Real hockey players skate in the better leagues, but don't worry if you are just a beginner or intermediate skater, because there are leagues for all ability levels. Nothing helps your skating ability more than playing in-line hockey. You will learn correct body form and even be able to take a hit and keep skating. Plus, hockey will teach you accelerations, cuts and stops, as well as build the leg muscles that make you a better skater. You get all this, and you can score goals as well.

In-line hockey requires additional equipment and padding. The stick will cost $11 to $15, padded gloves about $35, the helmet about $25, and the elbow and leg pads another $30. The fun will be worth the cost.

There is a free local magazine that will keep you up-to-date on all the in-line hockey news. *Northern California Hockey & Skating* can usually be found in any in-line skating store, and gives a complete listing of hockey leagues and information. The magazine can be reached at 701 J DeLong Ave., Novato, CA 94945, (415) 898-5414.

STUNT SKATING

Many acrobatic moves can be done on in-line skates. Cruising down a flight of outdoor stairs, banister rail slides, high jumps, half-pipe moves, and slalom courses are just a few of the radical stunts that can be pulled on these rolling machines. These moves are not perfected in a day, so don't be frustrated if they don't come right away. Be sure you are a proficient skater before even attempting any of these radical maneuvers, or you could get hurt. Be prepared for some falls on the stunt-skating learning curve, and wear all the padding you can find when practicing these wild moves.

SKATE NIGHTS

In-line skate shops throughout the Bay Area put on various skate nights during the week. Just call the shop that's closest to your house or hotel to find out when the next night is scheduled, and join as many as one hundred skaters, all wearing reflectors and carrying glow sticks, for a skate on the public roads of the area.

Because you will be part of a group, you will be able to skate on the urban roads that you would never be able to skate on your own due to car traffic. Automobiles and buses will stay out of sight because of the size of the rolling crowd. It's a great way to see your town, meet other crazy in-liners, and get a great skate workout as well.

In San Francisco, a huge skating group called the "Midnight Rollers" embarks from the Ferry Building (at the base of Market Street and the Embarcadero) every Friday night at 8:30 p.m. This skating event gets bigger by the week, and should be done by every in-liner at least once. The seventeen-mile route goes through all the best spots of the city, and can draw as many as 300 skaters.

In addition, all Nuvo Colour retail skate shops sponsor skate nights. These skates usually start from Nuvo Colour shops in San Francisco, Walnut Creek and San Mateo. Call each store individually for details on which night they roll.

SKATE MAINTENANCE

The in-line skates that you trust with your life are going to need some upkeep. You don't want to be coming down some steep hill and realize your brake pad, or wheels, are too worn for you to stop safely. We have been with some skaters that had wheels fall off on a Mount Tam descent. Talk about a bad day!

It is very simple to check your skates for brake-pad rubber wear and to replace it. New skates come with an instruction manual and skate wrench, so you can do your own repairs with no problems. Also, remember to rotate your wheels often, so they wear evenly. Wheel rotation will extend the life of your wheels and save you a lot of money. Watch the wheel bearings closely as well, to see if they show signs of excessive wear and tear. These bearings have a direct impact speed, stability and overall skating performance.

Skate supplies are available at any of the local in-line skate retail shops. Always explain the type of skating you expect to do when buying replacement wheels from the skate shop, so the skates operate at peak performance and safety. The cost for basic replacement wheels is about $40 but can go up to $80 for high performance wheels. In-line wheels will last a long time if they are treated right and rotated often. It also might be a good idea to add an additional brake pad and casing for the left skate if you skate a lot in the hills. This way, you will always have a backup brake, in case one breaks or wears down in the middle of your skate.

Be prepared for an epic skate right after putting on new wheels, bearings and brake pads. The skates will seem to just fly for you.

WHERE TO RENT

With the huge increase in popularity of in-line skating in the Bay Area over the past few years, there has also been an explosion of shops where you can buy and rent skates. Most of these stores are located in an area where you can skate right from the store, and after one rental session, you will probably want to buy a pair of blades and skate home.

There has to be a skating store close to you, so get out there and start rolling. Some of these stores offer lessons for beginners, if you are interested. A listing of the specialty rental shops of the area, along with their addresses and phone numbers, includes:

SAN FRANCISCO

Skates on the Haight: 1818 Haight St., San Francisco, (415) 752-8375.
Skates off the Haight: 384 Oyster Pt. Blvd., S. San Francisco, (415) 244-9800.
Nuvo Colours: 3108 Fillmore St., San Francisco, (415) 771-6886.
SkatePro: 27th and Irving, San Francisco, (415) 752-8776.
Achilles Wheels: 2271 Chestnut St., San Francisco, (415) 567-8400.
Magic Skates: 3038 Fulton St., San Francisco, (415) 668-1117.
Nomad Cyclery: 2555 Irving St., San Francisco, (415) 564-3568.

MARIN COUNTY

Any Mountain Sports Stores: 71 Tamal Vista, Corte Madera, (415) 927-0170.
Demo-Ski: 509 Francisco Blvd., San Rafael, (415) 454-3500.
Achilles Wheel: 167 Throckmorton Ave., Mill Valley, (415) 380-8333.

EAST BAY

Nuvo Colours: 1602 North Main, Walnut Creek, (510) 938-6886.
Willows Skate & Surf: 1431 Park Ave., Alameda, (510) 523-5566.
Wheels In Motion: 733 1st St., Benecia, (707) 746-8856.
Karim Cycle: 2801 Telegraph Ave, Berkeley, (510) 841-2181.
Any Mountain: 1975 Diamond Blvd., Concord, (510) 674-0174.
Any Mountain: 490 Market Pl., San Ramon, (510) 275-1010.

PENINSULA

Nuvo Colours: 1600 S. El Camino Real, San Mateo, (415) 571-1537.
Any Mountain: 2341 El Camino Real, Redwood City, (415) 361-1213.
Inline Sports: 19998 Homestead Rd., Cupertino, (408) 252-5233.
Palo Alto Sport Shop: 526 Waverly, Palo Alto, (415) 328-8555.
Pacific Mountaineering: 200 Hamilton St., Palo Alto, (415) 324-9009.

This is just a partial list of the local stores and it will change with new store openings. Your local *Yellow Pages* will have a complete and up-to-date listing under the "Skating" headline.

If you are interested in purchasing, in-line skates can now be bought at almost any sporting goods store, including the big chains, as well as at specialty skate shops. If you want to get serious about skating, buy from a store that knows something about the sport and the skates. The salespeople will be able to answer any questions you might have, as well as steer you in the right direction for your need. Also, find a store that carries supplies of brake pads, wheels and bearings. You'll need them in the not-too-distant future.

COST OVERVIEW

Cheap Budget:
Rent skates and protective gear every time you go. This way, you don't have to deal with the expense of skate maintenance, including buying new wheels and replacement brake pads. There are many places to rent in the Bay Area, and most are close to a good skating area. The cost will be $8 to $20 each time you go. If you start to go often, you should buy your own skates, so you don't keep throwing money away on rentals.

Moderate Budget:
This budget allows you to get your own pair of brand new skates. Yahoo! Expect to spend $150 to $299 for a nice pair that will get you stoked. Once you buy a pair, you can skate all the time and go anywhere you want. The protective gear adds about $60 to the total cost.

High-End Budget:
This is not applicable to the sport of in-line skating. This is a relatively cheap sport.

CHAPTER EIGHT

Trail Run

Season: All year long. Fun in all kinds of weather.
Learning Curve: Immediate. Just run.
Definitely easier if you are in shape.

To consider running an adventure sport, you have to step off the conventional track as well as the regular roads and hit the trails.

We don't intend to demean the ability of a 220-yard sprinter or marathon runner. These endeavors require awesome athletic ability, but there is not a lot of adventure. You can't exactly get lost or run out of water on a 220. A marathon is long and grueling, but you're on paved and marked roads. Adventure trail running is something different.

Trail running means dashing through a beautiful forest of redwoods on a single track trail, with rocks sticking up like land mines ready to take you out. Deer scamper in the background as you calculate your mile split times. You realize you probably went out at too fast a pace, and you are hurting badly now, with a mean cramp in your abdomen. You look up and there is a steep, one-and-a-half mile section of trail staring down at you. You dig in and gut it out to the top, hoping all along you're not lost because you weren't quite sure at the fork in the trail some five miles back that you followed the right track in the first place. The fog is starting to move in by now, bringing darkness and a drop in air temperature with it. If you have timed your run right and follow your trail map, you should be just about finished with another great open trail workout. If not, you are probably lost and have a long walk home. (Always carry a trail map for this reason). Welcome to the world of trail running.

Trail running on the Mount Tamalpais single tracks.
Photo: Scott Tucker

The Bay Area offers, quite simply, some of the best trail running in the country. There are miles of uncrowded, challenging single track paths that offer awesome country running. The best part is that most of these trails start only ten miles from the hustle and hassles of city life. And if you think you are in decent running shape because you've been jogging the flats to the Golden Gate Bridge and back, trail running will be a rude awakening. You'll be sore after the first couple of runs, but you'll also be hooked on the sport for life.

A great feature of this sport is that it's totally free of cost after you buy a pair of running shoes, a water bottle and a trail map. You won't need any instruction if you know how to put one foot in front of the other and go for it. The learning curve comes in the form of on-the-job training. With a little time and practice, you will understand what running pace you can carry, the correct form for running up and down the hills, and the science of reading a contour trail map, so you know of upcoming elevation changes. Studying maps is the only way to keep from getting lost or passing out from exhaustion on a huge climb that came as a surprise.

THE EQUIPMENT

The Running Shoe:
Since you're going to spend a lot of time in these sneakers, you might as well get some good ones. Most of the shoe companies today make a special trail-running shoe, if you want to take it that far, but any shoe with good ankle support and not too much padding on the heel should work fine.

Really expensive street running shoes with a lot of mushy heel padding are not good for trail running because the padding elevates the heel of your foot too high. This makes it really easy to twist your ankle on a trail's uneven surface. Laying on the side of the trail yelling in pain from a sprained ankle is no way to spend a Saturday morning, so choose your shoes carefully. The cost of shoes with adequate ankle support will range from $45 to $100.

Other Equipment:
The only other equipment you need is a water bottle and a trail map. Even if you know the trail like the back of your hand, you should carry a map. Maps are found at any local bicycle shop, or at the local park headquarters. You can get a water bottle fanny pack that will hold everything you need. If you are running in an area where the climate can change rapidly, which happens often around here, it would be advisable to carry a turtleneck or warm-up coat in your pack. Always carry some cash as well, just in case it's needed.

THE LEARNING CURVE

The learning curve in this sport simply depends on what kind of running shape you are in. If you are just starting out, we strongly recommend you get in decent shape on asphalt roads before venturing into the trails.

When you think you're ready, start on easy trails and work your way up. Make sure your trail map has the contour lines, so you can figure out the ups and downs and pace yourself accordingly. The key to successful trail running is finding a pace that will let you work hard on the uphills, get your stamina back on the flats, and coast with serious speed on the downhills. This pace might be six minutes a mile for some people and twelve minutes a mile for others. Find your comfortable running pace and push it as you start to get in shape.

In the beginning you might have to walk up a lot of the ascents. As you put in more time on the trails, you'll find yourself running them as well. In just a few weeks, you will be able to challenge and enjoy any trail in the area. Then beware, because there are an awful lot of trails to keep you busy and challenged. Trail running will get you in awesome physical shape.

WHERE TO GO

San Francisco: It's a little tough to find dramatic trail runs within the confines of any major city, but San Francisco does have some really nice trails. What the trails lack in elevation they make up in scenery. The *Coastal Trail* runs from the Golden Gate Bridge to the Cliff House along the water, and the trails inside Golden Gate Park are home of many cross - country championship races. *Sweeny Ridge Park* lies a little south of the city, near Pacifica, and offers beautiful trail running.

Marin County: The North Bay offers extensive trail runs on many square miles of parkland run by the Golden Gate National Recreation Area (GGNRA). The main areas include Muir Woods, Mount Tamalpais State Park, Marin Headlands, Olema Valley and Point Reyes National Seashore. Muir Woods and Mt. Tam offer you the classic Dipsea Trail run from Mill Valley to Stinson Beach. The Marin Headlands will test you with the Miwok and Wolf Ridge Trails. China Camp Park near San Rafael also offers some great trails. Point Reyes comes in with the Bear Valley Trail, which goes from the visitor center to the Pacific Ocean. The beautiful trails of Angel Island also offer some great trail running. The park service publishes a *Park Guide* that offers a detailed map of most of the trails in the area, along with some tidbits about the history, fauna, and bird watching. This book is available at most bookstores, or call the **GGNRA** at (415) 556-2920.

East Bay: The expansive parks east of the Bay Bridge offer too many miles of trails to list here. Some of the best trails are found in the *Wildcat* and *Tilden Regional Parks* in Berkeley, the *Redwood* and *Chabot Regional Parks* near Piedmont, Moraga and Castro Valley, and the *Del Valle, Sunol* and *Ohlone Regional Parks* of Livermore and Fremont. Of course, beautiful *Mount Diablo State Park* near Walnut Creek offers the most elevation in the area, if you want a good challenging trail run.

With thousands of acres of park lands, there is an awesome trail run close to you in the East Bay. Pick up the map *Trails of the East Bay* (Olmsted & Bros. Map Co., Berkeley) at any bicycle shop and most bookstores. Weather conditions tend to be a bit dry and hot in this area, so carry plenty of water.

Peninsula: There are challenging and beautiful trails south of the Golden Gate, in *Huddark* and *Wunderlich Parks* in Woodside. *Pescadero Creek, Castle Rock* and *Big Basin Redwoods Park* are a bit further south in less-populated residential areas; therefore, these trails are less crowded. Another great source of running trails are the more than 20 parks under the guidance of the Mid Peninsula Open Space District. These open space preserves are not developed, so you'll be lucky to find a bathroom. What they lack in convenience is more than made up for in beauty and remoteness. Some of the best include *Rancho San Antonio, Skyline Ridge, Windy Hill* and *Monte Bello*. Call the district office at (415) 691-1200 for more information.

Bay Area Trail Run Parks

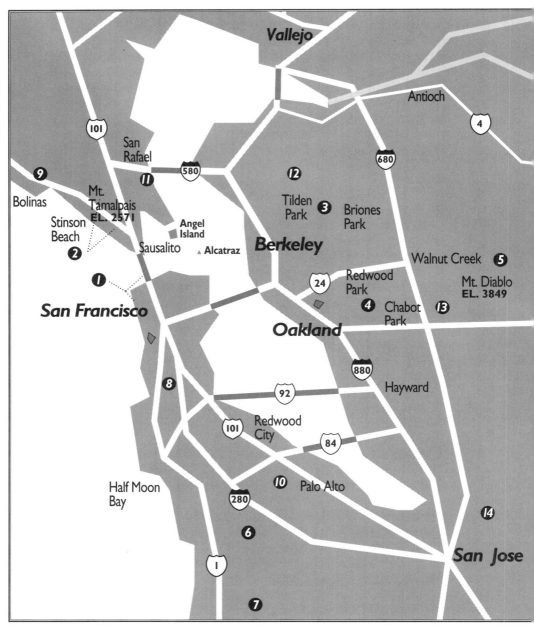

1 Coastal Trail & Golden Gate Park
2 GGNRA & Mt. Tamalpais
3 Tilden Park–Berkeley
4 Redwood & Chabot Park
5 Mt. Diablo
6 Huddart & Wunderlich Park–Woodside
7 Big Basin & Pescadero Creek State Park
8 Sweeney Ridge
9 Bolinas Ridge
10 Windy Hill Open Space
11 China Camp Park
12 Wildcat Canyon Park
13 Las Trampas Park
14 Sunol Wilderness

ADDITIONAL READING

The books listed below are an excellent source of information for great running trails. These books will also educate you on the history of the area parks, geology, flowers, birds, animal life, trees and climate. In addition, they will turn you on to some kick-butt trails that are way off the beaten track. These titles are usually available at local bookstores. The publisher's addresses are included, in case you have trouble locating these titles:

Mt. Tam; A Hiking, Running, and Nature Guide, Don & Kay Martin, Martin Press, P.O. Box 2109, San Anselmo, CA 94979.

Tamalpais Trails, Barry Switzer, Potrero Meadow Publishing, P.O. Box 3007, San Anselmo, CA 94979.

The Hiker's Hip Pocket Guide To Sonoma County, Bob Lorentzer, Bored Feet Publications, Mendocino, CA 95460.

The Park Guide, Golden Gate National Park Association, Fort Mason, Building 201, San Francisco, CA 94123.

South Bay Trails, Francis Spangle & Jean Rusmore, Wilderness Press, 2440 Bancroft Way, Berkeley, CA 94704.

Peninsula Trails, Francis Spangle & Jean Rusmore, Wilderness Press, 2440 Bancroft Way, Berkeley, CA 94704.

An Outdoor Guide to the SF Bay Area, Dorothy L. Whitnah, Wilderness Press, 2440 Bancroft Way, Berkeley, CA 94704.

TRAIL MAINTENANCE

Great trails are a precious commodity. Don't do anything that would harm them, like taking shortcuts through the untracked woods. This will damage the plants and cause erosion, and probably give you a bad case of poison oak as well. Don't leave energy bar wrappers or any other garbage out there. The local conservation groups sponsor volunteer trail-rebuilding and clean-up days during the year. These events are usually listed in the your local newspaper's outdoor section, so you'll have some advance notice. These cool environmental organizations could really use your help, if you can find the time.

RUNNING CLUBS

The popularity of running clubs in the Bay Area has soared in recent years. It's no wonder, since they welcome new members with open arms. It doesn't matter whether you are a beginner or expert trail runner. A running club is a great way to meet fun new people who also enjoy getting their butts kicked by a good trail. Club-sponsored runs also turn you on to new trails that you could never find on your own, and incorporate the safety of running in groups.

A list of some of the local running clubs follows. Make sure you are at least in some running shape before you make the call. It's a little embarrassing to show up for your first Saturday run and be dragging after only one mile of running. Most of the clubs have a low yearly dues of $15 to $25. For this, you get a newsletter, some good coaching and some training ideas. These clubs are great fun and you will definitely become a better runner by joining. Call for more information.

Fleet Feet Sports: (415) 921-7188, San Francisco.
Golden Gate Triathlon Club: (415) 434-GGTC, San Francisco.
Dolphin & South End Running Club (DSE): (415) 441-9329.
Tamalpa Runners: (415) 472-RACE, Marin County.
Palo Alto Run Club: (415) 328-4434, Palo Alto and Woodside.
Diablo Road Runners: (510) 906-8880, Contra Costa County.
Lake Merritt Joggers and Striders: (510) 601-7887, Oakland.
East Bay Frontrunners: (510) 482-4391, Contra Costa County.

RACING

A tremendous number of off-road running races are offered throughout the Bay Area. Getting involved will get you in great shape, allow you to run on some of the most beautiful trails in the area and introduce you to people as crazy as you, who can quickly become your best friends.

One of the toughest tickets in town is the famed *Dipsea Race*, held every June. This 7.1-mile scamper through the woods goes from Mill Valley to Stinson Beach, and has been around since 1905.

For a complete listing of other trail races, turn to the group **Enviro-Sports**, run by local former pro triathlete Dave Horning. The series competes on the Bay Area's most classic trails almost every weekend, offering races of different lengths and a low-key racing atmosphere. The group welcomes runners of all abilities and offers a great way for locals and visitors to get involved in trail running. Call for a schedule of races at (415) 868-1829. The address is P.O. Box 1040, Stinson Beach, CA 94970.

There are also a number of trail run races sponsored by other local groups. They are usually listed in *The Schedule*, a free monthly magazine available at any store that sells running shoes.

For the more competitive trail and cross-country runners, there is the NorCal Cross Country Championship Series, which offers prize money as well as fun. For information, call the **Pacific Association of US Track and Field** at (916) 983-4622, or write to 120 Ponderosa Court, Folsom, CA 95630. This very professional organization sponsors a complete series of championship races. The categories include cross country, long-distance road, and even the ultra grand prix series for the 50- to 100-mile crowd. The ultra grand prix series includes the epic *Western States* 100-miler, which runs from Squaw Valley to Auburn, if you are looking for a serious challenge. When you join the organization, you receive the bi-monthly publication *Pacific Athlete*, which lists a complete schedule of races and results.

COST OVERVIEW

Cheap Budget:
Use the running shoes on your feet now, change into a pair of shorts, and hit the trail. Total cost is zero.

Moderate Budget:
A new pair of running shoes will cost $40 to $110. Get a water bottle and trail map as well, and you're on your way.

High-End Budget:
This is not applicable to the sport of trail running. It's inexpensive no matter how you look at it.

CHAPTER NINE

Mountain Bike

Season: All year.
Learning Curve: Easy, if you remember how to ride a bike.

The Bay Area is a paradise for mountain bikers. It offers miles upon miles of desolate fire roads and single track trails to challenge any rider, beginner to expert. The beauty of mountain biking here is that you can go every day of the year. There are so many great areas that you can usually find a great trail only minutes from your front door.

It is generally accepted that mountain bikes were invented in the Bay Area. In the late 1970s, pioneers like Gary Fisher, Charles Kelly, Otis Guy and Joe Breeze took to the trails on Mount Tamalpais on paper-route bicycles refitted with nobby tires and extra gears for climbing. By the early 1980s, these "mountain bikes" were being mass-produced, and the craze of back country riding was born.

Today, the popularity of these bikes has grown to where the majority of the bikes sold in this country are the mountain variety. It's no surprise, considering the thrills you can experience on a fat-tired bike. And they are almost indestructible, so you don't have to spend much time fixing them.

The sad thing is that many of these solid bikes will never see the back trails because their owners only ride them on boring paved roads. This doesn't qualify as much of an adventure sport, and it's really a tragedy, because once you go for an off-road mountain bike ride, you'll be hooked for life. Get out there and try it. Go off-road or don't go at all.

THE EQUIPMENT

The Mountain Bike:
Mountain bikes are manufactured by every major bicycle company in the world. The sport has grown so much that it is no longer a specialized field, with only a few manufacturers selling to a niche buyer. Today, mountain bikes are ridden by all kinds of recreational riders. They come in all styles, colors and price ranges—even as much as $2,000.

But you don't have to sell the car or give up food to get into this great sport. You can get a lot of bike for a fairly reasonable price in today's market. Modern mountain bikes are light and sturdy high-performance machines. Newer bikes have shock absorbers to help you handle the bumps

Mountain biking on Montara Mountain.
Photo: Doug Acton

better, high-tech handle bars for easier climbing, and much better components than mountain bikes of just a few years ago. These bikes have come so far so fast that if you haven't been on one in awhile, you will be amazed.

The key is to find out which one of the many brands you should buy. Do your research at a real bike shop. Resist looking for a good off-road bike at the discount mega store. You are going to develop a pretty special relationship with your bike, so you need a sweet bike, a good repair shop and a nice deal when purchasing it. You'll find all of the above at a real bike shop (a listing follows). Go with an mind open and test drive as many brands, and price ranges, as you can.

We'd suggest you stay in the price range of $500 to $1,000 for your first mountain bike. The actual price, of course, depends on your budget restrictions. The bike you buy will probably be new; it's really hard to find good used mountain bikes that are in decent shape. Besides, finding a used bike is going to take time, which will cut into your mountain biking right now. Get a nice new bike—you deserve it so treat yourself.

So you are in this nice, shiny bike shop with about a zillion new bicycles all around. What now? The first thing to do is grab the bike shop worker and explain to this person exactly what kind of riding you want to do, as well as your price range. You will probably wind up spending a bit more than you want, but try to go for the best bike you can. You will be amazed at the huge selection of great mountain bikes in the $500-to-$1,000 range. The higher end will put you in a really sweet, lightweight, durable machine that you will never outgrow. The lower end will put you in a more basic, heavier bike that will work just fine, but won't have as much durability nor the higher-end components.

Mountain bikes that cost less than $400 tend to be far heavier and sport cheaper components. That's okay if you just want to ride it to the local video store and back on paved streets, but if you want to spend some time in the mountains, you will have to spend the additional money for a good bike. You don't want to be flying down a steep single track trail and have the derailleur, or worse, the brakes, foul up. Remember, if your bike does break down, for whatever reason, it could be a long walk home. The extra $50 to $200 on a better bike will be wisely spent.

As far as high-end mountain bikes costing $1,200 to $2,500, they are great bikes if you can afford them. These bikes will incorporate the latest technology, thereby stronger, lighter in weight, and made with the best components. This will make off-road riding easier for sure, but unless you plan to become a serious racer, we feel you won't need such an expensive machine. Most weekend riders, even if they are good, would not fully utilize the bike's potential. Besides the dollars saved could easily get you into a few of the other sports in this book.

It is also recommended, if you plan to spend any time off-road, that you avoid the temptation of getting a "hybrid" mountain bike. These are the semi-mountain bikes that look like nobby-tired road bikes. They are designed to give you a better ride on the paved roads than a regular mountain bike, but also allow you to go on some off-road trails. It appears you could use one as both a road bike and a mountain bike, saving the money of buying both kinds of bikes. In actuality, you wind up with a bike you cannot take on many of the fire roads and trails in this area. The bike is just not built for it. If you take one on local trails, you will be disappointed in the ride, and probably both destroy the bike and yourself. A hybrid will also disappoint you as a road bike, because it is heavier and slower than a real road bike.

Get a real mountain bike. If you need to ride the bike on paved roads for extended periods of time, get a set of smooth tires, which will give a more comfortable ride on the roads. Change them back to nobby tires before you head off on the trails.

Shopping for a new mountain bike can be a great experience and will surely put you in a fine mood. From your first test drive, you'll have a sense of what new-age mountain bikes can do. You will be amazed.

The Bike Frame:

Today's mountain bike frames have become a science unto themselves. They are made of aluminum, carbon fiber composites, or different types of steel. There are advantages and disadvantages to each. Frame designers are going for the lightest, strongest, most durable frame they can develop. The limits are being pushed daily and with every year frames get better and better.

Tubes of the material of choice are then tig welded together on most production bikes. On a $1,000 mountain bike the frame weighs 3.6 and 4.8 pounds, depending on the manufacturer. The complete mountain bike will come in around 23 to 27 pounds. Less-expensive bikes weigh 28 to 32 pounds complete, and high-end bikes come in as low as 21 pounds complete.

The Components:

Mountain bike components usually come in a set called a "gruppo," which includes everything from the derailleur to the cluster and brakes. Shimano components make up more than 90% of the market, so you will see it on almost every bike you look at. Shimano makes different levels of components for the different price ranges of bikes on the market. The LX model will be on $500 to $800 bikes, the XT on bikes costing $900 to $1,300, and the XTR model on high-end bikes running $1,500 and up.

The Helmet:
This is a mandatory piece of equipment for any bike rider, especially a mountain biker. You can be cruising along fine when a huge boulder or ditch jumps in front of you and sends you flying. *Too many people get seriously injured every weekend in bicycle accidents. Most of these injuries could be avoided by wearing a helmet.*

Don't become a victim. Today's helmets are light, comfortable, attractive and very reasonably priced, so there is no excuse for not wearing one. These helmets don't guarantee you to an injury-free ride, but they sure help. A good one costs $40 to $80.

ADDITIONAL EQUIPMENT

Water Bottle: A necessity. Install cages to hold two of them if you plan on long rides.

Gloves: These padded wonders are not a necessity, but they sure make riding a lot more comfortable. They cushion your hands when bouncing down uneven fire roads feels like handling a jackhammer. They're not very expensive, ranging in price from $10 to $30. Your hands will thank you.

Bike Pants: Again, these are not a necessary piece of equipment, but they promote more comfortable riding by putting extra padding right where you need it—between you and the seat. You might feel like an idiot the first time you wear skin-tight Lycra, but at least you will be comfortable, which means you will be able to ride longer. These tight pants are a blessing if you fall off your bike as well, because they help protect your skin. They range in price from $25 to $90.

Repair Kit: *You should carry a repair kit every time you go off road, because you're going to get a flat tire or break down at some point.* It can be a long hike out of the woods after a breakdown, especially if your friends keep riding and tell you later about the awesome ride you missed.

The repair kit should include an air pump, tire patch kit, spare tube and tire levers, so you can take a flat tire off the rim to patch it. Add a chain tool, some Allen wrenches, a screw driver and crescent wrench, and you should be able to handle a number of common mechanical problems.

The total cost will be about $30 to $40 for the lot. You'll probably have to buy the seat bag to hold the tools—that will be another $20. Don't worry, we are almost done spending money.

It is a good idea to learn how to use the tools before you bike into the great beyond. Bike shop employees can explain how to use them at the time of purchase. There is one enterprising company that put all the necessary tools into one multi-purpose tool called the **Cool Tool**. For $27, you get everything you'll need for bike repairs. This great product is available at any bicycle store. The company is located at 13524 Autumn Lane, Chico, CA 95926 (916) 893-3079.

Bike Shoes: Since mountain biking has become a lot more specialized in the last couple of years, the shoe question has become a bit more complex. If you decide to get quick-release binding pedals that require a specialized bike shoe, you will have no choice but to buy a pair. Such shoes can cost $40 to $100, and the pedals will be from $80 to $150 depending on the model. These shoes maximize your pedaling, but you have to wear the shoes every time you ride.

If you go with simple toe clips for pedals instead of the clip on system, you can wear all different kinds of shoes—even your flip flops if you ride to the beach. All bike shops carry specialized mountain bike shoes that will fit toe clips pedals, but you don't have to spend the money if you don't want to. Sneakers will do just fine. A good shoe to use for mountain biking is a lightweight, low-cut hiking shoe. They offer good foot protection and have deep grooves in the soles to lock into your toe clips.

Bicycle Computer: These computers are a nice addition because they will tell you all the important information you'll need as far as speed, pedal cadence, time in the saddle. The cost ranges from $30 to $65.

Trail Map: A definite necessity when riding the off-road trails in the Bay Area. You can get lost pretty quickly out there. Maps also give you elevations and a host of other valuable information. The cost is $4 to $7 per map.

Now that you're are all decked out and probably penniless, let's go ride. Everything else about this sport is free.

THE LEARNING CURVE

Getting Started:
Hopefully, you already know how to ride a bicycle, so the learning curve for riding off-road is easy.

The first difference you'll notice about these bikes, compared to what you might be used to, is the number of gears you now have at your disposal. There are at least 18 and as many as 24 gears, which enable you to climb hills that you would not even think of attempting on other types of bicycles.

The key to successful riding is to master the use of these gears. Get caught in the wrong gear on an uphill and you could lose your balance, resulting in an embarrassing fall (if you're locked into your toe clips). Flip the coin, and you'll find yourself pedaling so fast in too high a gear on a downhill that you'll lose control. This can lead to an even uglier crash.

Proper shifting will take a little practice to master. Concentrate on the technique called spinning. Think of your feet as a spinning wheel, equally dividing the leg muscle use between your thigh muscles and your hamstrings, in the back of the leg. Spinning the pedals as you climb is more efficient than trying to hammer on the pedals in a high gear. This bullheaded hammer method will cause fatigue very quickly. In essence, your goal is to have the same spinning speed at all times (unless it is super steep). The optimal range is 50 to 70 pedal revolutions per minute. A good method to count revolutions per minute is to count every time your right pedal comes to the top of the cycle for 15 seconds and multiply by four. Select the gear that keeps you at those revolutions per minute throughout your workout pace.

When you approach an incline, you should gear down to where you can maintain a steady, smooth and not too stressful spin, and vice versa on the downhills. Proper spinning technique will let you go on longer rides at faster speeds. Once you get the hang of spinning, which will become second nature to you in a week or so, you will never go back to the hammer method again. You also will be able to ride any trail this area can throw at you. The only thing that might slow you down is your physical condition. Conditioning will only come with time spent in the saddle. You would never think that getting in shape could ever be as much fun as riding a mountain bike.

Another thing you'll need to learn to take full advantage of a mountain bike is how to adjust your seat height for different conditions. On your old bike you probably kept the seat in the same position the whole time you owned it. Not so on a mountain bike.

When you ride uphill, you will want to extend your legs to maximize pedal power, so you will want your seat high. Your leg should be about 90% extended on the down stroke of the pedal. If your leg is fully extended, your seat is too high, and you will roll on your seat every time the pedal reaches its lowest point, which is not very efficient or comfortable. If your seat is too low when you pedal uphill, you will tire very quickly and may even pull an inner thigh muscle when you really push yourself.

If too low a seat on an uphill swing is wrong, the opposite is true when you start heading downhill—especially when it gets really steep and technical. When you are at the top of hill preparing to descend, get off your bike and push your seat down. This lowers your center of gravity, giving you a lot more balance when things start to get hairy. Your speeds can easily hit 30 mph, and you'll need to dodge boulders and pot holes.

Don't forget to make these adjustments. Once you master shifting and seat adjustment, you can ride almost any terrain the Bay Area offers with a maximum degree of efficiency and safety.

Intermediate Riding:
Once you feel comfortable on your mountain bike in all different types of terrain, and you are in the kind of shape that will allow you to climb long hills without feeling like you are going to die, you are ready to have fun on the many miles of trails and switchbacks this Bay Area mountain biking Garden of Eden offers. You can easily spend most of a Saturday tooling around trails on your new toy. And you will be smiling the whole way.

Some helpful hints to make your riding easier:
1) Stay in your seat while pedaling uphill as much as you can, especially when the terrain gets really steep. When you stand up off your saddle, the back tire will spin out and you might go over.
2) It is also a good idea to pick up a pair of the handle bar extenders to give you leverage on the uphills. A lot of the newer bikes come with extenders as standard equipment. You can add them to your bike for only $25.
3) On wild downhills, it is a good idea to quick-jump potholes so your front tire never gets bogged down. This takes practice.
4) On sharp turns, make sure the pedals are in a neutral position. If your left pedal is in the down position and you have to make a sharp left turn, the consequences could be ugly.
5) Learn how to shift your body weight to aid in steering. Sitting back a little bit on your saddle tends to help in balance as well. Some riders will go so far back they put their midsections behind the seat on really steep sections.
6) Never hit your front brake first or by itself when descending. This will send you flying over the handle bars so fast you won't know what hit you. Always put pressure on the back brake first, then bring in the front brake when it is needed.

Expert Riding:
Once you are so comfortable on your mountain bike that it feels like an extension of your body, you're an expert. This feeling does not come quickly, so don't be discouraged if you have not been riding that long. At this level, mountain biking becomes a part of your life instead of just recreational sport. It has gotten into your soul.

At this level, you are able to climb trails as steep as expert ski slopes, and ride down them smoothly. You may have to lock up your back brake and carry skids through the downhills when it's really steep, but try to avoid this, as it is very hard on the environment. It's quite a challenge to control your steering when there are some big obstacles, like steps, in front of you on the trail. The fun and excitement is almost indescribable.

You can also get into some big-time fun by riding at night. The headlights manufactured today are so good you will think it's noon inside the light beam in front of you. A complete set of night lights will not be cheap, but will open a new world for you. The price ranges from $150 to $250. These lights are especially great in the Winter months when it gets dark so early.

It's a special feeling to be out there on the trails at midnight with a couple of friends on a hard three-hour ride. You won't see many other people out there—it's a great way to avoid the crowds that populate regional park playgrounds on the weekends.

As with any sport you do in this area, make sure your mountain biking does not cause undue stress on the local environment. The parks of this area are a precious commodity so don't do anything to harm them.

TAKING A FALL

You'll fall as you begin to push yourself to the next level on the mountain bike learning curve. Falls tend to happen very quickly (one deep pothole can send you flying), which does not leave much time for planning. As in any sport, the key to not getting injured is to avoid falling. When you do fall, relax and use the old "tuck and roll" technique, so none of your appendages are sticking out as you hit the ground. *You should never ride without a helmet, no matter how hot and uncomfortable it gets.* Throw in some good common sense and the worst injury you'll get will be some minor scrapes that will sure hurt in the shower, but not prevent you from missing a day of riding.

RENTING MOUNTAIN BIKES

Whether you are in town visiting, or not yet completely sure this is a sport for you, it is easy to rent a mountain bike in this town. The cost will range from $15 to $20 for a half day, and run about $30 for a full day. Most of the shops that rent will credit the rental charges toward the purchase of a new bike should you decide to take the plunge.

The only concern when renting is making sure the bike is state-of-the-art, not some old clunker. Make sure the bike has good tires, modern gear and shifting components, and a strong, light frame to maximize your effort. When you rent, make sure to ask for a modern mountain bike. If you don't, your ride will not be as fun. A few of the shops that rent are listed below:

American Bicycle Rental: 2715 Hyde St., San Francisco, CA 94109; (415) 931-0234. At Fisherman's Wharf.

Park Cyclery: 1865 Haight Street, San Francisco, 94117; (415) 221-3777. Near Golden Gate Park.

Downtown Golden Bike Rental: 407 O'Farrell St., San Francisco; (415) 771-8009.

Start to Finish Bikes: *Marina area*—2530 Lombard St., at Divisdero St.; (415) 202-9830 *Golden Gate Park area:* 672 Stanyan St., at Haight St; (415) 221-7211 *Downtown area:* 599 2nd St., near Brannnan St. (415) 243-8812

Wheel Escapes: 30 Libertyship Way #210, Sausalito, CA 94965; (415) 332-0218. Located near Mt. Tam.

Trailhead Bicycle Rental: 88 Bear Valley Rd., Olema; (415) 663-1958. Located close to some great Marin County trails.

Encina Bikes: 2901 Ygnacio Valley Rd., Walnut Creek, CA 94598; (510) 944-9200. Located near Mt. Diablo.

Solano Ave. Cyclery: 1554 Solano Ave., Albany, CA; (510)524-1094.

Action Sports: 401 High Street, Palo Alto, CA 94301; (415) 328-3180. In Palo Alto for South Bay riders.

The Bay Area retail bike shops that sell mountain bikes are listed at the end of this chapter.

RULES OF THE TRAIL

Along with all the fun of mountain biking comes the responsibility of leaving the environment just the way you found it. It's easy to adhere to this by just following the **International Mountain Biking Association (IMBA)** riding guidelines. IMBA is a non-profit organization formed in 1988 in California to promote worldwide mountain biking through environmentally and socially responsible use of the land. Their address is is P.O. Box 7578, Boulder, CO 80306; (303) 545-9011. These riding guidelines are:

1) Ride on open trails only.
2) Leave no trace.
3) Control your bicycle.

4) Always yield to others ascending.
5) Never spook animals.
6) Plan ahead.

WHERE TO GO

Whether you are just starting out, or are an accomplished mountain biker, you'll find excellent trails and fire roads all over the Bay Area.

Always carry a trail map, not only so you won't get lost, but so you'll know what trails are closed to mountain biking. Over the past couple of years there has been a lot of controversy over this issue. Many of the single track trails are now closed to mountain bikers so you will have to get the majority of your fun on the fire access roads. Local trail maps will explain in detail which trails are open only to hikers, as well as give you tremendous information on elevation, distance and some history of the area you plan to ride. Maps are available at most bike shops and many book stores in the area. These maps are very reasonably priced from $5 to $8. Remember when mountain biking, you are sharing these trails with other hikers, horseback riders, and trail runners so don't bike out of control, or do anything to hurt the relationships between the groups. These parks are for everyone.

North Bay: This area encompasses everything north of the Golden Gate Bridge. Included in this mountain bike paradise are the *Marin Headlands, Mount Tamalpais area, Bolinas Ridge*, and a whole lot more. *Annandale State Park* near Santa Rosa offers excellent trails as well. You can spend years riding in this area and not begin to uncover all the trails waiting to challenge you.

East Bay: Hundreds of miles of trail await you in the many parks of this area. The climate tends to be a little hotter and dryer here, so carry plenty of water. There is exceptional riding in *Tilden* and *Wildcat Regional Parks* in Berkeley and *Briones Park* a bit north of Walnut Creek. *Mount Diablo State Park* near Walnut Creek presents a challenging ride to its 3,800-foot summit. Make sure to check out the *Coyote Hills* of Pleasanton Ridge as well. There is so much riding available around Berkeley that it supports some 14 bike shops.

Bay Area Mountain Bike Trails

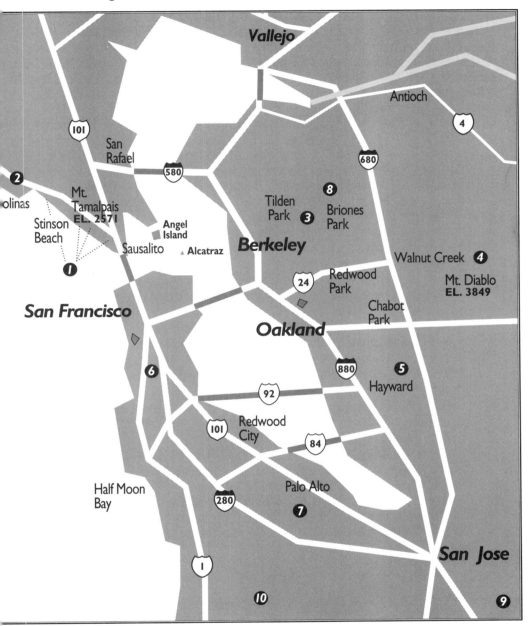

Vallejo

Antioch

101

San Rafael

580

Mt. Tamalpais
EL. 2571

Stinson Beach

Angel Island

Sausalito   ▲ Alcatraz

olinas

2

①

Tilden Park

8

Briones Park

3

Berkeley

680

Walnut Creek **4**

Mt. Diablo
EL. 3849

24 Redwood Park

Chabot Park

San Francisco

Oakland

880

5

Hayward

6

92

Redwood City

101

84

Half Moon Bay

280

Palo Alto

7

San Jose

1

10

9

① *GGNRA– Mt Tamalpais, Marin Headlands, Muir Woods*

② *Bolinas Ridge*

③ *Tilden Park & Wildcat Canyon Park*

④ *Mt. Diablo*

⑤ *Pleasanton Ridge*

⑥ *San Bruno Mountain State Park*

⑦ *Purisima Creek El Corte de Madera*

⑧ *Briones Park*

⑨ *Henry Coe Park*

⑩ *Gazos Creek*

Peninsula & South Bay: The good mountain biking starts just south of the city. The land begins to open up south of San Bruno and begins to get really good at Montara Mountain. The Woodside/Portola Valley area comes in with *Purisima Creek Preserve* and *El Corte De Madera Preserve*. Other great trails can be found in *Montebello, Los Trancos, Russian Ridge,* and *Skyline Open Spaces.*

Long Ridge, a beautiful single track for intermediate riders, is a bit further south on Skyline Blvd. There is enough riding available around the Palo Alto area to support more than 8 bicycle shops. The San Jose area offers *Henry Coe Park* for some sweet off-road riding as well.

This is just a small sampling of trails to ride in this area and does not detail the awesome mountain biking available outside the Bay Area in the Sierra Nevada mountain range near Lake Tahoe, the Santa Cruz Mountains to the South, and Sonoma Mountains to the North. Go into any mountain bike shop in the area you want to ride, and ask the workers where to go. They will point you to the that area's best trails, and maybe take you on their favorite rides.

ADDITIONAL READING

There are an abundance of very good local mountain biking books that explain the local trails and fire roads in more detail than this guide can because of space limitations. It is well-worth your time and money to invest in a few of these books. They suggest trails and detail elevations degrees of difficulty, so you can plan your bike outing for your ability. The books can be found at local bike or book stores. Some of the really good books include:

Bay Area Mountain Bike Trails, Conrad Boisver, Penngrove Publications, P.O Box 1017, Penngrove, CA 94951.

The Marin Mountain Bike Guide, Armor Todd, Wheel Escapes, 30 Libertyship Way, Sausalito, CA, 94954; (415) 332-0218.

Mt. Biking in the Bay Area, Michael Hudson & Mark Lord, Western Tanager Press, Santa Cruz, CA 95060.

Bay Area Bike Rides, Ray Hosler, Chronicle Books, 275 Fifth St., San Francisco, CA 94103.

Mt. Biking for Women, Robin Stuart & Cathy Jensen, Acorn Publishing, Waverly, NY 14892.

RACING

After you get into mountain biking, you might want to do some off-road racing as well. It is an excellent way to improve your riding skills, meet some fun people that are as crazy as you are, and seriously challenge yourself physically.

Races usually have categories for different ability levels, so don't worry if you are just starting out. Everyone starts in the *beginner* class. You move up in classes by gaining points in races; points are given depending on where you finish. Your next move up will be to the sport class, then expert, and finally to the *professional* class. You will know when you reach the pro class, because the paychecks and free equipment will start rolling in.

The races are put on and sanctioned by the **National Off Road Bicycle Association (NORBA)**. You can call for information and a schedule of races at (719) 578-4717, or write to One Olympic Plaza, Colorado Springs, CO 80909. Membership is a required to enter any NORBA race. The yearly dues are about $30 and include a subscription to *NorbaNews*. This monthly magazine will keep you informed of upcoming races as well as results of the race you might have just completed. The local racing district includes California, Nevada and Arizona, so you can have some fun traveling to the events.

An additional listing of just local races is available in the free monthly magazine *California Bicyclist.* The Northern California edition is available at any bike shop or call (415) 546-7291.

COST OVERVIEW

Cheap Budget:
A decent mountain bike will cost some money, so there is really no dirt-cheap method. You might be able to find a good used mountain bike for $300 that will get the job done. Renting bikes can cost as little as $20 for an afternoon, but if you plan to go more than a few times, it's cheaper to purchase your own bike.

Moderate Budget:
This budget bracket ranges from $500 to $1,300, and puts you on a sweet mountain bike. In the lower range you won't get front shocks and the bike will be a bit heavier; toward the high side, you get all the goodies. If you can find something used, you can get a really nice mountain bike for $400 to $700. Ask bike shop mechanics if they know of any good used bikes for sale. If you find a used bike on your own outside of the shops, get it checked out by a bike shop before you buy it.

High-End Budget:
Mountain bikes on the high end can easily cost $2,500 or more. These bikes will offer the best components, along with the lightest and strongest frames. If you really get into mountain biking and can afford one of these bikes, they are unbelievable riding machines.

Getting some air on the Mount Tamalpais fire roads.
Photo: Scott Tucker

THE MANY GREAT BICYCLE SHOPS OF THE BAY AREA

Since you'd be smart to make purchases for the sports of mountain biking and road biking in a full-fledged bicycle shop, we've included a thorough list of the many bicycle shops of this area.

There are over 120 local bike shops, which demonstrates the love Bay Area residents have for riding bikes. With the list below, you are sure to find a bike shop near your house, hotel or place of business. All of the bike shops listed carry assorted models of mountain bikes and road bikes, but they may specialize in one brand or another. It is a good idea to call to make sure the shop carries what you might be looking for.

SAN FRANCISCO

Golden Gate Park Area

Lincoln Cyclery: 772 Stanyan St., (415) 221-2415.
Park Cyclery: 1865 Haight St., (415) 221-3777.
Golden Gate Park Skates & Bikes: 3038 Fulton St., (415) 668-1117.
Start to Finish Bicycles: 672 Stanyan St., (415) 221-7211.
Presidio Bicycle Rentals: 5335 Geary Blvd., (415) 752-2453.

Avenue Cyclerly: 756 Stanyan St., (415) 387-3155.
Bike Nook Bicycles: 3004 Taraval St., (415) 731-3838.
Open Road Bicycles: 2555 Irving St., (415) 753-6272.
Mountain Avenue Bicycles: 1269 9th Ave., (415) 665-1394.
Pacific Bicycles: 4239 Geary Blvd., (415) 666-3377.
Fog City Cycles: 3430 Geary Blvd., (415) 221-3031.
Nomad Cyclery: 2301 Irving St., (415) 564-3568.
Nomad Cyclery: 1915 Ocean Ave., (415) 239-5004.
San Francisco Cyclery: 858 Stanyan St., (415) 221-2412.
Balboa Cyclery: 4049 Balboa Ave., (415) 752-7980.

Pacific Heights & Marina Area

City Cyclery: 3001 Steiner St., (415) 346-2242.
Marina Cyclery: 3330 Steiner St., (415) 929-7135.
Start To Finish: 2539 Lombard St., (415) 202-9830.

Downtown, Noe Valley, Fisherman's Wharf, & Mission Area

Bay Area Cyclery: 4537 Mission St., (415) 585-7480.
Noe Valley Cyclery: 4193 24th Ave., (415) 647-0886.
Start To Finish: 599 2nd St., (415) 243-8812.
Pacific Bicycles: 1161 Sutter St., (415) 928-8466.
Downtown Golden Bike Rental: 407 O'Farrell St., (415) 771-8009.
American Bicycle Rental: 2715 Hyde St., (415) 931-0234.

MARIN COUNTY

Sausalito Cyclery: #1 Gate 6 Rd., Sausalito, (415) 332-3200.
Bicycle Odyssey: 1417 Bridgeway, Sausalito, (415) 332-3050.
Mill Valley Cyclery: 369 Miller Ave., Mill Valley, (415) 388-6774.
Start to Finish: 116 Throckmorton Ave., Mill Valley, (415) 388-3500.
Village Peddler: 1161 Magnolia Ave., Larkspur, (415) 461-3091.
Any Mountain: 71 Tamal Vista, Corte Madera, (415) 927-0170.
Performance Bicycles: 369 3rd St., San Rafael, (415) 454-9063.
Fargo Bike Shop: 194 Northgate One, San Rafael, (415) 472-0253.
Marin Mt. Bikes: 16 Mary St., San Rafael, (415) 485-5100.
Mike's Bicycle Shop: 1601 4th St., San Rafael, (415) 454-3747.
Start To Finish: 1820 4th St., San Rafael, (415) 459-3990.
Pacific Bicycles: 275 Greenfield Ave., San Anselmo, (415) 457-9775.
Ceasar's Cyclery: 29 San Anselmo Ave., San Anselmo, (415) 258-9920.
The Bike Doctor: 5633 Paradise Dr., Corte Madera, (415) 924-6644.
Fargo Bike Shop: 175 San Marin Dr., Novato, (415) 897-0252.
Class Cycle: 1531 B South Novato Blvd., Novato, (415) 897-3288.
The Bike Hut: 459 Entrada Dr., Novato, (415) 883-2440.
Novato Cyclery: 1111 Grant Ave., Novato, (415) 892-5538.
Trailhead Bicycle Rentals: 88 Bear Valley Rd., Olema, (415) 663-1958.
Sunshine Bicycles: 737 Center Blvd., Fairfax, (415) 459-3334.
Otis Guy Cycles: 115 Ridge Rd., Fairfax, (415) 456-4132.
Sprockets Bicycle Repair: Mobile Bike Repair. Out of Fairfax, (415) 453-8682.
The Fat Tire Trading Post: 28 Bolinas Rd., Fairfax, (415) 258-9120.

EAST BAY

Carl's Bikes: 2416 Telegraph, Berkeley, (510) 835-8763.
Troy's Bikes: 5292 College Ave., Berkeley, (510) 658-6491.
Berkeley Bike Doctors: 1814 Euclid Ave., Berkeley, (510) 843-1427.
Square Wheels Bikes: 2135 University Ave., Berkeley, (510) 549-8350.
Velo Sport: 1650 Martin Luther King, Berkeley, (510) 849-0437.
The Bent Spoke: 6124 Telegraph Ave., Berkeley, (510) 652-3089.
Berkeley Cycles: 2114 Center Ave., Berkeley, (510) 845-7560.
Pacific Bicycles: 2701 College Ave., Berkeley, (510) 644-3751.
Karim Cyclery: 2801 Telegraph Ave., Berkeley, (510) 841-2181.
REI: 1338 San Pablo Ave., Berkeley, (510) 527-4140.
Missing Link Bike Shop: 1988 Shattuck, Berkeley, (510) 843-7471.
Hank & Frank Bicycles: 6030 College Ave., Oakland, (510) 658-1177.
Pioneer Bike Shop: 11 Rio Vista Ave., Oakland, (510) 658-8981.
Cycle Sports: 3241 Grand Ave., Oakland, (510) 444-7900.
Cycle Depot: 106 East 14th, Oakland, (510) 451-6245.
Alameda Bicycle: 1522 Park Ave., Alameda, (510) 522-0070.
Stone's Cyclery: 2320 Santa Clara Ave., Alameda, (510) 523-3264.
Cycle Sports: 2238 South Shore Center, Alameda, (510) 521-2872.
Encina Bicycle Center: 2901 Ygnacio Valley Rd., Walnut Creek, (510) 944-9200.
Diablo Bike: 2040 Mt. Diablo Blvd., Walnut Creek, (510) 932-2323.
Bicycle Connection: 554 Center Ave., Moraga, (510) 376-6060.
Concord Cycle Center: 3569 Clayton Rd., Concord, (510) 825-6666.
Clayton Valley Bike Center: 5411 Clayton Rd., Concord, (510) 672-0912.
California Peddler: 495 Hartz Ave., Danville, (510) 820-0345.
Danville Bike: 115 Hartz Ave., Danville, (510) 837-0966.
Lafayette Cyclework's Inc.: 3422 Mt. Diablo Blvd., Lafayette, (510) 284-1700.
John's Bicycle: 2836 Clayton Rd., Concord, (510) 798-8483.
F&M Cyclery: 37120 Freemont Blvd., Freemont, (510) 793-0566.
California Bike & Snowboard: 1469 Danville Blvd., Alamo, (510) 743-1249.
Witt's Bicycles Shop: 22125 Mission Blvd., Hayward, (510) 538-8771.
Dublin Cyclery: 7001 Dublin Blvd., Dublin, (510) 828-8676.
Solano Ave Cyclery: 1554 Solano Ave., Albany, (510) 524-1094.
El Cerrito Cyclery: 10400 San Pablo Ave., El Cerrito, (510) 524-8810.
M&J Bicycle Shop: 16884 East 14th, San Leandro, (510) 276-1132.
Robinson Bicycle Wheel Works: 1235 MacArthur., San Leandro, (510) 352-4663.
Cycle Depot: 471 East 14th, San Leandro, (510) 633-2453.
Contra Costa Cyclery: 2263 Contra Costa Blvd., Pleasant Hill, (510) 676-2666.
Orinda Spoke & Pedal: 17 Orinda Way, Orinda, (510) 254-1575.
Montclair Sports: 1969 Mountain Blvd., Montclair, (510) 339-6091.
Martinez Cyclery: 4990 Pacheco Blvd., Martinez, (510) 228-9050.
Danville Cal. Pedaler: 495 Hartz Ave., Danville, (510) 820-0345.
Danville Bike: 115 Hartz Ave., Danville, (510) 837-0966.
Sharp Bicycles: 2800 Hilltop Mall Rd., Richmond, (510) 222-8004.

Any Mountain: 490 Market Place, San Ramon, (510) 275-1010.
STD Cycle: 2550 San Ramon Valley Blvd., San Ramon, (510) 820-2998.
El Sobrante Schwinn Cyclery: 5057 El Portal Dr., El Sobrante, (510) 223-3440.
Cal Bicycles: 2106 1st St., Livermore, (510) 447-6666.
Livermore Cyclery: 2288 1st St., Livermore, (510) 455-8090.
CyclePath Cyclery: 22510 Foothill Blvd., Hayward, (510) 881-5177.
Pleasanton Bicycle Works: 525 Main St., Pleasanton, (510) 462-9777.

PENINSULA

Broadmoor Bike Shop: 150 San Pedro Rd., Daly City, (415) 756-1120.
Foster City Cyclery: 999 Edgewater Blvd., Foster City, (415) 349-2010.
Beach Park Bicycles: 1485 Beach Park Blvd., Foster City, (415) 349-1551.
The Bicycle Shop: 330 Grand Ave. South San Francisco, (415) 588-5111.
Cyclepath of San Mateo: 1212 S. El Camino, San Mateo, (415) 341-0922.
The Bike Doctor: mobile for house calls, (415) 327-0171.
Burlingame Cyclery: 1111 Burlingame Ave., Burlingame, (415) 343-8483.
California Sports: 1464 El Camino Real, Belmont, (415) 593-8806.
Performance Bicycle Shop: 2535 El Cam. Real, Redwood City, (415) 365-9094.
Pacific Bicycles: 665 El Camino Real, Redwood City, (415) 367-6094.
Redwood Cyclery: 1005 El Camino Real, Redwood City, (415) 364-6694.
Chain Reaction Bicycles: 1451 El Cam. Real, Redwood City, (415) 366-7130.
Any Mountain: 928 Whipple Ave., Redwood City, (415) 361-1213.
Menlo Velo Bicycles: 33 El Camino Real, Menlo Park, (415) 327-5137.
The Broken Spoke ReCyclery: 619 Laurel St., San Carlos, (415) 594-9210.
The Bicycle Warehouse: 428 S. Airport Blvd., S. San Francisco, (415) 588-1714.
Niles Bike Shop: 37469 Niles Blvd., Fremont, (510) 793-9141.
A Bicyclery in Half Moon Bay: 432 Main St., Half Moon Bay, (415) 726-6000.
Bike Route Inc.: 488 San Mateo Ave, San Bruno, (415) 873-9555.
The Bicycle Outfitter: 963 Freemont Ave, Los Altos, (415) 948-8092.
Action Sports: 401 High St., Palo Alto, (415) 328-3180.
Wheelsmith: 201 Hamilton Ave. Palo Alto, (415) 324-0510.
Garner's Pro Bike Shop: 3413 Alma Rd., Palo Alto, (415) 856-2088.
The Bike Connection: 2086 El Camino Real, Palo Alto, (415) 424-8034.
Campus Bike Shop: 551 Salvatlierra at Stanford Univ., (415) 325-2945.
Recyclery Bike Shop: 1955 El Camino Real, Palo Alto, (415) 328-8900.
Palo Alto Bicycles: 171 University Ave., Palo Alto, (415) 462-1127.
Klemens Bicycles: 3728 Carlson Circle, Palo Alto, (415) 813-9107.
Midtown Bike Shop: 2635 Middlefield Rd., Palo Alto, (415) 322-7558.

CHAPTER TEN

Road Bike

Season: All year long.
Learning Curve: Easy, if you know how to ride a bike.

If you haven't been on a road bike in awhile, you are in for a big treat. Today's productions road bicycles are lighter and stronger than you used to ride. And this makes them damn fast and high performance.

Road bikes on the market today are pounds lighter than those of only a few years ago—and the lighter the bike the faster you go. Technology continues to improve every aspect of the road bike, from the design, wheels, tires, components, and even the comfort of the seat. The newer form-fitting handlebars will make you a more aerodynamic rider. The shoe-binding systems will lock you into your pedals for better spinning ability, yet still provide the safety of being able to get out of them quickly. The components and materials that make up the gears, shifting systems, wheels and chain are vastly improved as well. All these improvements mean faster, smoother and more responsive road riding.

Though a new road bike can really fly, it is still driven by human power and there is no secret for getting in good shape to ride well. The only way to achieve that is by spending a lot of time in the seat putting in the miles.

The Bay Area offers hundreds upon hundreds of miles of smooth, uncrowded, beautifully paved roads to ride on. As you cruise, you will be able to take in gorgeous scenery. Road biking is great alone, with a friend, or with a local bike club (so you can draft off others). A list of the local clubs follows.

Road biking will also give you some great thrills—hitting 50 mph on a local downhill is tough to beat. Cranking down mile after mile of a beautiful stretch of road, in sync with your bike, is a feeling that every adventure athlete will cherish. Give it a try.

THE EQUIPMENT & COSTS

The Bike:

The first job is to go find yourself a road bike that fits. One of the worst mistakes you can make is to ride a bike that doesn't fit your body size. You will wind up with a bad back and maybe a knee surgery as well. To get the best fit, stop by a bicycle shop and talk with one of the shop workers. These people love to talk about bicycles—just stopping by to check out a line of improved road bikes and products can be fun. Explain your lack of knowledge about road biking and ask what frame size would be right for you. After a quick leg measurement, you'll know what size would fit you, and you can take your time finding the bike that's best for you and your budget.

Great downhill awaits in the Marin Headlands
Photo: R. Blick

Unfortunately, there is no rental market for road bikes, so you will probably have to buy a new one. This lack means you won't being able to rent and ride many different types before buying. There is a used market for road bikes, but it's not very large one because people tend to keep their older bikes for rainy days or sell them to friends. It is worth checking the local newspaper classifieds though if you are set on a used one.

Some of the local bike shops sponsor swap meets. These can be an excellent way to locate good used bikes. Check the monthly *California Bicyclist* magazine for swap dates and locations. This monthly publication is available free at any local bike shop and is great for announcements on swap meets, interesting bike articles, race schedules and classifieds. If you happen to find a used bike, it would be wise to bring it by a bike shop to have it checked out for you before you buy. The shop mechanics can usually tell you what it is worth and if the frame is too old or blown out.

Basically, road bikes fall into two main categories. The touring road bike comes with wider tires and a regular air valve (like that on your car tire). These bikes are very durable and good for touring, but they are on the heavy side (27 to 30 pounds). This means they are kind of slow and not as responsive as the racing bikes. Touring bikes are perfect for riding around Europe or the countryside, and you can carry a lot of luggage in saddlebags if you want to take a long bicycling trip. But the heavier frame, cheaper components and wider wheels limit speed and performance. These touring bikes are usually less expensive than the racing bikes, so they'll look like a good deal in the bike store. Just be aware they are not as much fun to ride. The price of a new touring bike will range from $199 to $450.

But if you want to fly down the road, you have to step up and get a racing road bike. It will open up the roads for you. You almost feel like you are test-driving a sports car when you first try one.

The bike usually weighs only 19 to 23 pounds (the frame is five to seven of those pounds), and they come with thinner, more performance-oriented tires that have special Presto valves, so you can't fill your tires with air at the local gas station. What these racing bikes lack in convenience they make up for in performance. You can easily hit 25 mph on the flat roads, and 40 to 50 mph on the downhills. Uphill riding is tough on any bike, but it is sure easier on these sleek racing machines.

A road bike will not be cheap, but the thrills will be worth it. For $500 to $700 you can get a pretty decent road bike that will last years. The cheaper ones work, but do not have the same performance of these bikes. On the higher end, racing road bikes can cost $2,800 or more. It all depends on your budget and how far into road biking you want to get. The higher end bikes have the latest technological advances and the strongest and lightest components. These bikes are beautiful, but unless you plan on becoming a pretty high-level road bike racer, the money might be better spent on something else.

The Frame:
Finding the right bike frame is a major part of the road-bike puzzle. Think long and hard before you decide which frame you want—this is the one piece that can't be replaced easily, or cheaply. Components, wheels, tires and the seat can be changed any time you want, but most bikers only have one frame.

Make sure the frame fits. The technological advances of these bike frames have been spectacular. In the last ten years, research and development think tanks have taken pounds of the weight off frames while at the same time making them stronger. They can be made of double-butted steel chrome molybdenum, aluminum, graphite or combinations of all three. Bike manufacturers also have discovered efficient ways to mass-produce bike frames, which has brought the costs down for all of us and made road biking accessible to everyone. The frame of a good road production bike in the $1,000 price range will weigh about four pounds. The complete bike will weigh 20 to 23 pounds. Less-expensive bikes will be considerably heavier.

Components:

Road bike components are sold in a "gruppo" package, which includes a complete set for each bike. The road bike market has three primary component manufacturers: Campagnolo from Italy, and Shimano and Suntour from Japan. Each maker has a line of components for every bike price level. The components on the high-end are the lightest and strongest, while components in the lower price range are heavier and will probably break down sooner. On road bikes in the $500 to $1,000 range, there are some really nice components. Only a serious bike racer will be able to appreciate the most expensive components. If you ever need to upgrade your components, or to replace some, these gruppos are available at most local bike shops.

Unfortunately, after you locate the perfect racing bike for you and your budget, you are not quite done spending money. To ride these sleek machines you will need a pair of bicycle shoes. You have two main choices. The older style works with cleated shoes that fit onto the pedal. You use them with toe clips. This is the less expensive way to go, but you give up some performance because your foot will still move around some, and you will have to reach down to adjust them all the time. You also have to remember to loosen the toe clip to get your foot out when you stop. Needless to say, this is a pain, especially when you have to make emergency stops and you wind up crashing because your timing is off. This toe clip-and-cleated shoe method costs between $50 and $70.

There is a better alternative. The newer bike technology has developed a shoe binding system that offers more performance and safety. With this system, your flat pedals are replaced by binding pedals, and the shoes lock in place. You simply step in, lock in, and you are off. To get out of them, you simply turn your foot hard to one side or the other, and the binding will release. This system works beautifully, but comes at a price. The complete set-up will run somewhere between $100 and $150. This system also means you can't ride the bike without the correct shoes—no jumping on your bike to ride to the store barefoot. But if you can afford it, you should get a shoe binding system. The added riding performance is well worth it.

Additional Equipment:

Now all you need is a bike pump, flat tire repair kit, water bottle, bike pants with the padded seat cushion so you can go on long rides, and a pair of bike gloves. This package will run you $90 or more, depending on the quality of the equipment you choose.

To get totally set up in the sport of road biking, with a new bicycle and all the necessary equipment, will cost from $600 on the low end, and up to $1,200 for a better bike and upgraded extras. The good news is that after the initial expenditures, the sport is totally free. As the dough rolls in you can buy some extra accessories, like a riding jersey, a bike computer that records distance, time, etc., and a whole lot of options to make your riding more enjoyable. This stuff will start to add up, but to justify the cost, you can always commute to work on the bike. You'll get in shape and save money on commuting costs.

Well, enough about the equipment. Now that you are probably busted broke, let's go ride.

THE LEARNING CURVE

Beginning Riding:
Before you start riding, make sure the bike is correctly fitted for you. You can do this at a qualified bike shop for about $25. Or you can get it done free if you have a friend that is a serious road biker.

This fitting includes the seat and handlebar height adjustments, shoe cleat or binding system fitting, and numerous other adjustments to the brakes, gears, and derailleur. Lastly, make sure the air pressure in the tires is correct. Resist the temptation to eyeball these adjustments, because you will regret it when your legs or back start to cramp up early in the ride.

Your first ride will be a little scary, because your feet will be locked into a performance machine that accelerates like a sports car and turns on a dime. Don't be intimidated. It is just a bicycle and you have been riding bikes since you were a little kid. The principles are the same. After a few miles you will begin to get the feel of your bike and to really enjoy the ride.

The correct body position on the flats is to have your arms slightly bent to absorb any bumps. Your head should be forward and down for better aerodynamics (less wind resistance). Your legs should be spinning (going around) at about 80 to 90 revolutions per minute.

Spinning is the most important aspect of road bike riding. Once you learn how to spin, you are no longer a hacker, but a real bike rider. The concept behind spinning is to maintain a steady pace of revolutions per minute no matter what the terrain. The steady pace is maintained by using your front and rear leg muscles equally during the pedaling process, which also prevents the overuse of one group of muscles and fatigue. Of course, your down stroke will always be the strongest, but the key is to pull up on the back stroke as well. This simple exercise will get you spinning.

The different gears on the bicycle are used to facilitate spinning. When you approach a hill, gear down to maintain the steady 80 to 90 revolutions per minute. If the hill steepness increases, keep gearing down till you run out of gears. If you are on the lowest gear and the hill still seems too steep, you have to gut it out. It helps to always be in a smaller gear than necessary before approaching a hill.

If the pedaling gets too easy gear back up. On the downhills, change to higher gears as you pick up speed, to keep the revolutions in the 80 to 90 range. When the road is flat, gear up when you want to pick up the pace, always trying to stay at 80 to 90 revolutions. This is a very simplistic explanation of spinning but it gets the point across. As you practice and develop this technique, you will understand how to use your gears better, and you'll become a better road bike rider.

As far as determining the stroke count while you are riding, there are some alternatives. The real nice way is to buy a new chronometers that, once installed on your bike, will tell you stroke count, bike speed, and number of miles ridden. These electronic wonders cost about $50 and are well worth it if your budget allows. If not, count each time your right foot reaches the apex of the spin as you pedal. Count for 15 seconds, then multiply that number by four. That is your strokes (revolutions) per minute. You hope to get 20 to 22 strokes every 15 seconds.

Once you become proficient at spinning, the whole sport of bicycling will become much more enjoyable. You will be able to ride faster, more efficiently and for longer periods of time. In other words, you'll be hauling butt on your bike and getting in great shape.

This ought to be enough technical jargon for you to think about for awhile. Don't be frustrated if, and when, you make mistakes in spinning. Just keep riding. Occasionally you will get caught in the totally wrong gear. When this happens on the uphills you will grind to an almost complete stop and may even fall over. When you are in too low a gear on the downhills, your legs will be spinning so fast (probably 120 or more revolutions per minute) that you will feel like you're about to disengage from your bike and fly away. As frustrating as it can be to learn spinning, don't quit trying and go back to a hammer pedaling stroke. You will never get good at road biking till you give that up. Use your gears effectively and practice till spinning becomes automatic, and it will become fun.

The other important part of the learning curve is turning. Since your vehicle has only two wheels, turning is primarily accomplished by leaning. At slow speeds, you have to turn the handlebars to accomplish turns. As you begin to pick up speed, leaning becomes more and more important. At higher speeds, you'll actually turn the handlebars less and less.

As you approach a turn, you have to know when to stop pedaling and keep your inside pedal up. Always enter a turn with your inside pedal in the 12 o'clock position and the outside pedal at 6 o'clock. This allows you to weight the outside leg and ensures you won't hit the inside pedal on the asphalt. Improper position means the pedal will scrape along the ground as you lean into your turn. This mistake can cause ugly accidents. On long gradual turns, it might be possible to pedal through the whole turn, but if you attempt this on a sharp turn, your pedal will hit the ground hard on the down stroke about halfway into the curve.

Use common sense and don't ride into turns at uncontrollable speeds. You actually want to start hitting the brakes before the turn and ease off as you go into the turn. This will keep your speed up as you pedal out of it and give you control all way through. As you ride more and more, leaning and pedal control will become almost second nature.

The last area of the road biking learning curve is braking. As you probably are well aware, bicycles come with a front and back brake. The key to understanding bike braking is to learn the correct "touch" when applying them. You want to apply enough pressure to slow you down, but not so much as to lock them up. Locking up the brakes will lead to skidding tires and you will probably lose control of the bike. Your goal is to apply pressure equally to the front and back brake, touching the back brake first a split second before the front one. Don't ever just apply the front brake, especially at high speeds. This action is usually followed by a free space flight over the handle bars and a crash landing when the front tire stops on a dime and you don't. Remember to apply equal pressure to both brakes, and you should have no problems.

Improved Riding:
Once you get into this great sport—and it will prove addicting—your riding will quickly elevate to new levels. You will want to learn more and more about road biking.

The first thing to master is the gears. By now, the elementary method that numbers the gears from low to high will not be specific enough for you, because there are many different sizes available for both the chainring, where your pedals are attached, and the freewheel on the rear wheel of the bike. To understand the gearing system on bicycles, simply count the number of teeth on the two big gears. Most road bikes come with 52 teeth on the big (high gear) chain ring, and 42 teeth on the smaller (low) one. The rear sprocket (freewheel) comes with a few more gear rings. Count the teeth on each one and jot the number down. On the rear sprocket, the higher the number the lower the gear.

On most production road bikes, rear sprockets come with a teeth arrangement of 14, 16, 18, 21, 24, and 28, but don't assume this. Now, you have to recognize which gear you are in while riding. For instance, 52 x 14 means you are on the largest chain wheel and the smallest gear on the sprocket. This is your bike's highest gear, and is reserved for serious speed. If you were in the 42 x 28 gear, it would be the lowest gear. This gear is reserved for climbing steep hills.

The reason this gear discussion is so important is because it will both help you train, and enable you to ride in the San Francisco Bay Area which offers the hilliest city on this planet. Road biking in the Bay Area means learning to handle hills. If you plan to ride in a very hilly area a lot, you might want to change your rear sprocket cluster to one that will give you even lower gears. Talk to the mechanic at a bike shop you like. This rear cluster can include rings with as many as 34 teeth. This change would make hill climbing a lot easier. If you are buying a brand new bike and you know you will be riding in a lot of hills, you might want to negotiate a change in the rear sprocket as part of your deal. This will save you money, because you won't have to go back to the shop complaining about the cardiac pain you've been experiencing on training rides, and then paying to change the sprocket. But don't get caught up in this gear thing too much. Being in better shape will usually allow you to ride a higher gear through the hills.

Another important aspect of improved riding is drafting. This is the fine art of letting the bike rider in front of you do most of the work.

If you watch any group of riders, whether they are in a race or just out for a training ride, you will notice that the poor rider out in front is doing all the work and everyone else is cruising along right behind them. The riders in the rear are drafting and it's something you should learn.

The front rider breaks down the wind resistance that can drive a solo bike rider crazy, and the rear riders take advantage of that break in the wind. On training rides, you will have to take your turn at the front of the pack, although this is not an exact science and can lead to heated arguments if one rider feels he/she has done too much of the work.

Be careful though. There is a learning curve to drafting. Make sure you have at least two fingers on the brake (without pressure) at all times while drafting. This way, you are ready to hit the brakes if you get too close to the forward biker. In the beginning, most novice riders sit 10 feet or more behind the forward bike. because they are afraid of being too close. Riding this far back does not help very much against the wind. As you get more comfortable on your bike, and are more confident in your friend in front, the gap will begin to narrow. Expert riders ride 12 inches or less from the back wheel of the rider they are drafting. This saves much more effort and energy.

Needless to say, you cannot space out when drafting. The consequences can be pretty ugly if you're not paying attention and can cause a crash. Concentration on the task at hand is the key to successful drafting. Always leave yourself an out as well, in case the forward biker has to hit the brakes. We have seen a whole column of riders go down when the lead rider had to hit the brakes to avoid an animal crossing the road, and the riders behind weren't concentrating. As long as you stay aware and leave yourself the ability to steer away, you can avoid accidents.

Drafting will let you go on longer rides, because you won't be fighting headwinds all the time. It's also good to learn if you want to get into racing some day. Road bike racing is all about drafting and positioning.

Another helpful hint is to get out of the saddle when riding uphill. This will give you a boost of energy and stretch out your muscles. As you probably can figure out, riding uphill separates the riders in good shape from those in mediocre and poor shape. Also on long downhills, it is helpful to sit back on your saddle. This will stretch out your body and keep your center of gravity lower, which helps reduce wind resistance. Make sure you always ride in control, and wear a bike helmet at all times because accidents can happen easier as speeds increase.

TAKING FALLS

There is little doubt that at some point you will go down and kiss the pavement on your road bike. This is why you always wear your helmet. It will happen so fast you won't have time to protect yourself. The key to not getting hurt in a fall is to relax and tuck and roll. As long as you are wearing bike pants and a shirt to protect your skin, a fall will look a lot worse than it is.

On almost every fall, you will just skip along the road and be fine. A good pair of bike shorts goes a long way in saving your skin from serious road rash. You can usually clean yourself up and be riding within a minute or two. The most common locations for road rash from the fall are along your hip and elbow. These patches will sure hurt in the shower, and the scar will give you something to show off to your friends, but they should not stop you from going out on a ride the next day. To make sure you never get anything worse than simple road rash, do not take unnecessary risks when riding.

WHERE TO GO

The Bay Area has many classic road bike rides. These rides are challenging, scenic, fast and fun. Just jump on any road that looks good to you and get out there pedaling.

Every town in this area has some desolate, nicely paved roads that are just waiting to be ridden. You will notice that some of the best road biking is in the same general areas as the best mountain biking. Don't be alarmed. You'll be riding different surfaces, and there is plenty of room for everyone. All the San Francisco Bay Area parks have beautiful maintained paved roads for road biking. It is a totally different experience to road bike an area you might have mountain-biked last weekend.

Do your best to stay off the roads with heavy car traffic, because they won't be much fun to bike on. There is no sense tempting fate with an accident, because many times, the drivers of cars will not see you. Always stay as close to the right shoulder as you can. Also, watch for clueless automobile drivers that open their car doors right in front of you after they park, or even worse, make a right turn into your lane. It is a good idea to wear brightly colored clothing, or even a day-glo vest, so you can be seen. Also, carry a map of the area you are riding in, just in case you get lost.

Listed below are some classic roads to ride while you are looking for your own favorites:

San Francisco: You will find some really nice riding throughout *Golden Gate Park,* on the *Great Highway,* in the *Presidio,* and along the *Marina Green.* Be very aware of automobiles, delivery trucks, pedestrians, traffic lights and other bikers. Also, keep a keen watch out for potholes, cable car tracks and crazy tourists buses. Remember you are in a crowded city. The popularity of road biking is so strong in this area that the city of San Francisco supports more than 28 specialty bike shops. It's no wonder why. Cruising the city streets with the Golden Gate Bridge in the backround offers spectacular rides. Areas just a bit south of the city offer for some good riding as well as the roads are less congested.

North Bay: Once you get out of the city, the roads start to open up and get less crowded, which is what you should be looking for. The area north of the city offers some classic road biking. Just a few highlights include biking the beautiful roads in the *Marin Headlands, Mount Tam State Park, Golden Gate National Recreation Area, Muir Woods* and *Paradise Loop* in Tiburon.

U.S. Route 1 out to Stinson Beach is a nice ride, and you can pedal all the way to Point Reyes if you're in good shape. Head a little farther north to even more great road biking throughout Napa and Sonoma Counties. This spectacular area includes excellent riding around Bodega, Healdsburg, Guerneville, Sebastopol, and St. Helena.

Peninsula & South Bay: The area directly south of the city offers exceptional road biking. Some of the highlights include U.S. Rt. 1 South down the coast through Pacifica, and all the way to Half Moon Bay if you've got the legs. *San Bruno Mountain* offers great riding as well. A bit further south is the beautiful *Pescadero Road.* There are also nicely paved roads outside Hillsborough, Woodside, in the Los Altos hills, and in Portola Valley that stretch all the way to the beaches of the Pacific Ocean.

More awesome riding awaits on the roads that take you through the *Santa Cruz Mountains,* and in the many state and county parks that fill this area. Closer to San Jose, there is great road riding in the *Mount Hamilton* area.

East Bay: This area comes in with miles upon miles of great road biking. Some highlights include the ride up the *Mount Diablo Summit Road* and a cruise around the *Black Hills. Diablo Park* is located just east of Walnut Creek. The Berkeley hills surrounding *Tilden Park* have some great roads, as does *Briones Regional Park,* which borders Orinda and Pleasant Hill.

More great rides can be found in Livermore, in the *Del Valle* and *Sunol Recreational Areas,* and the *Lafayette Recreational Area.* There are some 47 specialty bike shops in the East Bay to serve local riders.

Bay Area Road Bike Roads

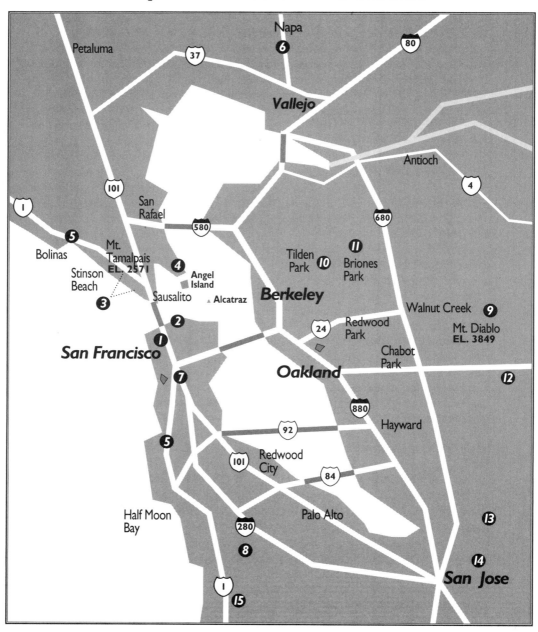

① Golden Gate Park
② Presidio & Marina Green
③ GGNRA—Mt. Tamalpais, Marin Headlands
④ Tiburon Area
⑤ Route 1 North & South
⑥ Napa County Area

⑦ San Bruno Mountain
⑧ Woodside & Portola Valley Area
⑨ Mt. Diablo Area
⑩ Berkeley—Tilden Park
⑪ Briones Park

⑫ Livermore Area—Del Valle Recreational Area
⑬ Sunol Wilderness
⑭ Mt. Hamilton
⑮ Pescadero Road

ADDITIONAL READING

There are some excellent books about road biking in this area. These books go into more detail on individual rides throughout the different parts of the Bay Area. They are usually available at local bike shops and book stores. Some of the best include:

Roads to Ride, Grant Peterson & Mary Anderson, Heydey Books, Berkeley, CA 94709.

S.F. Peninsula Bike Trails and East Bay Bike Trails, Conrad Boisvert, Penngrove Publications, Penngrove, CA 94951.

Sonoma County Bike Trails, Phyllis Neumann, Penngrove Publications, Penngrove, CA 94951.

The Pacific Coast Bicycle Trail, Bill Paul, Bittersweet Publications, Livermore, CA.94550.

Bay Area Bike Rides (Road & Mountain Bike Rides), Ray Hosler, Chronicle Books, 275 Fifth St., San Francisco, CA 94103.

The monthly magazines that serve the local road biking scene are also very good, offering a schedule of events and advertisements from the local shops. *California Bicyclist* and *CitySports* are available free at all bike stores.

RIDING CLUBS

Joining a road bike club can be a really good way to improve your road biking skills quickly. The clubs usually meet for Saturday morning rides, as well as offer great coaching and training advise to members.

Most clubs split the riders into groups with similar riding abilities, so don't be afraid to sign up because you're not an expert yet. There are more than one hundred bicycle clubs in the Bay Area. The best place to start is to ask at your local bike shop for information. The store probably has a club itself for you to join. If not, the shop will know of a club that offers just what you are looking for.

A complete list of weekly rides is available in *California Bicyclist* magazine. This publication is available free at any bike shop or health club in this area.

Some of the local clubs include:

Golden Gate Cyclist: (415) 788-2525. This group helps stage the San Francisco Great Bicycle Adventure, which attracts more than 10,000 bicyclists every year.

Berkeley Bicycle Club: (510) 540-6951. This club holds weekly rides and races as well.

Chain Reaction Cyclists: (415) 366-7130. These cyclists sponsor rides throughout Peninsula.

Diablo Cyclist: (510) 687-8370. The group holds rides throughout the East Bay.

Sierra Club: (510) 465-2193. This club holds weekly rides.

UCSF Cycle Club: (415) 476-0356. The cyclists sponsor weekly training rides in near Lake Merced or over the Golden Gate Bridge.

Valley Spokesmen: (510) 455-0558. The spokesmen offer weekly rides for all levels in Livermore.

Golden Gate Triathlon Club: (415) 434-4482. This group holds weekly rides in San Francisco.

RIDING CLINICS & SEMINARS

Many local bike shops will sponsor instructional clinics on road bike maintenance and repairs, riding skills and racing, and present guest pro riders when they are in town. The cost of these clinics range from $10 for a two-hour seminar to $950 for a complete five-day race clinic.

If you have the time, money and interest, the clinics are really worthwhile. There are clinics available for all ability groups, as well as women-only seminars in case you don't want to attend a co-ed clinic. All clinics and seminars are designed to make even a novice with the jitters feel welcome. Just taking the maintenance class alone will save you money, because you will be able to repair your own bike rather than paying the local shop to do basic maintenance. A schedule of helpful clinics appears in *California Bicyclist* magazine every month.

BICYCLE TOURING

There are a number of national, as well as local, companies specializing in weekend and week-long bicycles tours throughout the United States, Europe and beyond. The Napa Valley, Mendocino and a few other Bay Area locations are popular packages offered by active travel companies.

Taking a trip will be great for your biking progress, and more importantly, will be a great vacation. The company supplies everything—all you do is pedal. A listing of these companies can be found in any national bicycling magazine, usually in the travel directories in the back pages.

One of the best companies is located right here in Berkeley. The company, **Backroads**, can be reached at 1(800) 462-2848, or write to 1516 5th Street, Berkeley, CA 94710. The **Monterey area** offers Europeds, 761 Lighthouse Ave., Monterey, CA 93940l; 1(800) 321-9552.

RACING

The local road bike racing scene really falls into several different categories.

There are the fun century rides, low-key events that are generally 100 miles in length, although most organizers offer 25- and 50-mile options for less-experienced riders. Centuries are really fun; everyone is encouraged to finish and the overall winner is of secondary importance. Most of these events occur in beautiful countryside settings that will take your mind off of pedaling for 100 miles. These are good events to build up to as you start

Racers coming out a sharp turn in the Sausalito Criterium.
Photo: R. Blick

training. There are many centuries to chose from; they are held throughout the Bay Area and one is scheduled almost every weekend. A complete listing is available in *CitySports* and *California Bicyclist* magazines every month.

The second type of event is for the more serious competitor. This real road bike racing is under the jurisdiction of the U.S. Cycling Federation (USCF). The racing season runs from February till September, with races scheduled for almost every weekend. Women and men race separately and there are different age groups. There are usually juniors (under age 18), seniors (18-30), and the masters (over 30) classifications. The age groups are further broken down by ability. Everyone starts out racing in the beginner class, and moves up as they get better. You gain points by placing well in races, and the points enable you to move up to the next level. The competition gets harder and harder. Professional road bike races are in their own class, and you can only apply for a pro license after achieving the Class 1 category.

The breakdown of the classes at the amateur level are:
Class 1 Elite National caliber amateurs one step from professional riders.
Class 2 Expert Great riders that must work full-time, or ex-pro riders.
Class 3 Sport Really good riders on the way up.
Class 4 Novice Better riders than you might think.
Class 5 Beginner Where everyone must start out.

Some races offer a **citizen** class, which is for people who have never raced before. This class allows you to get the feel of a race without having to join the USCF or get your racing license. A racing license is required for all other classes of racers.

The USCF yearly dues run about $32 and allow you to race all you want. For about $10 extra, you can receive the USCF monthly newsletter, which will keep you informed of upcoming races, results and any other important developments in the world of road biking. For information, contact the **USCF** at One Olympic Plaza, Colorado Springs, CO 80909; (719) 578-4581. The federation divides the country into different racing regions; District 1 encompasses California and Nevada. **The Northern California/Nevada Cycling Association** (NCNCA) publishes a monthly newsletter that provides racing information for the local district. Write 18684 Vineyard Road, Castro Valley, CA 94546 for a copy.

Another monthly publication you will want to start reading is *VeloNews*, available at any bike shop for $3.50. This will keep you informed of all the big national and international races.

Each race you enter will have a entry fee, which ranges from $10 for the small-purse races to $70 for a big-purse race. Once you get really good, you might get a sponsor to pay these entry fees for you. That is incentive enough to get out there training!

The smart thing to do if you are interested in bike racing is to watch a race and see if it's for you. It can be a lot of fun, and challenging. If you get hooked watching, then get in damn good shape, pay the dues to USCF, and give it a shot. The experience of screaming along a patch of road on your bike racing a pack of others is pretty hard to match.

COST OVERVIEW

Cheap Budget:
The only really cheap way to get into this sport is to pick up an inexpensive bicycle and start pedaling. You can find bikes for as little as $50 at garage sales. They will not be a great ride, and won't give you the full experience of riding a serious road bike, but so what? You'll still be out riding and getting in great shape. If that is all your budget allows, then start here and get a better bike down the road.

Moderate Budget:
This budget starts at about $300, which will get you a good used racing bike if you can find one. Ask the mechanics at the local bike shop if they know of any for sale. For a new bike, expect to spend $500 to $1,200. The low-end bike will be a bit heavier and the components will not be as good; the high-end road bike will be worth every cent, especially if you really get into road biking.

High-End Budget:
This is where a serious racer can spend the big bucks. The cost of a top-end road bike is $2,500 or more. They are beautiful machines, but probably not worth the cost unless you are a very serious road biker.

CHAPTER ELEVEN

Rock Climb

Season: All year long, except when it is raining or wet rock persists.
Learning Curve: One weekend for the basics. Lifetime to master.

A rock climber enjoys the face of Summit Rock off Skyline Blvd. in Saratoga
Photo: Dan Nelson

If you liked climbing trees as a kid, you can relive that experience and more, by rock climbing in the Bay Area.

The feeling of being 40 feet off the ground, fastened to the side of a sheer rock face by small but strong protective gear, balancing on quarter-inch outcrops with your fingertips and toes, is an adrenaline rush that is tough to beat. Climbing chimneys and overhangs is pretty sweet as well. Once you get into this sport, you will feel like a spider inching up the tiniest cracks with agility and strength you never thought you had.

This sport offers on the edge fun. The Bay Area is not on the cutting edge of climbing, like Boulder, Colorado—you won't be able to go on multi-pitch climbs right outside your front door. Around here, one-pitch climbs and top-rope bouldering are more the norm. This translates into about 40 feet of elevation for most local rock climbs, although a few sites offer 80- to 100-foot elevations.

Still, San Francisco offers climbers excellent instruction and training a mere 150 miles from Yosemite National Park. Yosemite is considered one of the best rock-climbing areas in the world. There is also some phenomenal climbing in the nearby Sierra Nevada Mountains, which are only a three-hour drive from the Bay Area.

Because of its proximity to some of the best climbing walls in the world, the Bay Area has become home to a large number of very skilled climbers who live in a metropolitan area because of work and family obligations. If not for these obligations, they would be living in tents at Camp 4 in Yosemite. That's how addicting this sport can be.

There are many challenging outdoor rock formations in the area that rate up to 5.12 in difficulty on the climber's standard rating scale. The demand for good climbing is also filled by three large challenging indoor climbing wall facilities. You can climb to your heart's content in a rock gym, no matter the weather or darkness outside.

There is definitely enough rock in this area to challenge climbers of any level, and rock climbing is an adventure sport you should look at getting into. Climbing evokes the whole spectrum of human emotions. You will experience anxiety at the bottom before starting a route, gut-wrenching fear about halfway up when you feel like you are stuck, total fatigue three-quarters of the way up, as your arms give out, and complete exhilaration when you reach the top. The best part of rock climbing is that all this adventure comes at minimal risk, if it's done right. And make sure you always do it right—with the proper protection. What more could you ask for in an adventure sport?

Be advised that rock climbing should never be attempted without first taking classes of instruction from an expert. You need to learn the correct knots, equipment and belaying techniques from an established rock climbing school. The margin of error is way too steep to forego professional instruction. Rock climbing is not supposed to be an aerial sport. But it is real easy to fall in this sport, and falling from an elevation of more than five feet without safety backups is no way to go. At best, the result will be you on the way to some hospital emergency room. Do not take stupid chances like trying to teach yourself rock climbing. The $50 or $100 you'll save is not worth getting hurt. A complete list of local climbing schools is included later in this chapter.

EARLY ROCK CLIMBING IN THE BAY AREA

The Bay Area is steeped in climbing history. Rock climbing and bouldering has been very big in the Bay Area since the 1930s. Early pioneers in the sport were local Sierra Club members Dick Leonard and David Brower, who climbed at Berkeley's Cragmont Rocks. They made huge advances in the manufacturing of climbing rope (they started with clothesline and advanced to nylon) and belaying techniques. They had to wear basketball sneakers a size too small to feel the rock, because climbing shoes were not yet available. These adventurers and their mates went on to make many successful first ascents through out the West, and Berkeley continues to be the center of bouldering in the area. The **Sierra Club** maintains its World Headquarters here in San Francisco, and still does a lot for the sport of climbing. It is well worth checking out their bookstore or library for excellent climbing books. The address is 730 Polk St., San Francisco, 94109; call (415) 923-5600 for hours.

TYPES OF CLIMBING

The adventure sport of rock climbing is broken down into six major types. They are not mutually exclusive, meaning you will eventually use all of them. On some climbs, you might use two or three different methods to get to the top. It all depends on what the rock face throws at you.

The different types of rock climbing are:
Bouldering: This is where every rock climber starts out, and practices for the rest of his/her climbing career. A climber must boulder to keep muscles in climbing shape. Bouldering also lets you try out new climbing moves and refine old ones, while only a few feet off the ground. All you need is a good pair of climbing shoes and some chalk.

Try to traverse a whole rock face, while touching the ground two feet below. This is not as easy as it sounds. On the same boulder, there can be many different routes, all with different degrees of difficulty. Mastering moves in bouldering will give you the confidence to execute them later when you are 100 feet up. It's the same move, just at a higher elevation.

Add a top-rope if you decide to get more than five feet off the ground, just in case you slip. Accidents in bouldering are by far the number-one cause of injury in rock climbing. They happen for only one reason; the climber went too high and should have had protection in place. This protection can be in the form of a top-rope, anchored belay, or another climber spotting you.

Free Climbing: This means you are climbing free, but with a rope firmly attached for safety in case of falls. In true free climbing, the rope is never used to help you over a tough section, or hung on for a rest. To free-climb a section of rock, you must not use the rope or any other device for aid, and of course, you can't fall. The rope is strictly for protection. You will be doing a lot of free climbing as you get into this sport.

Aid Climbing: This means you are using aid to get over a certain section of rock that can't be free climbed (at least by you). This aid can come in the form of the rope, pitons, anchors, etc. In approaching a new and difficult rock face, it may be necessary to first climb it with the use of aid, then free climb it after you have practiced the moves. Most of today's climbers use this technique on new routes. They free climb the line after they figure out the best method.

Free Solo Climbing: This is the high-risk climbing, because no protective ropes are used. It is just you and the rock. With every foot in elevation, the dangers increase. Once the climber gets above 10 feet, any slip or fall will present a major problem. In the last ten years, this type of climbing has gotten a lot of media exposure because of the dangers involved. Needless to say, free soloing should not be attempted till you are a really, really good rock climber. Even then, think hard and know your own abilities before embarking on a free solo climb. The margin of error is very high and you only get to screw up once, so be careful.

Traditional Climbing: In the old days, this type of climbing involved aid in the form of pitons or bolts that were hammered or drilled directly into the rock face. This method permanently scarred the rock face, but it was felt to be a necessary evil to reach the summit.

In the last twenty years, with increased concern for the environment, climbers have shifted to the use of temporary protection, which is slipped into cracks in the rock for protection, and taken out when it is no longer needed. This modern method leaves no mark on the rock face, and has mostly replaced permanent anchors in rock climbing. The traditional climbing method is still practiced to some degree in the sport of mountaineering, where permanent protection and anchors might need to be set. There are also a lot of permanent anchors set in many of the local bouldering spots. Do not use these anchors unless you have thoroughly tested them. Even then, put in a backup anchor. These anchors can be very old, and have been known to slip out.

Sport Climbing: This area of climbing has had unparalleled growth since the early 1980s and has turned rock climbing into a large spectator sport. Climbers compete head-to-head on bolt-protected routes (indoor and outdoor), often in front of big crowds. The best climbers are able to obtain sponsorship from climbing equipment manufacturers, and can make a real living from the prize money. Heck, maybe you can give up your day job and just climb. These competitions are fun to watch, and you will learn something from the experts every time you watch them climb.

NATURAL ROCK vs. INDOOR CLIMBING WALLS

To rock climb in the Bay Area, the option of climbing real rock versus artificial rock is a decision that must be faced every day. Obviously, in bad weather or at night, the decision is a little easier to make—go right to the gym. On the nice sunny days the decision is a bit harder.

There is a distinct difference between climbing on natural rock and climbing on an artificial climbing wall. As you will soon discover, each just "feels" different to your fingers. Climbing walls are also in a controlled environment, where the hand and foot holds are strategically placed on the route. This does not exist on real rock and is something you have to get used to if you have only been climbing indoors. Outdoor rock is also subject to erosion, so a hold that looks really firm may actually be pretty brittle, and may not support you.

The fact is, to become a good climber around here you have to spend a lot of time on both natural and artificial rock, so you might as well enjoy them both.

Another important difference between fake rock and real rock is in the education of the climber. Due to the huge increase in the popularity of the artificial climbing walls, a whole new class of climber has emerged. This group is made up of people who have done all their climbing and training on indoor rock. A large number of climbers fall into this group and some of them have developed into some very good rock jocks.

But problems can arise when these climbers head into the great wide open to climb on real rock. Outdoor climbing means setting up your own protection, instead of using the preset belays and top-ropes at the gym. It is really easy for this type of climber to be overconfident when he/she approaches an outdoor climb that appears less technical than indoor climbing. This overconfidence can lead to not setting the correct protection, and injuries. Do not let this happen to you. Make sure you take the proper precautions in regard to setting up protection, safety ropes and belays. Set and reset belays indoors as well, so you stay in practice.

EQUIPMENT

Rock climbing equipment has made astounding technical advances in the last twenty years. It was not long ago that climbing was done with a hammer, pitons and crummy ratline rope. Today's rock climbing equipment is nothing short of phenomenal. You get to employ great rope, comfortable harnesses, sticky shoes and so many different kinds of carabiners, runners, chocks, spring-loaded cams, Friends, nuts and bolts that you will feel very comfortable while climbing.

The climbing equipment is included in the class when you sign up for a basic rock climbing course, but you will want your own when you get into this sport. You can purchase this equipment at many specialized climbing retail stores around town these days, due to the gaining popularity of rock climbing in this area. These specialty stores include REI, North Face, and Marmot, which have multiple locations so there's probably one near you. Used climbing equipment is sometimes available at swap meets and from climbing friends. Be very careful when you purchase used equipment—always have it checked out by a climbing expert. Remember, your life depends on this equipment. This is not a place to get cheap.

The first piece of necessary safety gear is a sit harness. They come in many styles, cool colors and different weights. All harnesses have basically the same features. There are two leg loops sewn solidly into webbing straps connected to the waist belt. A belay loop is sewn into the waist belt so the climbing rope can be tied on. A further protection feature is the tie-back waist buckle. A harness will cost $60 to $120.

Next come spider climbing shoes. If you have only climbed in a pair of old sneakers, these shoes will be quite a treat. They come with a specialized sticky rubber sole that adheres to the rock face exceptionally well. They should be worn tight and with no socks, so you get a good sense of the rock through the soles. The cost of sweet climbing shoes ranges from $80 to $140. Local climbing shops will rent just about everything else you'll need to climb, but buy your own shoes. Then you can get out and start bouldering.

Climbing rope is very specialized and comes in many styles, thicknesses and colors. Make sure the rope you use is, in fact, designed for rock climbing. Climbing ropes have some "give," and will stretch slightly in a fall. This stretch helps prevent jarring stops when you come to the end of your line. The stretch also lessens the strain on the rope, so it will last longer.

Treat your rope like gold, because your life depends on it. Always watch for signs of damage, and do not climb with a damaged or worn-out rope. Ropes are available in two standard lengths: 150 and 165 feet. The cost will range from $120 to $180 per rope.

As far as the different thicknesses of the rope, your everyday rope should be of the half-inch size. You will learn all kinds of knots to use with these ropes—ring bends, figure 8s, bowlines and clove hitches will start you off.

Protection is last, but definitely not least, on the equipment agenda. The working end of the protection is placed securely into cracks in the rock face, with a rope or wire sling protruding. You must simply attach a carabiner to the sling and run the climbing rope through it. In case of a fall, the protection will hold you if it is set correctly, and the fall will end when the climbing rope becomes taut.

Because of the innumerable different sizes and configurations of rock cracks, there are many types of protection. This "pro" will range from the basic chocks and Hexcentrics to spring-loaded camming devices called Friends. Additional pro includes stoppers, rocks, Camalots and nuts. You will also need slings, carabiners and belay devices to round out the climbing equipment portfolio. The technological advances in the protection equipment area will blow your mind. Just head into a local climbing store to see the many species of protection devices.

The only way to get comfortable setting and using different types of protection is with the proper instruction and practice. With experience, you will be able to look at a crack and instinctively know exactly what type and size protection to use. As you get serious about climbing, it will become necessary to build up a good inventory of protection pieces. All this stuff will not be cheap. Pieces of pro can cost up to $50 each, so start slow. One cost-effective alternative is to get into climbing with some friends, so you can split the cost.

THE LEARNING CURVE

Beginning Climbing:
The first thing to do is go to a bouldering area and start horsing around on the rock. You won't have to go out and spend a lot of money right away on a rope and harness; all you'll need are shoes. You can get the feel of rock climbing by bouldering at any of the local climbing spots.

And bouldering is so much fun. You get to work on all kinds of climbing moves—finger jamming the cracks, smearing on the rock face, stems in the chimneys, laybacks, and more. Make sure to have a spotter when practicing the more technical moves just in case you fall. *The more time you spend bouldering the better climber you will become.*

After a few sessions at the boulder playground, go sign up for a basic rock climbing course (a list of schools follows). You will be far ahead of the rest of the class because of the bouldering practice you've had. The cost of the basic climbing course can be as low as $60 and as much as $150. Most basic courses involve a two-day or weekend school. On the first day, you will learn knots, equipment and basic climbing moves. These basic moves will add to your vocabulary a whole new climbing jargon, including moves like edging, smearing, undercuts, jugs, and jams. The second day of class will consist of top-rope climbs, rappels, belaying techniques and a lot of smiles. After you finish the course, some schools will let you rent equipment at very reasonable costs. This keeps the expense down and makes it easy to stay with climbing. The learning curve in this great adventure sport progresses quickly for those who climb often.

Intermediate Climbing:
Once you are in pretty good climbing shape, you'll have a radically changed body. To climb successfully you have to be pretty lean, and develop some serious upper body strength to go along with strong legs. All this will have you feeling pretty good about yourself (modestly, of course).

You can take intermediate rock climbing courses from the Bay Area schools, but we'd suggest taking weekend road trips, which can include courses and multi-pitch climbs on some bigger walls located out of town. These weekend get-away classes are offered by local climbing schools and will take you to such great climbing spots as Joshua Tree, Yosemite or Lake Tahoe.

For the Yosemite area, you can call the **Yosemite Mountaineering School** (209-372-1335) direct and order a class schedule. For the best climbs in the Lake Tahoe region, call **Alpine Skills** (916-426-9108). This school is located near Donner Summit. It is best to call ahead to arrange an instructor for the class you'd like to take. These classes sell out quickly on many weekends. These schools will provide experienced guides to lead multi-pitch climbs. The classes are very reasonably priced and a whole lot of fun. Go with a few friends to keep the costs reasonable. Three of you can hire a guide to lead you on an eight- or nine-pitch climb (about 500 feet of elevation) for about $40 each. You will return home a much better climber.

As you advance through this intermediate stage, you will also begin to learn about leading. This is when rock climbing gets really interesting, because you are putting in your own protection and anchors as you climb. This protection is not only responsible for your safety, but it also has to support the climbers that follow. You want to execute this stuff right.

As an intermediate climber, you will also be spending a lot of time bouldering on the local rocks and climbing at the indoor gyms. Have fun trying the overhangs at the gym. They will humble you pretty quickly in the beginning.

By this point in the learning curve, you'll have decided how far you want to take this climbing gig. *This sport is capable of inciting thrills and adventures that are not attainable in other sports.* Because of this, you have to pay your dues. To get really good and take this sport to the major big-wall climbing level, you must be really committed. To climb big walls, you will also have to get in great shape, both physically and mentally, because situations can get dicey pretty quickly. You have to know what you are doing. To get this good, you will have to dedicate some money, a lot of energy, and most of your free time to climbing. If you can swing this, the adventure road of climbing will be long and satisfying.

CLIMB RATINGS

Different climbs are rated for difficulty under a unified rating system in America. The system is called the Yosemite Decimal System. The right to name and decide the level of difficulty for a line is usually reserved for the first person to climb it.

Things start to get interesting on the climbing scale at about 5.1. This system rates increasing difficulty in tenths to 5.9. When you get into the next set of numbers, things begin to get delightful. The 5.10a rating starts the difficulty curve, which progresses in increments labeled a, b, c and d, followed by 5.11a, b, c and d, and so on. This madness makes its way to 5.15a for some serious human-fly antics. The beauty of this system is that all climbing guidebooks for a particular area will list the various crags, climbs and their ratings. With this system, you can get a very good idea of the difficulty of the climb you are thinking about doing. It is also easy to judge your improvement as a climber, because when you move from 5.8 climbs to 5.9 climbs, you'll know you're getting better. Also, knowing the difficulty of a route ensures you never get too far over your head by attempting a climb that is too difficult for you.

LOCAL CLIMBING SCHOOLS AND WHERE TO GO

The Bay Area has some great climbing schools and options where you can learn the sport and not have to destroy your bank account. Most of the basic rock climbing courses include an hour-long class on climbing gear fundamentals, safety, and the basic moves. This intro-class is usually given on a weeknight before the full day weekend course. The weekend consists of hands-on training and instruction from qualified instructors on the local rock where the belays and anchors are set. By the end of the first day, you will be doing some pretty technical rock work and loving it. By day two, and the conclusion of the basic course, you will feel like a spider and be hooked on rock climbing for life. Additional further courses to facilitate the rock climbing learning curve are offered by the schools as well.

The best local places to learn are:

Outdoor:

There are two main schools for outdoor instruction in this area. Both are inexpensive and really good. All equipment is included in the cost of the course. Call for a complete catalogue of courses.

Cal Adventurers: 2301 Bancroft Way, Berkeley; (510) 642-4000. This school, associated with UC Berkeley but open to all, offers a variety of classes from basic to advanced multi-pitch climbs. The cost is roughly $65 per course. The group also offers weekend get-away classes to Yosemite, Lovers Leap and Lake Tahoe for about $150. This great school even has an outdoor climbing wall. A three-month pass is only about $35, and includes unlimited use of the wall.

Outdoors Unlimited: 633 Parnassus Avenue on the UC San Francisco campus; (415) 476-2078. The school is open to all and offers inexpensive, good instruction through a variety of courses.

The other alternative for basic rock climbing instruction is to hire an experienced guide to teach a group in a private lesson. This method might lower the student-to-teacher ratio, offering more specialized instruction. Ask at any of the local climbing centers for more information.

Indoor:

The beauty of indoor climbing gyms is you can go climbing regardless of the weather or time of day. You can practice your technique, or take instructional climbing courses relatively cheaply. All routes on the indoor walls are rated on the Yosemite Decimal System, so you can chart your progress as you go from 5.3 to 5.10.

The climbing wall routes will also change constantly, with the addition or deletion of holds that gym personnel deem appropriate. This keeps the gym rat climbers challenged. Since these gyms are usually staffed by expert climbers you can expect some damn hard routes, and a lot of variety. And don't think the climbing is any easier inside. The walls have ratings up to 5.11 and higher. Climbing shoes and harnesses usually can be rented at a small cost from the gym, in case you do not have your own equipment yet.

CityRock: 250 45th St., Emeryville; (510)654-2510. This is the biggest climbing wall around, at more than 40 feet and with more than 5,000 square feet of rock to play on. The cost for a monthly pass is roughly $45. The gym also issues day passes for roughly $10. Being located in the East Bay, **CityRock** serves the hot climbers out of Berkeley and the surrounding area. It's great to just go there and watch some of these human flies perform.

Class 5 Fitness: 25b Dodie St., San Rafael; (415) 485-6931. This gym serves North Bay climbers. Classes are offered for all levels, and to join the club there is a small initiation fee. Monthly dues are only about $40.

Arete Rock Climbing: 1400 Oka Road, Los Gatos; (408) 358-3576. Arete is the newest climbing wall facility in the Bay Area and serves those living south of San Francisco.

There are also some smaller climbing walls around town, at some of the health clubs and specialty climbing stores. **REI** (510-527-4140) and **Marmot Mountain Works** (510-849-0735) offer walls at the retail climbing stores in Berkeley, as does the **Palo Alto North Face** store (415) 327-1563). Some of these artificial walls are thirty feet tall. **Club One**, a health club at the One Sansome St. in San Francisco (415-399-1010) also has a short wall. Call these clubs and stores directly for information.

Bay Area Outdoor Climbing Spots:
There are a number of very good climbing crags around the Bay Area offering climbs with ratings of 5.10 and higher. The elevations can climb to 80 feet in some places, but 25 to 40 feet is the norm. Many spots have what appears to be permanent aid in place. Test this aid very well and do not count on it without backup aid or anchors.

There is a very good local guide by Jim Thornburg called *Bay Area Rock*, available at local climbing stores like North Face, REI, Patagonia and Marmont. This is the updated version of Mark Jensen's book, *Bouldering in the SF Bay Region*. Check your local climbing shop's book section to find a copy of either guide. They are both very well done and reasonably priced (from $8 to $10). The route descriptions include driving directions to the crags, and a detailed map of each face with ratings. These books act as every local climber's manual.

A few local climb spots are listed below, along with the crag's vertical and highest-rated routes, so you can plan your trip. The Bay Area's best spots include:

San Francisco: There are some great buildings and cement walls on which to practice your bouldering techniques located all around town. Climbing can be legal on some walls, and totally illegal on some others, so make sure you pick your spots and stay out of jail. There is also some totally legal good climbing at the *Sea Wall* (25 feet/5.9) at Ocean Beach, and *Glen Parks Miraloma Rocks* (25 feet/5.9 with some overhangs).

North Bay: Up in Marin and Sonoma Counties, there are many places to climb. *Mickey's Rock* (50 feet/5.12) out at Stinson Beach offers excellent climbing. *Split Rock* (25 feet/5.11) and *Turtle Rock* (35 feet/5.11) in Corte Madera, and the rock formations at the top of *Mount Tam* (40 feet/5.10) are all in Marin County. Sonoma comes in with rocks in the *Mount St. Helena* area that reach 60 feet and a 5.11 rating.

East Bay: People have been rock climbing in this area for more than sixty years. Berkeley comes in with *Indian Rocks* (35 feet/5.10), as well as Cragmont Rock (30 feet/5.10). These crags represent the most popular climbing spots in the whole area.

There is also some good climbing in the Mt. Diablo region as well, especially at the *Tiers*. Another good spot is *Pine Canyon*, which is located in the Castle Rock Area of Mount Diablo Park. This challenging face has a 120-foot pitch with some 5.9 rock, which ought to keep you busy for awhile.

Peninsula & South Bay: This area comes in with Stanford University, where you can boulder legally on the art building. There is also natural rock at *Handley Rock* (35 feet/5.10) in the Palo Alto area, and at *Woodside Road Rock* (45 feet/5.11), located near the intersection of U.S. Rt. 280 and Woodside Road.

A bit further south, you'll find *Castle Rock* and *Summit Rock*, both near Saratoga, for some good 5.8 to 5.12 climbing. Lastly, the Santa Cruz Mountains offer additional great climbing.

Always climb safe and check with local climbing stores in each area; the locals will turn you on to some of their favorite local outdoor climbing spots. They might even take you climbing with them if you ask nicely.

Bay Area Rock Climb Areas

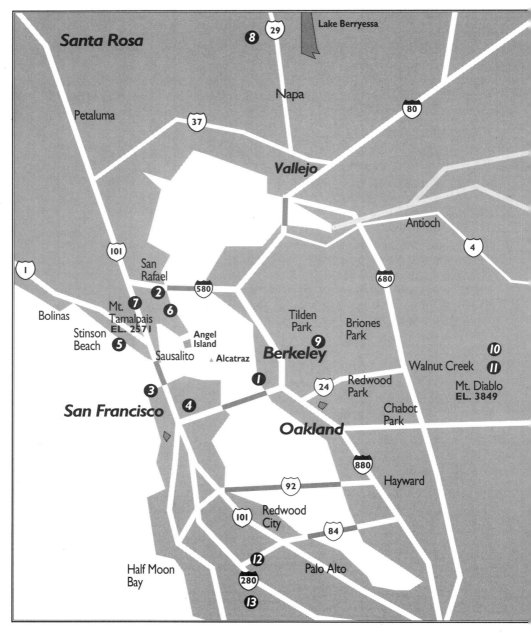

INDOOR FACILITIES
- ❶ City Rock Climbing Wall
- ❷ Class 5 Fitness Climbing Wall

OUTDOOR CLIMBING SITES
- ❸ Sea Wall
- ❹ Glen Park
- ❺ Mickey's Rock
- ❻ Split Rock
- ❼ Mt. Tamalpais Peak
- ❽ Mt. St. Helena
- ❾ Indian Rocks–Berkeley
- ❿ Castle Rock Area
- ⓫ Tiers
- ⓬ Handley Rock
- ⓭ Woodside Road Rock

COST OVERVIEW

Cheap Budget:

You should never think about picking up really cheap climbing gear, because your life depends on this stuff. The least expensive way to get into the sport is to take a basic rock climbing lesson ($80), and then rent equipment from the school after that. The other choice is to keep bouldering, which is free after you buy climbing shoes ($80 to $140).

Moderate Budget:

This budget enables you to go for a comprehensive rock climbing course for about $180. You can also join one of the local climbing gyms for about $40 a month, and do all the climbing you want. Building a climbing equipment repertoire will cost you $300 for the rope, climbing shoes, harness and some protective gear. Additional equipment will add up pretty fast.

High-End Budget:

You can spend as much as you want on climbing equipment. The budget limits also depend on where you are climbing, because different equipment is needed at different climbing sites. A complete set of a few climbing ropes, many carabiners, a lot of protection, a few harnesses and two pairs of shoes (one for bouldering and one for multi-pitch climbs) will cost you $1,000 or more.

Part 3
AIR

The air above the San Francisco Bay Area is a playground that is alive and well, offering crystal-clean air for bungee jumping, hang gliding, paragliding, and parachuting.

The one common thread that runs through all air sports is that they require professional instruction. Given the severity of any mishap at the altitudes involved, you would not want it any other way. This instruction will obviously cost you some money. The amount will vary depending on the particular sport and how far you want to take it. It will be money well spent, because you'll find these air escapades will give you some serious, gut-wrenching, off-the-chart thrills.

It is impossible to describe the feeling of hang gliding off Mount Tamalpais, or stepping out of an airplane door at 10,000 feet with a parachute strapped on your back. You have to experience it yourself. A bungee jump off the Golden Gate Bridge will also get the butterflies moving in your stomach, as will paragliding off Mount Diablo.

In some cases, the thrills will be more than you bargained for, but that's where the expert instruction you've received will come in very handy. With the proper instruction, you will be able to handle anything these sports throw at you like a pro. And when your feet finally touch down onto the safety of Mother Earth, you will sport a smile from ear to ear. You will also have an insatiable appetite to get back up there for some more. So go get some air.

RISKS INVOLVED

To assume that these air adventure sports—or land or sea sports for that matter—do not involve some degree of risk would be a mistake. When you defy gravity, even for a little while, there is a chance of being injured when you land on the ground. This is a fact whether you are elevated six inches walking off a curb, or flying at ten-thousand feet in a hang glider.

It has always been said that it is not the fall that hurts you, it's the landing. Falling off a curb can blow out the ligaments in your ankle just as easily as landing a parachute jump. Obviously, any fall from the elevations reached in these sports may lead to more than just an injury, which is why the sports mentioned here should never be attempted without professional instruction and supervision.

As you know, mistakes in aviation can be lethal. That is why no detailed explanations are included in the learning curve sections of the chapters on air sports. You cannot teach yourself to hang glide, like you can mountain biking or open-water swimming, but with the correct classes taught by a pro the risk of injury, or worse, is actually quite low. The technological advances in the equipment used in each of these sports have come so quickly in the last ten years that it is very unlikely equipment failure will cause a mishap. More likely, human error will be the cause of any problem. And it's usually something that could have easily been avoided.

As shown in some interesting statistics from the U.S. Hang Gliding Association, the fatality rate for these sports is actually quite low, especially compared to some popular occupations that some of you might work in.

These statistics show the fatality rate for:
• A fireman is 49 per 100,000;
• A roofer is 32 per 100,000;
• A Peace Corps volunteer is 43 per 100,000;
• A truck driver is 40 per 100,000;
• Driving an automobile in America is 20 per 100,000;
• The sport of parachuting is 2 per 100,000;
• The sport of hang gliding is 22 per 100,000.

The fatality statistics for bungee jumping and paragliding are even lower than those for hang gliding.

This means that if you have the interest in trying any of these great air sports, you should go for it. Just make sure you are aware of the risks and take the proper safety precautions for each sport. Ask a lot of questions of the instructor before the class starts, and during the learning process, and only take lessons from a qualified school.

Never try to save money in these sports by taking free lessons from a friend of a friend. Be smarter than that.

This section of the book has no cheap budget overview sections because you should not think about saving money in these sports. There will be some expenses involved, but the experience will be worth every cent.

If you get uncomfortable with the risks involved at any point in the learning curve, don't do it. You don't have anything to prove to anyone. Know your own abilities and stay within them. Don't ever downplay the risks involved, but understand reports in the news media of accidents in these sports are presented to shock viewers. Accidents are not the norm. Just be smart, and you won't have any problems.

Now that you understand the risks involved, let's go get some air play.

CHAPTER TWELVE

Bungee Jumping

Season: All year long.
Learning Curve: A 10-minute lecture that covers the basics, followed by the jump.

The history of Bungee Jumping can be traced to a native tribe on the isolated island of New Hebrides. The tribe was first brought to public attention in a famous *National Geographic* article in 1970. Story has it that the first bungee jump was the result of a domestic squabble between a tribal woman and her husband. The woman fled to the sanctuary of a near-by tree top. The husband found her, and started climbing the tree after her. When he got close she jumped, and he leaped after her. Unbeknownst to him, she had tied a tree vine to her ankle. Needless to say, her flight had a bit softer landing than his, which supposedly ended in his death.

After this, the rest of the tribe decided to get into flying. Full-fledged platforms were built, reaching heights of 80 feet, and the stakes were increased to where the full extension of the cord brought the head of the jumper within inches of the ground. One missed calculation in the cutting and tying of these rudimentary vines brought severe consequences.

The modern version of this sport goes back about 30 years, to some renegades from England who formed the Oxford Dangerous Sport Club. They proceeded to bungee jump off some of the world's best known bridges. The Golden Gate Bridge was first jumped by these maniacs during rush hour in 1979. Jumping off the bridge is now done under cover of darkness and is kept very quiet to avoid arrest by the local authorities.

The sport of bungee jumping looks kind of wild, but advances in equipment in the past few years have made the sport a lot safer. This safety factor has opened the sport to the masses—that is, those in the mass that are just tilted enough to do it. In other words, people just like you.

We are fortunate in the Bay Area to have several companies that will instruct and supervise your entrance into the sport of bungee jumping. One of the local companies, Bungee Adventures, was actually the first bungee jumping company in the United States that taught this crazy sport.

The wild Bungee Adventure Kockleman Brothers take a plunge.
Photo: Mike Krieger

A really nice feature of this great sport is that the learning process is simple. After you sign your life away on the waiver forms, you will find that the expert instructors will, in fact, make you feel very comfortable. Then, you take your plunge from 100 feet or higher, from either the bridge or jump structure. Yahoo!

EQUIPMENT

The bungee cords used for jumping are actually designed to military specifications. The Army uses these types of cords to drop tanks and other heavy equipment, which are attached to parachutes and dropped from airplanes.

The cords have a minimum static breaking strength of 4,500 pounds each. An individual weighing 150 pounds will produce a maximum force on the cord of three Gs, which is about 450 pounds. Several cords are used in each jump, for even further safety and better rebounding. The number of cords used depends on your body weight. Two cords are usually used for jumpers that weigh around 100 pounds, and as many as four cords are used for those weighing more than 200 pounds.

The other equipment used in bungee jumping includes a chest harness, a seat harness and heavy-weight carabiners. All this equipment is rated to withstand a force of more than 4,000 pounds and is supplied by the jump school. All the above-mentioned equipment is included in the price of the jump. So, do you feel safe yet?

THE LEARNING CURVE

The beauty of this sport is that the whole instructional period will take about 15 minutes. Another nice thing is that it really does not take very much athletic ability to become an accomplished jumper. The mechanics of the sport, equipment explanations and safety requirements will be explained by the jump master in no time. You are then qualified to take the plunge and experience the thrill. Not a bad learning curve, heh?

THE JUMP

As you ride up to the 120-foot or 240-foot elevation of the jump platform, the confidence you showed on the ground begins to fade. In a short minute, you are perched on a rickety platform listening to a countdown from five to zero supplied by other jumpers on the firm ground below you. A part of you hopes this countdown never ends.

But, of course, the inevitable zero comes and the next thing you know you're swan-diving into the open blue yonder. You will actually enjoy this free fall for a few long seconds. Then, you sense that land is coming up quick. You are then rudely jolted to your senses by the cord, which stops you cold within spitting distance of the hard ground.

This nice little break will last for about one half-second before you are catapulted at a screaming speed back up toward the platform. Thankfully, your ascent will end about twenty feet from the pulpit, where others can see your eyes bulging out of their sockets. Your nerves will be as stretched as they have ever been at this point.

Throw in the fun of some four to six more bounces, each decreasing in strength, and then your ride comes to an end. As you hang like a spider, waiting to be dropped back onto the safety of land, you desperately try to regain your composure. You'll want to act like this bungee jump was not that big a deal when you confront your friends waiting on the ground. After all, you're a cool customer, and not that easily fazed by some little jump with a cord attached to your chest. Walking away after you have been disconnected from the cord, you almost pull it off—till someone notices the wet spot on your pants.

This bungee jumping is one great thrill.

After your first jump, which will be from about 100 feet, it is up to you how far you want to take this sport. One thing is for sure: the higher you go the more thrilling the ride. The next plunge is usually from 200 feet (double your fun). The bungee cord jump record is somewhere around 2,500 feet. Picture that rebound.

You can also opt for a special double-ankle harness, which allows a head-first jump. This will let you experience the thrill of seeing the rock-hard land coming at your face even better than the conventional chest-and-waist harness. Yes, the strange things we do for fun.

WHERE TO GO

The places where you can bungee jump in this area have come full circle in the last 10 years. Initially, local jumping companies utilized the many desolate bridges around Northern California for jumps. Even though many of these bridges were located in thinly populated and remote areas, local authorities did not look kindly on these jumping activities, and started issuing bridge-jumping citations. There were even some arrests, and confiscation of expensive cords and other equipment.

After multiple jump cancellations due to these hassles, the companies got smart and moved operations to privately owned lands closer to the Bay Area. This trend lasted for a few years. First came jumping from balloons, and then cranes. The only problem was these local jumping sites ran into insurance problems, which eventually shut them down.

But because of the public's demand for bungee jumping, a small number of cool companies have gone back to the bridges. The scenery and adrenaline rush involved in these bridge jumps is just spectacular. This time around, the local authorities have been a lot friendlier, and the jumps go off without any hitches. The bungee jump companies listed below all have favorite bridges located around our area. All the companies are based in the Bay Area, and they do their jumping from desolate bridges in the Sierra Nevada's. Most jump sites are only a two- to three-hour drive from the Bay Area. The thrills will more than warrant the drive.

LOCAL BUNGEE JUMP COMPANIES

Bungee Adventures: (415) 903-3546. These kooks started the first bungee jumping company in America back in the late 1980s. The two brothers/owners, Pete and John Kockleman, were featured in the Reebok sneaker commercial for the pump shoe that was shown on television a few years ago. They have held the world record for bungee jumping elevation at various times.

They have been known to jump near the Shoreline Amphitheater in Mountain View, but the jump site moves around. These guys have built a reputation on safety and on their ability to take small groups on midnight jumps off the Golden Gate Bridge. That's an experience sure worth looking into. Write for information at 2218 Old Middlefield Way, Mountain View, CA 94043.

At press time, B.A. had stopped giving basic instruction in Bungee Jumping. The brothers have decided to concentrate on stunt bungee jumps and theme park jumping. The phone number still is operational, and they will refer you to other bungee jumping schools.

Bridge Bungee Jumping: (415) 855-9143. This "boing" business is based out of the South Bay, and has taken over for **Bungee Adventures**. They are well versed in all the methods of modern bungee jumping. It is owned by former B.A. instructor and jump master Mike Krieger. The school will give you choice of wearing the standard chest/waist harnesses, or you can go for the ankle harness, and dip your head in the river. Krieger has recently come upon a 220-foot jump from a cement-arch railroad trestle over a flowing river; the jump will blow your mind. Jumps should be booked in advance so call ahead.

Icarus Bungee: (510) 521-5867. This adventure bungee company specializes in bridge jumping with small groups. The cost is roughly $85 for two jumps, and the group offers an even better deal for groups of five or more. This company is also well-versed in the different harness options of modern bungee jumping. The address is P.O. Box 801, Alameda, CA 94501.

Squaw Valley USA: (916) 583-4000. Although not exactly local, these guys are located at the top of the tram at Squaw Valley Ski Resort in beautiful Lake Tahoe. A nice bungee jump will add to your trip in the mountains.

Over the years, a few other jump companies have opened, but the business does change rapidly due to the insurance requirements and local laws. It is a good idea to look in your local Yellow Pages under the heading Bungee Jumping to see if new companies have opened.

ADDITIONAL READING

There is an excellent book about bungee jumping called ***Bungee Jumping for Fun and Profit***, by Nancy Frase, (ICS Book Publishers, Merrillville, Indiana). This book goes into a lot more detail on the sport than we have space for here. The book is available at most bookstores, or call the publisher at 1(800) 541-7323.

COST OVERVIEW

Do not think in terms of trying to bungee jump cheaply. Always pay the going rate at a qualified school. If somebody knows a friend who has bungee equipment and would let you jump for free, forget it!. This sport would have dire consequences if something went wrong.

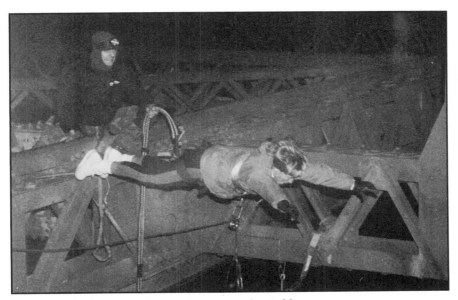

No turning back now—A bungee jumper on the Golden Gate Bridge.
Photo: Bungee Adventures

The costs involved in bungee jumping have come down dramatically in the last few years. Jumps are now very reasonably priced. You can get started for about $59 for one jump. A second 200-foot jump will cost $79 to $100. This price sometimes includes a videotape of your big jump. Additional jumps can be purchased that same day for even less. The costs involved will seem very reasonable given the thrills you are guaranteed to receive. Grab a few friends and make a day of it.

CHAPTER THIRTEEN

Parachute

Season: All year long, weather and wind permitting.
Learning Curve: Jump on day one after a six-hour course.
Lifetime to master.

The fine art of parachuting has been around some 200 years. The first known air descent with a chute was back in 1785, when one J.P. Blanchard harnessed a crude parachute onto a stray dog he kidnapped off the streets of Paris. The poor canine test pilot was tossed out of a balloon piloted by Blanchard to test his theory on the aeronautics of air travel with a canopy attached. The dog landed safely, and a new sport was discovered.

Blanchard himself even took the parachute plunge a few years later, hoping to get the humans into the act. He never jumped again, even though his first jump was a success. Many others did follow, with some gaining international daredevil fame. The balloon continued to be the launch dock from which this new group of adventurers practiced and refined their art. Parachuting became the main event at various carnivals and festivals all over Europe up into the mid-1800s. Crowds showed up to watch these brave air pirates jump from as high as 5,000 feet.

The chance of survival was not that good in the early days. This was a high-risk profession, because the odds of the chute opening were about 50/50 in those days. Event promoters even adopted the practice of refusing to pay the parachutist till after the jump was completed successfully. That way, the promoter saved the money in case the dive ended in failure. Fortunately, the sport of parachuting is a whole lot safer these days.

The safety of parachutes did not progress much till the early 1930s. It really took a couple of World Wars, and full acceptance of the parachute by the airplane pilots, to get aeronautical engineers involved. For some crazy reason, fighter pilots disdained the parachute till after World War 1. Before that, they felt it was safer to stay with the plane if problems developed. For a pilot to want to stay with a burning plane instead of jumping out tells you the odds of the chute deploying were not very good in those days.

The huge government military expansion during the World Wars, and the spending that came with it, is the real reason for improvements in parachute kites and deployment engineering. This research, and

Another happy student during a tandem parachute jump.
Photo: Tara Fitz-Gerald

continuing parachute development, helped us gain a military victory back then, and also gave us the sport of parachuting as we know it today. Advances have come so far that the sport of parachuting in no way resembles the daredevil escapades of parachute pioneers.

Gone are the old round canopy chutes. These have been replaced by the controllable and safer square chutes. Modern parachute technology also has developed an automatic ripcord device that deploys the chute at certain altitude, in case of a major debacle, like the parachutist being unconscious. Although not perfected yet, this device has aided many a parachutist that has gotten into trouble. In addition, all parachutists wear a reserve chute, just in case the main one doesn't open. These safety improvements have helped the sport become more popular.

In the modern sport of parachuting, the fatality rate has dropped to two per one hundred-thousand jumps. The odds that anything would happen to you while parachuting are extremely low. This safety record has made the sport more popular in recent years. Last year alone, there were more than 2.6 million jumps made in America. That represents a whole lot of air time.

And the thrills are so fine. Every parachute jump you make is a great experience. You get a great plane ride up to the air playground, which includes an awesome view of the local scenery from 10,000 feet or more. Next, you plunge through an open door for a ride through open space. The ride seems like it lasts for hours but actually lasts less than a minute. Then, you pull the ripcord to deploy the chute, and you cap the ride off with a nice, mellow, controllable descent. The finale is a sweet touchdown on Mother Earth, which brings a big, fat smile to your face.

THE LEARNING CURVE & COST OVERVIEW

There are really only four types of jumps on the parachute learning curve. You must start with a static cord jump or the more popular tandem jump. Your ultimate goal is the free fall jump. A description of each follows:

Static Cord: This involves a tether that runs directly from your chute to the plane. As soon as you jump out of the plane door, the tether will become taut. The tension will automatically deploy your chute (assuming all goes well).

It used to be that everyone embarked on the parachute learning curve with the static jump. You then had to successfully complete seven to 10 more static jumps before moving up to the free fall jumps. Not anymore; tandem jumping enables you to start with the free fall experience. Still, the static jump is practiced at some jump centers. Ground school will last about five hours, followed by a jump from around 3000 feet. The cost is about $75 for the first jump and $35 for additional jumps. All jumps must be done with the same school. Ground school classes usually not transferable to other jump sites.

Tandem Jump: For this jump, the student is strapped to the jump instructor before the plane leaves the ground. After lift off the instructor and student exit the plane door harnessed together, jumping from about 10,000 feet. The student then acts out the commands of a free fall as if he/she were alone with the instructor observing and able to take immediate action if needed. The instructor pulls the rip-cord on the special tandem chute, which is bigger and more stable than a regular chute, at about 2,500 feet. After chute deployment, instructor and student drift to earth together.

The proximity of the instructor makes the jumper feel very safe. This tandem method also allows first-timers to experience a free fall right from the start. Tandem jumping is for anyone who has ever wanted to free fall. The costs range from $100 to $150, and the ground school course will last three hours. You can usually take the class and jump in the same day, weather and wind conditions permitting.

Accelerated Free Fall Jump: This program has been developed in the last few years, and allows students to bypass both the static cord and tandem jumps, and go directly to free falling. After extensive ground school instruction and technical training, which will take most of the day, you are escorted out of the plane by two expert jump instructors who hold on to you as you free fall (you are not attached to the instructor as in the tandem jump). You jump from about 10,000 feet, and pull your own ripcord at about 2,600 feet. You finish the float down alone, but the experts are nearby should any difficulties arise.

If you want to get serious about parachuting right away, this is the way to go. You have to do at least three jumps with two instructors and four jumps with one instructor before you can move on to free falling alone. The costs for all jumps with instruction is about $1,000, after which you graduate to the solo free fall rating. All classes and jumps are done from the same jump school airport location, and all equipment rental costs are included in the price of the jump program.

The Free Fall Jump: This is what the sport is about. You will jump alone, deploy your own chute, and fully experience the free fall adventure. Instruction continues with each jump, covering mechanics, body form, and even re-packing your own chute.

By now, your jump master is your best friend. After eight to 10 successful jumps with instructor supervision watching your every move, you will receive a Class A parachute license. As a Class A pilot, you can go to any parachuting facility under the regulation of the United States Parachuting Association (which is just about all of them), and complete unsupervised jumps on your own.

What a great thrill to add to any vacation or business trip. Imagine parachuting in Hawaii, Europe or back in your hometown. Call the **USPA** at (703) 836-3495 for a listing of parachute jump centers in the area you are visiting. The cost to jump after you are Class A certified will drop dramatically, to $16 to $20 per jump, at most parachute centers in the United States.

As you get better and better at free falling, you can jump from greater elevations. This will increase the size of your air playing field and let you participate in aerobatics and group jumps as well. The more you go, the more fun the sport becomes. This sport of jumping out of planes is a great way to spend a Saturday or Sunday after a stressful work week. Go give it a try.

WHERE TO GO

Bay Area Jump Centers & Schools:
Because of the large number of adventure seekers who live and visit the Bay Area, this region supports a number of very good parachute jump schools. The schools are located at small airports in less populated areas for obvious reasons; usually you must drive for an hour to get to a jump center.

The major Bay Area parachute schools are listed below. In almost all cases, an appointment is necessary. If you have a number of crazy friends interested in parachuting as well, group rates are available and usually less expensive. Call for a free brochure today. They will all be happy to send you the information.

All of these jump centers listed are members of the United States Parachuting Association, which sets guidelines for instructors and safety requirements for the schools. Never parachute at a jump center that is not sanctioned by the USPA.

Local jump schools include:
Bay Area Skydiving: 3000 Armstrong Rd.; Byron, 94514; (510) 634-7575. This school is located about 35 miles east of downtown San Francisco, off

Interstate 580 in Byron. Hours are Wednesday through Sunday from 8 a.m. till sunset. This school has a fleet of three planes and excellent instruction.

Adventure Aerosports: Located at the Hollister Airport, which is a short drive just south of San Jose; (408) 636-0117. Stop by here for a nice parachute jump, then continue on to Santa Cruz for some surfing or mountain biking.

SkyDance SkyDiving: 24390 Aviation Ave., Yolo County Airport, Davis, 95616; (916) 753-2651 or 1(800) 752-3262. These jump masters are located about an hour's drive east of the Bay Area. The school is open Wednesday through Sunday. The jump school is run by the capable, experienced jump master Alasdair Boyd. The facilities are so good that many national parachute teams train here. Teams from Denmark, Norway, Japan and England, along with the our national team, have trained and participated in exhibitions at the site. It's great to see professional skydivers perform if you ever get the chance. .

Parachute Center: 23597 N. Highway 99, Lodi; (209) 369-1128. This jump center is owned by legendary sky diver Bill Dawse, who has over 20,000 jumps to his credit.

West Coast Skydiving: Located on the grounds of Petaluma Airport in Petaluma, which is about 35 miles north of the San Francisco; (707) 765-2325. The school offers jumps on Wednesday and Friday afternoons, and all day on Saturday and Sunday.

EQUIPMENT AND COST OVERVIEW

Rental of parachute equipment is usually included in the price of the instructional courses. You can always continue to rent equipment if you have no interest in buying, but you might want to eventually purchase your own equipment.—like after you qualify for a Class A parachute license.

Be aware this stuff doesn't come cheap, and purchasing used equipment is only recommended if it is thoroughly checked out and certified by someone you trust with your life, like your jump master. If a deal on a used parachute looks too good to be true, it probably is. Don't buy it. Buy the best stuff you can.

First, you will need a primary parachute, which will run about $1,000 new. A reserve chute will cost about $500 or more, and the harness set-up comes in around $500 as well. Throw in the necessary helmet, goggles, altimeter, and the cool jumpsuit, and you can add another $300 to $400 to the total. As an estimate, the complete parachute set-up, including new top-of-the-line equipment will run you $2,000 to $2,500. A complete used set-up, if available, can be purchased from your local jump center for about $1,500.

Bay Area Parachute Centers

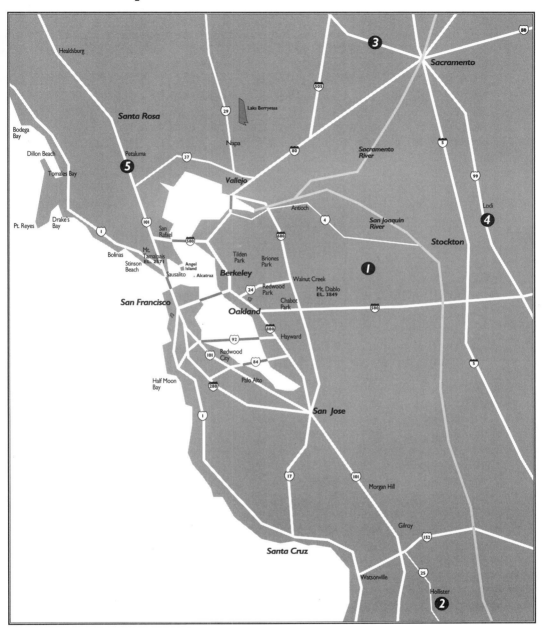

1. *Bay Area Skydiving*
2. *Advanced Aero Sports*
3. *Skydance Skydiving*
4. *Parachute Center*
5. *West Coast Skydiving*

This may seem like a lot of money to start, but after the initial cash outlay, the only costs associated with this great sport will be the actual price per jump of about $16 to $20 each. Over the long term, this sport is not that expensive. The jump cost is a pittance to pay for the immeasurable thrills each jump in this sport brings.

It is strongly recommended that you get the advice of your jump master before purchasing any equipment. Jump masters have a wealth of information on the best equipment, and they will be more than happy to share this information with you. Just ask them. Most schools can sell you the right equipment from their jump center retail shop. The shop will usually offer discounts for those who took the basic instruction at their site.

THE NEXT STEP

After you obtain your Class A license, you can jump all over the world. A complete list of jump centers in the U.S. is available from the **USPA** (703) 836-3495; or write 1440 Duke Street, Alexandria, VA, 22314. The USPA has also developed the parachutist rating system that is adhered to by all jump schools in the industry. The rating system is broken down into four different classes, with the basic requirements listed below:

1) **Class A-Novice:** Completion at least 20 free fall jumps, with three of them 40 seconds or longer. Passage of a written exam given by a certified jump instructor, and the ability to pack your own main parachute.

2) **Class B-Intermediate:** Completion at least 50 free fall jumps, with three of them more than 45 seconds long and all 50 jumps totaling more than 10 minutes of free fall time. Passage of a written exam that is not easy.

3) **Class C-Advanced:** Completion at least 300 free fall jumps, with at least 10 of them 45 seconds or longer, and totaling at least 20 minutes of free fall time. Passage of an even harder written exam and a few more fun, secret goodies to make sure you know what you doing up there.

4) **Class D-Master:** Completion at least 200 additional free fall jumps (the jumps from Class C don't count), with at least 10 of them longer than 60 seconds. At this level, each applicant is judged individually. Not many Class D ratings are given. You are essentially a grand master of parachuting if you qualify for this rating.

As you see, moving up in ratings will take a commitment of time and money on your part. It's worthwhile if your schedule and budget permits; if not, stick with your Class A license. Make sure to keep it current by jumping at least once every six months, or you'll have to repeat some of the classes. By keeping your license current, you can jump whenever you need an 'air fix.' Remember to always jump safe and smart.

CHAPTER FOURTEEN

Paraglide

Season: All year long when weather and wind conditions permit.
Learning Curve: Short flights the first day after three hours
of instruction. Lifetime to master.

Paragliding at the Stables in the Fort Funston area.
Photo: Andy Whitehall.

Paragliding was the brain child of adventure-seeking French mountain climbers who wanted to find an easy way down from various high altitude peaks in the French Alps. They imagined, and later designed, an uncomplicated, lightweight "flying parachute" that was light in weight and could be launched by foot. This new flying machine allowed these adventure-seekers to climb all day long, then simply step off the peak and float down to the valley below. This meant they could day climb longer and not worry about getting stuck up on the mountain. What took eight hours to ascend could be descended in about 20 minutes by paragliding. Plus the flight offered as much fun (if not more) as the climb up.

Luckily, this experiment became a practical reality in a very short period of time and a great new sport was found. It is now a mega-sport in its own right and growing more popular by the day. This thrilling sport is now practiced in almost every country of the World. It is no wonder why. Paragliding is really flight in its simplest form, the costs are not unreasonable, and the learning curve is simple. Plus the flights are so much fun. Modern paragliders bear little resemblance to the early canopies that were pioneered only some 20 years ago. Gone are slow, square canopies that offered poor performance and could be a bit unsafe at times.

The old-canopy design permitted only low glide flight angles. These glide angles are expressed in lift-to-drag ratios. Early paragliders had about a 3-to-1 ratio, which meant you would fly three feet forward for every one-foot drop in elevation. This meant the flights were fast and the elevation drop was pretty dramatic. Today, thanks to modern technology, canopies are now more aerodynamic, safer and more performance-oriented. The lift-to-drag ratio can now be as high as 7-to-1 on modern paraglide kites. This means you are in the air a lot longer. And the longer you are up, the more chance you will catch some thermals. Now that many of the risks have been removed from the sport through better equipment, paragliding has become a sport for everyone who has the desire to fly.

Imagine for a moment the thrills and adventures this awesome air sport offers. You are standing on a mountain peak with a view that belongs on a postcard. After unpacking the canopy and going through a short pre-flight check list of equipment and weather conditions, you are ready for flight. Lift-off is easy, you simply pull the canopy up into the wind to fill it with air. Then, you step off the mountain to soar through the great blue yonder. The ride is, for all intensive purposes, indescribable. Because paragliders fly slower than hang gliders (or any other flying machine for that matter), they are able to circle tighter, and that means you can remain within the strong core of thermal lifts. These thermal lifts offer the pilot the opportunity to ascend straight back up into the blue yonder. These thermal lifts are so much fun they will blow your mind. Then you get to float around for a while before coming to a feather touch landing back on the ground. Paraglide flights can easily last thirty minutes or longer.

The beauty of this sport is the learning curve is not steep. Flight instruction is a lot less intensive than learning to fly a hang glider, for example. You will get some form of flight from the first lesson, and the first goal is achieving a solo rating, which can be accomplished with five short days of instruction and some ground school. Pay attention in school, because you are going to learn an awful lot in a short period of time.

In a nutshell, paragliding is an adventure sport that is easy to learn, not that expensive, and capable of giving you more thrills than you've ever imagined. Everyone has a buried desire to fly. Let that desire surface and go sign up for some classes.

BAY AREA PARAGLIDING SCHOOLS

We are fortunate to have outstanding schools staffed with expert instructors. It speaks well for the Bay Area that there are enough adventure seekers living here to support three paragliding schools. These excellent local schools facilitate the learning curve—you don't have to waste a lot of time driving for two or three hours to learn the sport. The schools also make you feel very comfortable as you progress. All paragliding equipment is provided for you by the school and included in the cost of the beginning classes.

The Bay Area paragliding schools include:

Chandelle SF, Inc.: This local school is one of the oldest hang gliding establishments in the world. They also teach paragliding. The school has been in business more than 21 years and represents one of the most experienced schools in the country. Being the air maniacs that hang gliders are, they caught the paragliding bug several years ago, and formed an excellent training school run by Norma Jean Marsh, a renowned paragliding instructor and examiner with more than ten years experience in this relatively new sport. Their flight training hill is on some private land up in Marin County, so it's very convenient. This site usually offers great weather conditions year-round as well as privacy. Call (415) GLIDING (454-3464), or stop by to visit at 1595 E. Francisco Blvd., San Rafael, CA 94901. They offer a retail shop for paragliding and hang gliding equipment as well.

    Airtime of San Francisco: The ground school and office of these paragliders is located near Ocean Beach, within the San Francisco city limits. **Airtime** offers a flight training site just down the road from the office on the beach near Fort Funston, which is also a hang gliding hot spot. This place also offers open ground-school lectures with some hot local pilots (usually on Thursday nights) on many paragliding subjects, ranging from weather to soaring. Call them for a schedule and stop by a lecture to see if this great sport is for you. They offer equipment sales as well. Call (415) 759-1177 or stop by at 3620 Wawona, San Francisco, CA 94111.

    Glidell Limited: 555 Bryant Road, Palo Alto, CA; (415) 424-9704, Located down the Peninsula, only about an hour's drive South from the city, Glidell offers expert instruction in paragliding to facilitate your learning curve. Plus the weather is usually a bit better in this part of the Bay Area so you'll get a good tan while flying. They offer equipment sales as well.

THE PILOT RATING SYSTEM

All launch sites, as well as individual paragliding pilots, are rated on a flight ability scale that is standard throughout the country. This unified rating system is governed by the **United States Hang Gliding Association** (phone 719-632-8300). There used to be a separate paragliding association that governed paragliding exclusively, but this caused confusion because many of the launch sites and schools were hang gliding sites and school first. By incorporating the two sports under one governing body, the USHGA, has helped unify hang gliding and paragliding pilots, who now work together to promote the popularity and safety of both sports.

The paragliding rating system was established to guide a pilot's progression, and rate each flyer and launch site so no pilot launches from a site too advanced for his/her skill level. This successful system has kept accidents to minimum because it prevents a pilot from flying at a site over his/her ability level.

The different levels are broken down into three classes:

Class 1-Solo Rating: This represents the novice class of pilots. To qualify for this rating, a student must first complete a thorough ground school instruction course. Then, the student has to fly at least five days, with a minimum of 25 flights, under the guidance of a certified instructor. Additionally, the student flyer has to demonstrate a comprehensive knowledge of all the equipment used in paragliding, as well as the ability to read weather conditions, and execute basic flying maneuvers.

The Class 1 rating will enable a pilot to solo fly (after an instructor has conducted an orientation), and practice on a training hill without direct supervision. There are some restrictions for Class 1 pilots; these include no flying when the wind is more than 12 mph, and only flying a canopy designed for a Class 1 pilot. These canopies are more forgiving than the high-performance ones that will come later.

Class 2-Pilot Rating: By the time you achieve this rating, you are a full-fledged pilot of paragliding. The minimum requirements include at least 100 flights, some 50 flying days, ridge-lift flights of at least 15 minutes, and thermal flights of at least 30 minutes. Upon successful completion this rating, you are cleared to fly at more launch sites locally, and around the whole country.

This Class 2 ranking opens the adventure doors of this sport. More than 85% of the launch sites throughout the 50 states are rated Class 2. There are still some restrictions for the pilots at this level, to ensure their safety. These limitations include showing caution when flying in winds that exceed 15 mph, not flying alone, and demonstrating the ability to judge when a site and conditions are unsafe for you to fly.

Class 3-Advanced Pilot Rating: This is the expert class of paragliders. A pilot who has obtained this rating will have logged at least two years of flying experience (with the last 12 months injury-free), completed at least 500 flights over some 200 flying days, and booked a total of at least 150 hours of flying time. A Class 3 pilot is able to fly from technically demanding sites, and in strong soaring conditions. This is the highest rating the USHGA offers, other than an instructor's license, which is even harder to get. Class 3 pilots are the cream of the crop; they are, in general, knowledgeable, safe, and all-around cool flight jockeys.

EQUIPMENT & COSTS

One of the main attractions of paragliding is the simplicity and lightness of the equipment involved. These attributes are not made at the expense of safety or performance. For example, the canopy you fly will weigh about 15 pounds. This makes it easy to carry in a big backpack during the hike to the top of your favorite mountain top. You then simply set up your equipment, wait for the right wind conditions, step off the peak, and fly down to the base. What an awesome sport!

The basic equipment and costs aren't cheap at first look, but remember, you are buying a flying machine, not a toy. Think of it as an investment in an aerospace machine. If the costs prohibit you from getting involved, you can continue to take lessons from the local paragliding center where you took the basic course. You can also purchase used or demo equipment, which will save you a lot of money. With the continued popularity of this sport, more used equipment has become available as pilots move up the learning curve and upgrade flying canopies. Just make sure all used gear is thoroughly tested and certified by a qualified service center. Your paragliding instructor will be the best source for any equipment purchases, whether new or used. Do not purchase anything in paragliding without consulting your flight instructor.

A list of the basic paragliding equipment includes:

Canopy: This sweet flying machine is made of a woven polyester and nylon fabric, supported by many lines of Kevlar, aramid and polyethylene. These support lines are firmly attached to a group of webbed nylon risers. The risers are then connected to your harness with strong, locking carabiners. Canopies come in many different models with different performance ratings, ranging from recreational models to advanced competition canopies. A new one will set you back about $3,000 to $3,400, and a quality used one will cost $1,800 to $2,000. Used paragliders are readily available from your flight instructors.

Harness: This specialty designed harness will securely attach you to your canopy with locking carabiners. This strong connection, with its solid webbing, will make you feel very comfortable. Harnesses also have a built-in seat, so you automatically assume the right flying position when in flight. They range in cost from $300 to $600 for a new one. Used ones do exist for considerable cost savings.

Helmet: A specially designed paragliding helmet will cost $100 to $300. They are worth every cent, so don't get cheap—this is your head we are talking about. Buy a good one.

Reserve Chute: This piece of equipment is, of course, not an option but a requirement. A reserve chute will range in price from $300 to $600.

Instruments: These are the vitally important gadgets that tell you what is going on during the flight. The *altimeter* registers your altitude. The *airspeed indicator*, or *windmeter*, shows wind velocity, and the *variometer* will keep you informed on your ascent and descent rate. Total cost for all of them will range from $600 to $1,000 depending on the models chosen.

Basically, purchasing your own complete set of used paragliding equipment will cost you $2,500 to $2,800. The new stuff will set you back $3,500 to $4,500. This may seem like a lot, but remember this is an investment in a flying machine. And this sport is so much fun it will surely be worth the initial cash outlay if you can swing it. Plus, after the gear is bought, all your flying is free of charge.

LEARNING CURVE & COST OVERVIEW

Let's face it, you are not going to learn this sport in one afternoon or one weekend. You will have to make a serious time commitment to become proficient at paragliding. That commitment is pretty easy to make considering what this sport offers. You'll soon find yourself at a beautiful flying site in a nice breeze, flying high above the countryside.

Before you know it, you will have qualified to become a Class 1 pilot. This process will take anywhere from 10 to 12 flying days. Most local schools are very user-friendly in scheduling course time. The schools also offer full-package deals on lessons, which can save you considerable money over taking the classes on a hourly basis.

Introductory Course: This five-hour day will give you a basic understanding of the equipment and aerodynamics. This instruction is followed by nice low-level flying under the guidance of your expert instructor. This class is designed to get you hooked on paragliding, and it will. You will probably schedule your next lesson right then. The cost for the introductory course is about $150. Sometimes, local paragliding flight schools run specials offering introductory classes for as low as $99.

Five-Day Basic: Every beginning paraglide pilot starts here. This course takes you through all the basics of the sport. There will be many low-level flights, extensive instruction and lots of fun. The cost ranges from $500 to $700, depending on the school. The class may include two to four other students, who will quickly become your best friends.

Five-Day Advanced: This specially designed course focuses on giving you your Class 1 Novice rating, so you can go solo. The course will run you about $1,000. You will learn fast by performing many flights each day, and sitting in on an extensive ground school on all facets of paragliding. If you know for sure that you'd like to get seriously into this fine sport, this is the way to go.

Private Instruction: The alternative to group lessons is to go private. One-on-one instruction will cost a bit more, but you will improve a lot faster than in a group lesson. This means you'll get your Class 1 rating faster. Private lessons to the Class 1 rating level will run $1,500 and up. Call the local paraglide centers for more information.

Canopy Purchase Method: Most paraglide schools offer discounts on the lesson package if you commit the purchase of a paraglide canopy through their retail shop. Technically, the school cannot sell you a canopy till you obtain your Class 1 license, but your commitment to the sport will go a long way in saving you money. For those who know paragliding is the sport for them from the onset, this can be an exceptional deal. The deal you get on the kite is almost like getting all the lessons for free. Plus, the shop proprietors will think you are a nice person because you spent some of your hard-earned money there, and you might get some special attention in the classes. That way you will learn to fly quicker. The cost of such a program ranges from $2,200 to $3,000, which includes the cost of the canopy and lessons to get to the Class 1 rating.

WHERE TO GO

The Bay Area offers some outstanding paraglide launch sites. Throughout the early part of the learning curve, most of your flying will be limited to the school's training site, where the basic lessons are taught. These sites tend to be secluded for safety reasons, and the hills are not too steep. This way you will work out any mishaps of the beginning learning curve at lower elevations, so you won't get hurt or embarrass yourself at the higher-elevation launch sites.

All the sites mentioned below do require at least a Class 1 rating, and most are Class 2. This provides you with even more incentive to get the beginning lessons out of the way so you will be flying at these great Class 2 sites sooner.

A special thanks should go out to all the local paraglide clubs and members, who have had to tread through the red tape of the local municipalities, insurance companies, and police forces to open these great flying sites to paraglide pilots (and hang gliders as well).

Make sure you are confident in your abilities as a pilot before attempting to fly at any of these sites. Always fly safe, know your limitations and never get in over your head. Be especially aware of changing weather and wind conditions. Optimal wind conditions for paragliding range from about 8 to 14 miles per hour. When the wind starts to pick up, conditions get a bit unsafe.

Also, be aware that paragliding is a fairly new sport. Most of the flying sites in the Bay Area were strictly hang gliding spots before paragliding came on the scene. Sometimes, small confrontations can occur between hang glide and paraglide pilots. These confrontations are similar to those between surfers and boogie boarders out in the surf, or skiers and snowboarders on the snow. If a squabble erupts, it is usually because someone has an ego a bit too big. Respect the space of other flyers, whether they be paragliders or hang gliders. Follow that common courtesy rule and you will never have any problems.

The best local paraglide launch sites include:

San Francisco: The city offers some choice parargliding at the *Stables* launch site, located close to the Fort Funston hang gliding launch site. This area is a bit south of San Francisco city proper, just past Ocean Beach and Golden Gate Park off U.S. Rte. 1. Pull onto the Fort Funston road, opposite Lake Merced, and you are in the Mecca of paragliding and hang gliding for the Bay Area. The ridge soaring offered here is usually optimal in spring, summer and fall months. Be careful during June and July, when west winds might be too strong to allow safe flying conditions. The AirTime paragliding school, located nearby, utilizes this launch site.

North Bay: The expansive open spaces north of the Golden Gate Bridge offers excellent paragliding launch sites. There are many lower-level sites in Marin County. The San Rafael-based Chandelle SF, Inc. paragliding school utilizes most of these sites for both classes and experienced pilot flights. Call them for details. *Mount Tamalpais* is in the process of being opened to paragliders, who will join the hang gliders who are already approved for launches here.

An open local peak that is currently open to paragliding is *Mount St. Helena* (elev. 4,343 ft.), located in Robert Louis Stevenson State Park just north of Calistoga in Napa County. This launch site offers enticing flying for Class 2 approved pilots.

East Bay: The center for paragliding activity in this area is beautiful *Ed Levin Peak* (elev. 2,594 ft.) located in Milpitas. There is also some great flying off *Mission Peak* in Freemont. Another hot spot is Mount Diablo (elev. 3,849 ft.). This sweet peak is just east of Walnut Creek, and offers great paragliding for Class 2 pilots or better.

Bay Area Paragliding Centers & Sites

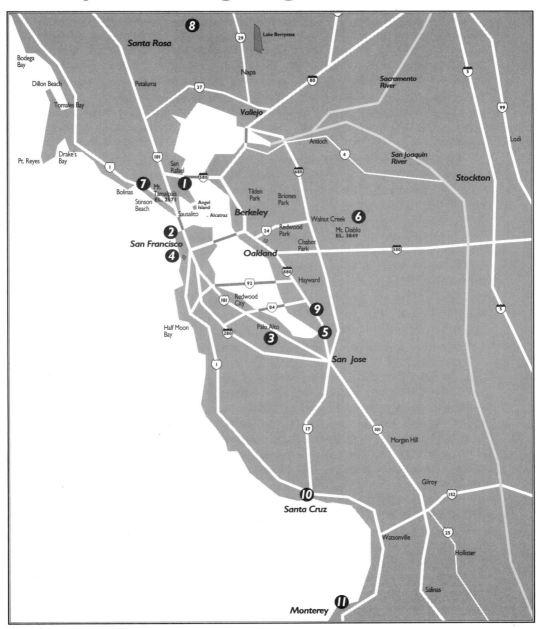

SCHOOLS
① Chandelle SF, Inc.
② Airtime of San Francisco
③ Glidell Ltd. Paraglide School

FLY SITES
④ Fort Funston
⑤ Mountain Peak
⑥ Mt. Diablo
⑦ Mt. Tamalpais
⑧ Mt. St. Helena
⑨ Mission Ridge

⑩ Waddell Creek
⑪ Marina

Peninsula & South Bay: The area south of San Francisco comes in with some nice launch sites near Palo Alto. These sites are utilized by **Glidell Limited** paragliding school. There is also some great flying along the coast at *Waddell Creek*, near Davenport. The Santa Cruz mountains, located a bit further south, offer additional great launch sites. *Marina*, located south of the Bay Area toward Monterey, comes in as a real nice paragliding spot as well.

This list represents just some of the local paragliding spots. As you can see the Bay Area has no shortage of great flying sites to practice this great adventure sport. You will learn of more sweet spots as you progress through the paraglide learning curve.

After obtaining your Class 1 and 2 ratings, you can take your paraglider on some road trips to some exceptional flying spots just a few hours drive from the Bay Area. These spots include *Big Sur* (located just south of Monterey) and *Slide Mountain* (near Lake Tahoe) to name a few. Check at your local paraglide center for when they are all planning a road trip. The views and flying are truly epic at some of these sites.

For even more paraglide launch sites out of town, call the **USHGA** in Colorado Springs at (719) 632-8300. The address is 599 E. Pikes Peak, Colorado Springs, CO, 80903. This governing body of the sport is staffed by really nice people, and they will be happy to supply you with detailed information on any flying sites throughout the country and the World.

BAY AREA PARAGLIDING CLUBS

Each Bay Area launch site for paragliding and hang gliding is supervised by a local club close to the site. Basically, it works like this. A municipality won't let a launch site open unless it is insured. The insurance companies won't write a policy unless there is a supervising club to govern the site. The site has to be overseen by a stated club administrator who takes his/her job very seriously. You need the approval of the site administrator before you can fly a site. This successful process has kept mishaps to a minimum.

All efforts are made by club members to keep the risks natural to this sport to a minimum. If you are an experienced paraglider just visiting town, or if you've just moved here, once you have clearance to fly you will be welcome by everyone. These local clubs do a tremendous amount of work to further the growth, and safety, of both paragliding and hang gliding. They also do a fair amount of post-flying socializing as well. At these functions is when the real flying stories start to expand with each additional beer. On the whole, paragliders are a fun loving bunch.

For information on any of the local clubs, contact the **Bay Area Paragliding Association** by calling Ken Davis at (415) 756-7560. A lot of the local hang gliding clubs maintain paragliding memberships as well. A complete listing of these clubs is in the hang glide chapter.

ADDITIONAL READING

Paragliding, A Beginner Guide, Mark Wright, 14080 Highway 215, Moreno Valley, CA 92553 (909) 697-4466. An excellent basic paragliding book well worth looking over before you enroll in any lessons.

PARAGLIDING: The Magazine, 8901 Rogue River Hwy., Grants Pass, OR 97527; (503) 582-1467. Published six times a year. A cheap subscription rate of only $26 a year will keep you up-to-date on all the latest news, equipment introductions, great trips and launch sites, and training methods in the world of paragliding.

CHAPTER FIFTEEN

Hang Glide

Season: All year long, weather and wind permitting.
Learning Curve: Long, but with a lot of flights and fun the whole way.
A lifetime to master.

Although hang gliding as we know it has only been around some 30 years, the real story of hang gliders goes back a lot further in time.

Inventors have been obsessed with human flight since the beginning of civilization. Legend has it that during mythological Greek times, the brilliant architect Daedalus and his son Icarus took the first glider flight. The legend has it the King imprisoned both of them on the island of Crete, separated from Athens by some 145 miles of the Mediterranean Sea. Daedalus concluded the only way off the prison island was to fly off, so he applied his architectural brilliance to studying birds inhabiting the island. This led to the creation of a lightweight craft that could soar in air thermals.

After many prototypes, he succeeded in building two gliders, one for him and one for his son, by using bird feathers waxed onto wings made from wooden spars. On one windy, stormy day, the unseasoned pilots launched into the wind from a steep cliff and soared into clouds. They headed toward Athens, riding in the thermals at elevations above 10,000 feet. Daedalus's successful flight (the legend states that he actually circled Athens, but it was cloudy so he flew to Sicily to land) was marred by the death of his son, Icarus, who smashed into the sea. Supposedly, he lost control of his glider while doing some stunt flying too close to the sun. This melted the wax binding the feathers to the wing, and caused the glider to fall apart. The moral of that story is always stay within your flying limits.

This legendary flight success story is not that unrealistic. The current world record of hang gliding distance flying is more than 308 miles, and the altitude hang gliding record is over 20,000 feet.

Man's fascination with flying kept the dreamers busy for thousands of years more, though there aren't many documented success stories. Then, in the late 1800s John J. Montgomery accomplished the first controlled flight right here in California. The gliders of this time produced some legendary flying pioneers. The most famous of the group was Otto Lilienthal of

Germany, who made more than 2,000 successful glider flights. The serious inventors of that time, however, forsook gliders to work full time on the principles of powered flight, and by 1903, the Wright Brothers had staged the first successful engine-powered flight on the beaches of Kitty Hawk.

From that famous flight, the flying world broke into two camps. A small number of purists felt flying had nothing to do with engines. So, while the masses of aerospace engineers and plane builders went full force at improving the engine-powered plane, these purists continued to try and perfect the glider.

Many years later, a glider with a flexible wing was designed by Francis Rogallo in the mid 1950s. Rogallo was a NASA aeronautical scientist who tinkered with his flexible wing concept at home. NASA was experimenting with a directional parachute theory at the time. This flexible wing was a major development, because it made "sky sails" easily transportable. Rogallo's kite design, which stretched the sail over a frame of aluminum tubing to create an air foil, was one of the major advancements of flying history. He also designed a control bar, which let the glider pilot actually steer the wing.

Riding the ridge lift above Fort Funston.
Photo: Andy Whitehall

Now armed with government funds from the NASA program to study different uses, the Rogallo wings technology progressed rapidly. One study looked at them for use on the re-entry flight of a spacecraft. Word of aeronautical glider improvements started to leak out and Rogallo's design was soon copied by flying enthusiasts all over the world.

The early 1970s marked the beginning of the adventure sport of modern-day hang gliding. And California has been a hot-bed from day one. The aerodynamics of the Rogallo sky sail let flyers launch from a cliff into the wind, and drift down on a 4-to-1 lift-to-drag ratio, which means that for every 4 feet of forward travel, the pilot will lose 1 foot of altitude. This was substantially higher than any previous L/D ratios. Because of these longer flights, the popularity of hang gliding really started to boom. More money was pumped into the sport for research and development of the kites, and this has led to dramatic improvement in the performance and safety of modern-day hang gliders. Thanks to technological improvements, today's gliders are able to fly up to a 12-to-1 L/D ratio. This 12-to-1 ratio was unheard of only eight years ago.

The sport of hang gliding has continued to grow and improve into the 1990's. According to current statistics put out by the United States Hang Gliding Association, the fatality rate is a low 22 per 100,000 flights. It's statistically safer to fly a hang glider than to be a fireman, truck driver and roofer. If you use common sense, take the right lessons and fly smart, the chances of getting hurt (or worse) are actually quite low. The biggest cause of accidents in hang gliding is human error; the pilot forgetting to hook in is unfortunately a common one. Remember to always pay attention in this sport. As with any adventure sport, and especially this one, screw-ups and getting in over your head can hurt you, so be careful at all times.

Now that the risks have been explained, let's daydream about what this great adventure sport offers. You will be able to launch a beautiful flying kite off a ridge or cliff, and soar up to 10,000 feet once you are an accomplished pilot. You'll have the ability to fly for hours on end. And while in flight, you'll be treated to an amphitheater of resplendent scenery just below you. Eventually, you will float down toward Mother Earth and a feather soft landing—and a feeling of flight that will remain in your soul forever.

You will have to invest a little money (about $150 for a ground lesson and tandem flight) to give hang gliding a try. If you are like most adrenaline junkies, this sport will find its way into your life shortly thereafter.

For any general information on the sport of hang gliding, feel free to contact the **United States Hang Gliding Association (USHGA)** by phoning (719) 632-8300. Their address is 559 E. Pikes Peak Ave, Colorado Springs, CO, 80903.

HANG GLIDING IN THE BAY AREA

The Bay Area is steeped in modern hang-gliding history. Back in the late 1960s, when gliders were still launched from tow lines, one of the first foot-launched flights ever was made in the local Coyote Hills by fearless Dave Kilborn. With his successful flight, pilots began foot launching off ridges and mountain tops all over the world. This helped bring the sport of hang gliding to adventure seekers everywhere.

The popularity of hang gliding in the Bay Area began to really boom in the mid 1970s, when two of the sport's early advocates, Jan Case and Lee Sterios, relocated here from Denver. They brought with them a bunch of gliders and a shell of a company named Chandelle Sky Sails. They quickly started selling hang gliders and offering instruction to locals from the beaches near Fort Funston. As students progressed, they moved up in launch elevation till they were soaring off the local cliffs.

With the sport's sudden growth in popularity, some rules had to be established at Fort Funston to make sure pilots were not getting over their heads and flying in conditions they were not qualified for. Ms. Case, along with other dedicated members of the local hang gliding club, called the Fellow Feathers, developed a rating system to monitor the launch site. To launch from the site, a pilot had to be approved by three members of the club. This program was so successful at preventing accidents and injuries that it was adopted by the United States Hang Gliding Association (USHGA) as the standard flying site rating system for the country.

Hang gliding has continued to boom in the Bay Area. As testament, there are four successful hang gliding schools operating out of this area to fill all the flying needs of the adventure seekers who live and work here.

LOCAL HANG GLIDING SCHOOLS

The great state of California is home to far more hang gliding schools than any other state in the country. There are some excellent schools and soaring centers right here in the Bay Area. All hang gliding schools are governed by the USHGA, but each one has its own special teaching method. It is worth getting information on all of them to figure out which school would be best for you.

Chandelle SF, Inc.: This is one of the oldest hang gliding schools in the world. The instructors have taught all levels, from novice to expert, for over 20 years. The training site is on a beautiful lush green hill in Marin County, which offers easy access just up Highway 101 North to anyone in the Bay Area. The retail shop and class scheduling office is located at 1595 E. Francisco Blvd., San Rafael, CA 94901; (415) 454-3464.

Mission Soaring Center: This school and retail shop is located at 1116 Wrigley Way, Milpitas, CA 95035; (408) 262-1055. This location serves the needs of pilots who live and fly in the eastern and southern sections of the Bay Area. The training site is on a private ranch about an hour south of San

Francisco near Hollister. The training hill offers consistent winds and a lot of flying room. This site also offers higher launches than most of the other training hills of the area.

Natural Flying: This place serves the many adventurers of the South Bay, with a fine hang gliding school. They are located at 17506 Hoot Owl Way, Morgan Hill CA; (408) 779-7976.

Western Hang Gliders: Reservation Road & Highway 1, Marina, CA; (408) 384-2622. This southernmost group offers a hang gliding school and pro shop just North of the city of Monterey. You can go see the Monterey Bay Aquarium in the morning, and then go hang gliding in the afternoon.

Instruction in hang gliding is also offered by some independent teachers, clubs and shops throughout the area. Ask at any of the local hang gliding shops for more information.

Make sure you feel comfortable with your instructor and never take any lessons from a pilot who is not a certified instructor. It is not worth the risk. Pay the money for the best lessons you can find. It will be safer and you will learn faster.

THE PILOT RATING SYSTEM & COST OVERVIEW

Hang gliding operates under a national rating system by which a pilot's ability level is judged and the different launch sites throughout the country are rated. This way a Hang 2 (Novice) pilot knows his or her ability level, and won't be permitted to launch from a more difficult Hang 3 (Intermediate) site.

The rating system is taken very seriously by instructors, who administer the required field and written exams by which hang glide pilots move up to the next level. A description of the basic requirements for each level follows. Because every student learns at a different pace, the time frame for each level is just an estimate. The six categories are:

Student: *A new pilot remains in the student stage until he/she achieves the Hang 1 (Beginner) rating.* At this stage, you will learn the basics of hang gliding, including safety features and requirements of the equipment, important weather and wind information, and how to rig and de-rig the hang glider. Lessons are given on fairly flat ground in the beginning, with the training site increasing in pitch and elevation as you get more comfortable handling the glider.

Your initial flights will involve 10 feet of elevation. This will increase to 50 to 75 feet by your second or third lesson. After some time, you will begin to understand the basic maneuvers, how to steer with your body weight, launching and executing safe landings into the wind.

At this point, hang gliding gets fun. Up till now, your day usually consisted of trudging a 50-pound glider up the training hill over and over again, with little action on the flight down. After five training-site classes, your flights will start to go up to 100 feet in elevation.

For those who do not want to commit to the cost of a complete Hang 1 lesson package right away, a less-expensive introduction lesson package is offered by most schools for around $200. This great introductory package includes two days of basic lessons and then an awesome tandem flight with a certified instructor from one of the higher local Bay Area launch sites (like Fort Funston or Mount Tam for example). These tandem flights are a great way to experience the thrills of hang gliding (tandem flights are a bit less stressful as well, because you are strapped onto your very qualified instructor) without waiting weeks and months to obtain your Hang 2 rating. Once you are a Hang 2, you will be experiencing the thrills of this great sport on your own.

Hang 1-Beginner: To achieve a Hang 1 rating you must be able to set-up and do a preflight check of your glider, hook in correctly, launch yourself, and demonstrate glider handling abilities while in flight. You also must know the wind conditions at a given site, including velocity, direction and the effect of the wind on the glider. Upon becoming a Hang 1 pilot, you can fly up to 150 feet in elevation, and in winds up to 15 miles per hour. The complete cost of lessons to become a Hang 1 will be about $500.

Hang 2-Novice: This Hang 2 rating should be your goal from the beginning, especially if you plan to get into this sport at all.

You can usually make the jump from Hang 1 to Hang 2 with 15 hours of additional instruction. In these classes, you will learn 'S' turns, designated landing spots, and more practice and tidbits that will make you a way better pilot. You also must pass a written test that will make sure you know what you are doing up there.

After you achieve a Hang 2 rating, your elevation capabilities jump to 300 feet and you will be able to fly in winds up to 18 mph. Most local schools offer a class and cost structure with this Hang 2 rating as the goal for a price of $850 to $1,000. This cost includes the complete ground school, many training hill sessions, and the glider rental. With the Hang 2 rating, you can soar off many of the beautiful local peaks. *Ed Levin Peak* (elev. 1,750 feet) in Milpitas is a really nice Hang 2 launch site, and every first year Bay Area hang gliding student's goal.

Hang 3-Intermediate: The jump from Hang 2 to Hang 3 will require some serious air time. Most instructors estimate it will take a full year to graduate from a Hang 2 rating to this Hang 3 level. And you'll have to fly fairly frequently.

By the time you receive this Hang 3 rating, you have become a fairly serious hang glider pilot. This means you have probably purchased your own glider by now. At this level you will able to launch off most of the great flying sites in the area, including *Fort Funston* and *Mount Tamalpais*.

To achieve this rating, you must successfully complete 30 more flying hours with instructor supervision. You also must have at least 90 flights and a minimum of 30 flying days. This translates into about ten hours of solo airtime. What a blast!

Complete understanding of all of the elements of hang gliding is also required to obtain this rating. This includes understanding stalls, 360s, thermals, spins and 180-degree turns. You will also have to execute consecutive landings within 50 feet of a chosen landing spot.

After achieving a Hang 3 rating, you can fly in winds up to 25 miles per hour and will be welcome at most intermediate spots around the area, and throughout the world.

Hang 4-Advanced: By the time you get to the Hang 4 level, you are an expert pilot who can handle just about anything.

To get to this stage, you will have committed a lot of time to the sport, and it will have been well worth it. Hang 4s spend an awful lot of time flying around in the thermals, soaring up to 15,000 feet. With this advanced rating, you'll be welcomed at just about any site, including the epic launch atop *Mount Diablo* as well as some of the beautiful out-of-town sites like *Glacier Point* in Yosemite and *Mount Haleakala* (elev. 10,000 ft.) on Maui, in Hawaii, as well as the many peaks in the Alps near Chamonix, France. Your flying options will be endless.

Hang 5-Master: There are not many of Hang 5 ratings handed out by the USHGA. Basically, this master level is about the same as Hang 4, but the Hang 5 distinction is a special honor reserved for those awesome hang gliding pilots who also put a lot back into their sport.

EQUIPMENT & COSTS

As with many other adventure sports, the technological advancements in the equipment used in hang gliding over the past 15 years has been nothing short of phenomenal. Gone are the home-made kites of bamboo, plastic and cheap sails. Because many early wings were homemade in the early days of the sport, there were no manufacturing controls. This led to some unsafe gliders which caused accidents. In today's world of hang gliding this is no longer the case. Gliders today are high-tech flying machines manufactured from only the finest aluminum compounds. These sturdy frames are then surrounded with lightweight Mylar sails, and are manufactured under a strict safety code.

Hang gliding equipment continues to improve as far as performance and safety. This nice equipment does not come without cost, but look at it as investing in a personal flying machine. Hang gliders are sure a lot cheaper than private planes, or even used automobiles for that matter. And they sure are a lot more fun.

The best source of any hang glide equipment purchases is your flight instructor. He/she will know your exact ability and can steer you into the right equipment for your flying level and budget.

A basic equipment list with the costs associated includes:

The Glider: Choosing the model of kite depends primarily on your ability level at the time of purchase, as well as what kind of budget you are working under.

It is advisable not to buy a beginner glider, because you will not be in it long enough to get much value from it. Instead, save your money and rent the school's gliders till you progress as a pilot. Training gliders are for teaching the basics and are used up to a Hang 2 rating. Once you reach the Hang 2 or 3 level, you can buy a performance kite that will supply outstanding flying capabilities. And you won't have to worry about the time and hassles of first selling the beginner kite.

Higher performance gliders are designed for the different levels of pilot ability based on the national hang glide rating system. As you continue to improve, so do the capabilities of your glider. A new, nicely designed glider for a Hang 2 pilot will cost between $3,300 and $3,500 new. These gliders will offer such flying capabilities and performance that they will blow your mind.

There is a used market for gliders at retail shops and through some of the different local hang gliding clubs. The cost of a decent used glider will be about $2000. Make sure it has been maintained and serviced. *Don't ever buy any new or used glider that is not certified by the Hang Glider Manufacturing Association.* The HMGA certification tells you that the glider has been tested to meet specific strength and stability requirements. The certification also designates a minimum pilot hang level as well, so no pilot ever gets in over his/her head by flying too advanced a glider. This minimum hang level should never be compromised. Make sure you have any used equipment thoroughly checked over by your flight instructor.

Harness: There are basically four types of harness used to attach the pilot to the glider. Most schools will start you out in an *apron harness* that is good for short flights. At the next level, you'll move into a spaghetti harness, which distributes your weight more evenly. Moving up to the next level brings you the *cocoon harness*, which will enclose you from shoulders to toes for maximum comfort on longer flights. Finally, the *pod harness* offers more protection from the wind and cold, which will be necessary for those 10,000-foot soaring climbs. A good harness will run from $400 to $800 new, and roughly $250 to $550 used.

Reserve Parachute: This chute is a necessary piece of equipment for high-altitude hang gliding. The two basic types are a *manual launch* reserve chute and a *rocket-deployed* variety. The cost ranges from $300 to $1,200 new. Buy the rocket-deployed variety if your budget allows. This will blow the safety parachute away from the glider, so it doesn't get caught up and will open freely.

Helmet: This is not an area to be frugal, since your head is at stake. Good helmets cost $100 to $300. Invest in the best one your budget allows.

Flight Computers: First comes the *variometer*, or "vario," a high-tech instrument that tells you the vertical speed at which you are climbing or descending. A good vario is also a necessity, and costs $300 to $500. Other instruments include an *airspeed indicator* and an *altimeter*. The cost of these will run about $200 for each.

Again, the best source for any hang gliding equipment will be your flight instructor, and at the school where your ground lessons are given. Ask a lot of questions, so you know you are purchasing the right equipment for your budget and flying ability.

WHERE TO GO

The Bay Area has always been considered a great spot for hang gliding and this area has been home to many world-class hang glide pilots. Not only are there some outstanding sites right in this area, but San Francisco is close to some epic soaring sites like *Glacier Point* near Yosemite, the *St. Lucia Mountains* near Big Sur National Park, and *Slide Mountain* in Nevada near Lake Tahoe.

All of the local hang gliding schools offer tandem flights off these peaks, so anyone can get the sensation of hang gliding right away. Time's a wasting, so go sign up and get some flight if you have the urge. Some of the best local soaring sites include:

San Francisco: *Westlake*, a group of cliffs a bit south of Fort Funston, lie right along the coast near Pacifica. This beautifully maintained flying spot is only a short twenty-minute drive from downtown. The spring, summer and fall months offer some great flying at this Hang 3 spot, where ocean breezes rocket into the hills, creating an awesome upward lift.

Fort Funston is located just off the Great Highway across from the Olympic Club Golf Course and just south of Ocean Beach. This is the center of hang gliding activity for the Bay Area. On any given afternoon when the conditions are right up to 40 hang gliders are sharing the ridge thermals here with spectacular views of the Pacific Ocean.

North Bay: Marin County comes in with some good flying off *Mount Tamalpais*, a Hang 3 site with an elevation of around 2,600 feet. With normal winds from the west and no fog, this site offers a beautiful flight to a soft landing on Stinson Beach. Drive a little further north to *Mount St. Helena*, near the town of Calistoga, which offers a 4,343 foot peak and some beautiful hang gliding as well.

East Bay: This area comes in with *Mount Diablo*, located just east of Walnut Creek, with an elevation of 3,849 feet and a Hang 4 launch site rating. You can see the entire expanse of the Bay Area when flying at this great site.

Bay Area Hang Gliding Schools & Launch Sites

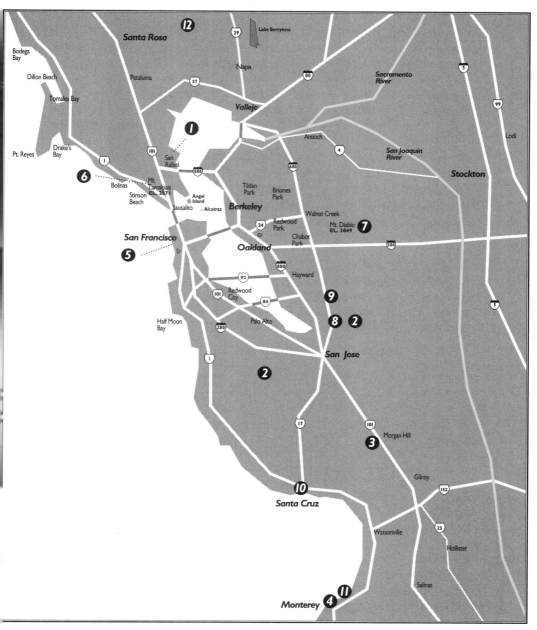

Bodega Bay
Dillon Beach
Tomales Bay
Pt. Reyes
Drake's Bay
Bolinas
Stinson Beach
Sausalito
Half Moon Bay

Santa Rosa
Petaluma
Napa
Vallejo
San Rafael
Mt. Tamalpais EL. 2571
Angel Island
Alcatraz
Berkeley
Tilden Park
Briones Park
Redwood Park
Oakland
Chabot Park
Hayward
Redwood City
Palo Alto
San Jose
Walnut Creek
Mt. Diablo EL. 3849
Morgan Hill
Gilroy
Watsonville
Hollister
Salinas
Santa Cruz
Monterey
San Francisco

Lake Berryessa
Sacramento River
San Joaquin River
Stockton
Lodi
Antioch

Lake Berryessa

SCHOOLS

1 *Chandelle SF, Inc.*
2 *Mission Soaring Center*
3 *Natural Flying School*
4 *Western Hang Gliders*

LAUNCH SITES

5 *Fort Funston*
6 *Mt. Tamalpais*
7 *Mt. Diablo*
8 *Ed Levin*
9 *Mission Ridge*
10 *Waddell Creek*

11 *Marina*
12 *Mt. St. Helena*

Peninsula & South Bay: This area offers a Hang 2 site at *Ed Levin County Park,* located in the town of Milpitas. To soar off this 2,600-foot peak is every local beginner pilot's dream and goal for the first year of flying. *Mission Peak* in Freemont offers a nice launch site, as does *Waddell Creek* near Davenport. You can also drive a bit further South to many good launch sites near *Santa Cruz* and *Marina,* near Monterey.

Do not ever attempt to fly at these spots until you are a qualified hang glider. Special thanks should be given to the local hang gliding pilots and shop owners who work hard with the local government agencies, authorities and insurance companies to keep these great flying spots open.

Don't do anything stupid or jeopardize the availability of these flying sites. Always know your hang gliding ability and never get in situations you can't handle. Obey those rules and hang gliding will offer you more enjoyment than you thought humanly possible.

CLUBS

All of the above mentioned hang gliding sites are maintained and supervised by the club in that area. If you are an experienced pilot who is looking to fly in the Bay Area for the first time, you have to get checked out before you are allowed to fly these sites. Most of the local hang gliding clubs are listed below. For a further listing, contact the **U.S. Hang Gliding Association** at (719) 632-8300.

Marin Hang Gliding Association: Don Saito, (510) 482-2913. For Mt. Tam.

Sonoma Wings: Todd Robinson, (707) 875-2633. For Mt. St. Helena

Wings of Rogallo: Ed Klein, (408) 371-4084. For South Bay launch sites.

Fort Funston HG Association: Contact Enzo Fatica, (415) 342-9042.

Monterey Bay Hang Gliding: Steve Espinosa, (408) 462-2351.

ADDITIONAL READING

Hang Gliding Magazine: Published monthly by the U.S. Hang Gliding Association, Inc., 559 E. Pikes Peak Ave, Suite 101, Colorado Springs, CO 80903; (719) 632-8300. This is the Bible for all hang gliding pilots. A yearly subscription is included in your dues to the organization, which run about $54 a year.

Hang Gliding For Beginner Pilots, Peter Cheney, is the official training manual of the U.S. Hang Gliding Association. The book is available from Turner-Milner Printing, 201 Armour Dr. Northeast, Atlanta, GA; (404) 872-4411.

Local Environmental Organizations

To keep the San Francisco Bay Area the outdoor sports paradise that it is, a monumental effort has to be maintained to protect the environment from pollutants, oil spills, garbage, and general overuse. These are just a few of the problems confronting our local, national and world environment.

A list follows of the major local environmental groups fighting the battles that protect this beautiful little piece of Eden known as the Bay Area. They could use your help, either through monetary contributions or by volunteering your time. Write or call for information on any organization you'd like to support.

A list of additional environmental organizations is in your local Yellow Pages. For an even better source of environmental information, pick up a copy of the *Bay Area Green Pages*, published by the Green Media Group, P.O. Box 11314, Berkeley, CA 94701. This excellent publication offers a complete digest of local environmental issues and explains how you can help.

Local environmental groups include:

Surfrider Association
122. South El Camino Real #67
San Clemente, CA 92672
(714) 492-8170
Local Chapter
Bill McLaughlin
750 LaPlaya, Suite 620
San Francisco, CA 94121
(415) 665-1444

BayKeeper
Building A, Fort Mason
San Francisco, CA 94123
(415) 567-4401

Bay Area Ridge Trail Council
311 California Street, Suite 300
San Francisco, CA 94104
(415) 391-0697

Bay Institute of San Francisco
10 Liberty Ship Way
Sausalito, CA 94965
(415) 331-2303

Save San Francisco Bay Association
P.O. Box 925
Berkeley, CA 94701
(510) 452-9261

Sierra Club
730 Polk Street
San Francisco, CA 94109
(415) 776-2211

San Francisco Boardsailing Association
1592 Union St., Box 301
San Francisco, CA, 94123
Additional chapters in North Bay, East Bay, and Peninsula

The Bicycle Trails Council of Marin
P.O. Box 494
Fairfax, CA 94978
(415) 456-7512

Greenpeace
139 Townsend St. 4th Floor
San Francisco, CA 94107
(415) 512-9025

Land Access
Mountain Bikers for Open Trails
P.O. Box 422
Fairfax, CA 94978

Ocean Alliance
Fort Mason Center, Building E
San Francisco, CA 94123
(415) 441-5970

International Mountain Biking Association IMBA
Promoting environmentally
safe mt. biking
PO Box 7578
Boulder, CO 80306
(303) 545-9011

People for a Golden Gate National Recreation Area (PFGGNRA)
3627 Clement St.
San Francisco, CA 94121
(415) 752-2777

Local Playgrounds

There are a few really special places in the San Francisco Bay Area where you can play at four or five different sports in the same park. It is worth noting these great outdoor playgrounds. They allow you to throw everything in your car and spend the day participating in a lot of different adventure sports without wasting time.

After you get into some of these great outdoor sports, it might be worth relocating to a residence or hotel closer to one of these awesome parks, or any of the other more than 40 parks throughout the Bay Area. That way, it will be easier to for you to get to these playgrounds after a day of stressful work, boring sightseeing, or doing errands.

A list follows of some of these best Bay Area parks, along with the adventure sports associated with each. Some big fun days await you at any of them.

Mount Tamalpais Area & Stinson Beach: Located a short 30 minute drive from downtown San Francisco. Take Lombard St. or 19th Ave. to the Golden Gate Bridge and follow the signs for Stinson Beach. Your outdoor sports options include:

Trail Run the Dipsea Trail.

Surf or **Boogie Board** the waves at Stinson Beach.

Mountain Bike all around Mt. Tam.

Road Bike along Rt. 1 to Bolinas, Pt. Reyes and back.

Rock Climb the 5.10-plus overhang at Mickey's Rock.

Hang Glide off Mt. Tam as soon as you're a Hang 3, or do a tandem flight now.

In-line Skate down from the summit of Mt. Tam to the Pantoll parking area.

Sea Kayak right from Stinson or Muir Beach.

Marin Headlands & Rodeo Beach: This great recreational area is even closer to the city. Just take the first Sausalito exit on the north side of the Golden Gate Bridge and go left into the headlands. You can drive all the way to the beach, or park along the side of the road to run or bike the trails. This expansive park offers city-weary San Franciscans the next best thing to an escape into the real wilds and it's only minutes away. Your choice of adventure sports for this area include:

Surf or **Boogie Board** the waves of Rodeo Beach.
Trail Run the Miwok, Wolf Ridge, Chaparral or Coastal Trail.
Mountain Bike trails like the Bobcat and Springs.
Road Bike on all the paved roads.

Mount Diablo State Park: This expansive park serves as the playground for residents of Walnut Creek, Danville and Clayton. From San Francisco, take the Bay Bridge to Rt. 24 East and then take Rt. 680 south to Diablo Road. From there, just follow the signs to the park. Your play choices here include:

Rock Climb Boy Scout Rocks or the Tiers area.
Mountain Bike up Pine Canyon, the Stage trails, and others.
Road Bike the freshly paved South Gate Road to the summit.
Hang Glide from the mountain's 3,849 foot peak, which carries a Hang 4 rating.
Trail Run the many miles of trails all through the park.
In-Line Skate from the top when there are no cars around.

Golden Gate Park & Ocean Beach: You can play to your heart's content right inside the city limits at this great park. On weekends, the park reaches its full playground potential when many roads are closed to automobile traffic. This area offers some great thrill-sport opportunities, including:

Road Bike the rolling hills, or do laps on the track at the Polo Fields.
Trail Run the trails located all through the park.
In-Line Skate the silky smooth paved roads and rolling hills.
Surf the many beautiful breaks off Ocean Beach.
Rock Climb some of the climbing spots on Ocean Wall

Marina Green & Presidio: Another great city playground with spectacular views of the Golden Gate Bridge. To get there, follow the signs that point to Marina Green. This area offers some epic conditions to:

Windsurf the screaming summer winds off Crissy Field.

In-Line Skate the hills of the upper Presidio or get speed on the run-away flats.

Surf the great left wave of Fort Point.

Road Bike the thrilling hills of the Presidio out to Ocean Beach.

Trail Run the many miles of Presidio trails.

These represent just of few of the great local areas where you can indulge in several sports inside the same park.

There are well over 600,000 acres of open land set aside for recreational use in the Bay Area. This vast play land makes up more than 40 state, regional and national parks. Just grab a map and go outside and play.

And don't worry. There is probably nothing you can do in the park that hasn't been done before. With all the sports maniacs living in this area, somebody has probably already skated down it, climbed up it, sailed or surfed it, or jumped off it. And that's nice to know, because sometimes you will get in situations where you have to stretch a bit, and you might be damn scared. It's very reassuring to know that whatever it is you're trying, someone has probably done it successfully before. And lived.

Bay Area Health Clubs

L et's face it, there are going to be days and nights when you have to play inside. Since you have to get in shape to have fun in the many adventure sports detailed in this book, it is appropriate to include a list of local Bay Area health clubs.

These clubs come with different facilities and membership rates, so the best strategy is to call the clubs closest to your work, hotel or home, for information, and compare to find which will best serve your needs.

There are more than 150 successful health clubs operating throughout this area. Most of these clubs also offer day-use rates for visitors, or if you just want to try it out. These clubs are great when the weather is bad or when you have to sneak in a quick workout into a crazy schedule. Health clubs are also pretty sweet for Jacuzzis, saunas, or massages to ease those aching bones after an afternoon of windsurfing, trail running, or any of the other great sports in this book.

Another tough weekend of book research.
Photo: Susi Watson

CITY OF SAN FRANCISCO

Downtown Financial District, Nob Hill, & Northpoint Area
SF Bay Club: 555 California St. (BankAmerica Bldg.), S.F., (415) 362-7800.
S.F. Bay Club: 150 Greenwich St., San Francisco, (415) 433-2200.
Golden Gate Tennis & Swim Club: 379 Drumm St., San Francisco, (415) 616-8800.
Nob Hill Club: 950 California St., San Francisco, (415) 397-2770.
Northpoint Health Club: 2310 Powell St., San Francisco, (415) 989-1449.
Telegraph Hill Club: 1850 Kearny St., San Francisco, (415) 982-4700.
24 Hour Nautilus: 350 Bay St., San Francisco, (415) 395-9595.
24 Hour Nautilus: 100 California St., San Francisco, (415) 434-5080.
Dolphin Club: Jefferson & Hyde St., San Francisco, (415) 441-9329.
South End Club: 500 Jefferson St., San Francisco, (415) 776-7372.

Downtown South of Market St. & Mission Area
Club One: Museum Park, San Francisco, (415) 512-1010.
Pinnacle Fitness: Hills Plaza, 345 Spear St., San Francisco, (415) 495-1939.
Pinnacle Fitness: Sharon Bldg., 61 New Montgomery St., San Francisco, (415) 543-1110.
Gold's Gym: 501 2nd St., San Francisco, (415) 777-4653.
YMCA: 169 Stuart St., San Francisco, (415) 957-9622.
The Sports Palace: 828 Valencia St., S.F., (415) 550-9216.

Upper Market St. & Civic Center Area
City Athletic Club: 2500 Market St., San Francisco, (415) 552-6680.
Golden Gate Fitness: 358 Golden Gate Ave., San Francisco, (415) 776-7113.
Market Street Gym: 2301 Market St., San Francisco, (415) 626-4488.
The Muscle System: 2275 Market St., San Francisco, (415) 863-4700.
The Muscle System: 364 Hayes St., San Francisco, (415) 863-4701.
Navarro's Gym: 3470 Mission St., San Francisco, (415) 550-1694.
Newman's Gym: 142 Leavenworth St., San Francisco, (415) 775-7020.
San Francisco Athletic Club: 1755 O'Farrell St., San Francisco, (415) 776-2260.
24 Hour Nautilus: 1335 Sutter St., San Francisco, (415) 776-2200.
YMCA: Central, 220 Golden Gate Ave., San Francisco, (415) 885-0460.
YMCA: 4080 Mission St., San Francisco, (415) 586-6900.

Marina & Pacific Heights Area
InShape: 2328 Fillmore St., San Francisco, (415) 346-5660.
InShape: 3214 Fillmore St., San Francisco, (415) 922-3700.
Advantage Fitness: 3741 Buchanan St., San Francisco, (415) 563-3535.
Cathedral Hill Athletic Club: 1333 Gough St., San Francisco, (415) 346-3868.
SF Fitness: 1528 Union St., San Francisco, (415) 749-0642.
Marina Club: 3333 Fillmore St., San Francisco, (415) 563-3333.
Pacific Heights Health Club: 2358 Pine St., San Francisco, (415) 563-6694.
Mindful Body: 2876 California St., San Francisco, (415) 931-2639.
Jewish Community Center: 3200 California St., San Francisco, (415) 346-6040.

Castro & Noe Valley Area
World Gym: Showplace Square, 260 DeHaro St., San Francisco, (415) 703-9650.
25th Street Work Out: 1500 Castro St., San Francisco, (415) 647-1224.
Purely Physical Fitness: 1414 Castro St., San Francisco, (415) 282-1329.
Cole Valley Fitness: 957 Cole St., San Francisco, (415) 665-3330.

Golden Gate Park Area
9th Ave. Muscle & Fitness: 1247 9th Ave., San Francisco, (415) 564-4343.
Taraval Fitness Center: 645 Taraval Ave., San Francisco, (415) 664-0074.
Parkside Fitness Club: 1647 Taraval St., San Francisco, (415) 731-0880.
Powerhouse Gym: 1850 Ocean Ave, San Francisco, (415) 239-9340.
Alex's Gym: 49 Ocean Ave., San Francisco, (415) 563-3535.
Fitness USA Health Spa: 3251 20th Ave. San Francisco, (415) 681-2500.
YMCA: Stonestown, 333 Eucalyptus Dr., San Francisco, (415) 759-9622.
MegaFlex Gym & Fitness Center: 3119 Vicente, San Francisco, (415) 753-5177.

SOUTH SAN FRANCISCO & PENINSULA
Powerhouse Gym: 950 King St., Daly City, (415) 878-0100.
Fitness USA Health Spa: 386 Gellert Blvd., Daly City, (415) 755-0600.
Gideon's Gym & Fitness: 30 Hill Ave., Daly City, (415) 994-5679.
What A Racquet: 2945 Junipero Serra Blvd., Colma, (415) 994-9080.
Gym West: 121 Beech St., Redwood City, (415) 364-0933.
D. Nelson Health & Spa: 515 Veterans Blvd., Redwood City, (415) 365-3800.
She Fitness For Women: 363 Main St., Redwood City, (415) 366-2777.
Pacific Athletic Club: 200 Redwood Shore Pwky., Redwood City,
    (415) 593-9100.
Schoeber's Athletic Club: 425 Eccles Ave, South San Francisco, (415) 873-8500.
Supreme Athletic Club: 975 Industrial Rd., San Carlos, (415) 593-1671.
World Gym: 1119 Industrial Rd., San Carlos, (415) 595-2707.
California Athletic Club: 1650 Industrial Rd., San Carlos, (415) 595-3000.
Royal Athletic Club: 1718 Rollins Rd., Burlingame, (415) 692-3300.
World Gym: 888 Hinckley Rd., Burlingame, (415) 259-1555.
24 Hour Nautilus Fitness: 225 Baldwin Ave, San Mateo, (415) 343-7922.
Jazzercise Fitness: 711 South Blvd., San Mateo, (415) 347-2250.
NorCal Gym: 1475 Old Country Rd., Belmont, (415) 595-1948.
YMCA: 1877 S. Grant Ave., San Mateo, (415) 286-9622.
New San Mateo Spa & Fitness: 83 21st Ave., San Mateo, (415) 572-8575.
Colony Swim & Tennis Club: 2000 Fairway Dr., Half Moon Bay,
    (415) 726-2849.
Prime Time Athletic Club: 1730 Rollins Rd., Burlingame, (415) 697-7311.
Donnelly Sq. Fitness For Women: 1208 Donnelly, Burlingame, (415) 347-1706.
Foster City Athletic Club: 1159 Chess Dr., Foster City, (415) 377-1991.
Reach Fitness Club: 377 2nd St., Los Altos, (415) 949-3730.
Spa of Los Altos: 371 2nd St., Los Altos, (415) 948-8898.
Fitness 101: 40 Scott Dr., Menlo Park, (415) 321-7900.
Gold's Gym: 1400 Shoreline Blvd., Mountain View, (415) 940-1440.
YMCA: 4151 Middlefield Rd., Palo Alto, (415) 856-3955.
21st Point Fitness: 199 E. Middlefield Rd., Mountain View, (415) 969-1783.
24 Hour Nautilus: 2550 W. El Camino, Mountain View, (415) 941-2268.
Twisters Sports Center: 2639 Terminal Blvd., Mountain View, (415) 967-5581.
Mt. View Athletic Club: 444 Castro Ave., Mountain View, (415) 961-8085.

MARIN COUNTY

Elan Fitness Center: 230 Greenfield Ave. San Anselmo, (415) 485-1945.
Fairfax Health Club: 713 Center Blvd., Fairfax, (415) 459-9000.
Class 5 Fitness & Climbing Wall: 25 Dodie St., San Rafael, (415) 485-6931.
Coast Fitness Center: 625 Grand Ave, San Rafael, (415) 459-8668.
Marin Jewish Center: 200 N. San Pedro, San Rafael, (415) 479-2000.
Nautilus of Marin: 734 A Ave., San Rafael, (415) 457-8944.
YMCA: 1500 Las Gamos Dr., San Rafael, (415) 492-9622.
Rolling Hills Club: 351 San Andreas Dr., Novato, (415) 897-2185.
Nautilus of Marin: 1530 Center Rd., Novato, (415) 898-2582.
Stinson Beach Health Club: 3605 Rt. 1, Stinson Beach, (415) 868-2739.
Original Gym: 941 Sir Francis Drake Blvd., Kentfield, (415) 455-8018.
Symmetry: 555 Redwood Hwy., Mill Valley, (415) 383-3436.
Studio Dance Fitness: 237 Shoreline Hwy., Mill Valley, (415) 388-6786.
24 Hour Nautilus: 1001 Larkspur Landing, Larkspur, (415) 925-0333.
World Gym: 5651 Paradise Dr., Corte Madera, (415) 927-9494.
Nautilus of Marin: 3020 Bridgeway Ave, Sausalito, (415) 331-3020.

EAST BAY

Alameda Athletic Club: 1226 Park St., Alameda, (510) 521-2001.
Bay Island Gymnastics: 2317 Central Ave., Alameda, (510) 521-1343.
Beyond Aerobics: 1207 Park St., Alameda, (510) 523-5944.
Harbor Bay Club: 200 Packet Landing Rd., Alameda, (510) 521-5414.
Mariner Sq. Athletic Club: 2227 Mariner Sq. Loop, Alameda, (510) 523-8011.
Iron Island Gym: 2306 Encinal Ave., Alameda, (510) 522-9837.
CityRock Gym & Climbing Wall: 1250 45th St., Emeryville, (510) 654-2510.
Every Women's Fitness: 5800 Shellmound Ave., Emeryville, (510) 654-9990.
World Gym: 6101 Christie Ave., Emeryville, (510) 601-1141.
Courthouse Athletic Club: 2935 Telegraph Ave., Oakland, (510) 834-5600.
Fitlab: 5335 College Ave., Oakland, (510) 547-6636.
Fitlab: 1183 Solano Ave., Albany, (510) 524-9323.
Fitness Center 1800: 1800 Harrison, Oakland, (510) 893-2041.
Gym Masters: 3008 McArthur Blvd., Oakland, (510) 530-1046.
Inside Out Health Club: 4444 Piedmont Ave., Oakland, (510) 655-8308.
YMCA: 2350 Broadway Ave, Oakland, (510) 451-9622.
Lakeview Ladies Fitness: 344 20th Ave., Oakland, (510) 465-0900.
Norman Marks Health Club: 298 14th Ave, Oakland, (510) 452-3755.
Oakland Athletic Club: 1418 Webster St., Oakland, (510) 893-3421.
Oakland Hills Tennis Club: 5475 Redwood Rd., Oakland, (510) 531-3300.
Park Exercise Studio: 3810 Park Blvd., Oakland, (510) 530-6937.
Sports Club: 1200 Clay St., Oakland, (510) 835-2000.

The Spa: 7850 Edgewater Dr., Oakland, (510) 568-2000.
24 Hour Nautilus: 40910 Freemont Blvd., Freemont, (510) 226-6900.
Club Sports: 46650 Landing Park Way, Freemont, (510) 226-8500.
24 Hour Nautilus: 1505 Willow Pass Rd., Concord, (510) 674-8412.
24 Hour Nautilus: 1507 E. 14th St., San Leandro, (510) 278-9744.
24 Hour Nautilus: 3901 E. Castro Valley Blvd., Castro Valley, (510) 733-6448.
Walt's Health Club: 1660 Wash. Ave., San Leandro, (510) 351-1830.
Works Exercise Studio: 2640 College Ave., Berkeley, (510) 841-1373.
World Gym: 1270 San Pablo Ave, Berkeley, (510) 527-5070.
Premier Fitness World: 1776 Arnold Industrial Way, Concord, (510) 674-9940.
Fitness Matters: 4330 Clayton Rd., Concord, (510) 827-9922.
Big C Athletic Club: 1381 Galaxy Way, Concord, (510) 671-2110.
Clayton Valley Athletic Club: 5294 Clayton Rd., Concord, (510) 682-1060.
Crow Canyon Athletic Club: 2460 Old Crow, San Ramon, (510) 838-0660.
Club Sports: 350 Bolinger Canyon Lane, San Ramon, (510) 735-8500.
Linda Evans Fitness Center: 2074 Treat Blvd., Walnut Creek, (510) 938-2120.
Body Beautiful Women's Fitness: 2885 Ygnacio, Walnut Creek, (510) 945-7767.
24 Hour Nautilus: 2033 N. Main, Walnut Creek, (510) 930-7900.
Gold's Gym: 1853 Ygnacio Valley Rd., Walnut Creek, (510) 935-1132.
Valley Vista Club: 3737 Valley Vista Rd., Walnut Creek, (510) 934-4050.
Walnut Creek Fitness: 1908 Olympic Blvd., Walnut Creek, (510) 932-6400.
World Gym: 2150 N. Broadway, Walnut Creek, (510) 933-9988.
YMCA: 350 Civic Dr., Pleasant Hill, (510) 687-8900.
Supreme Court Fitness: 100 Coggins Dr., Pleasant Hill, (510) 938-5370.
Pleasant Hill Ladies Fitness: 1 Mayhew Way, Pleasant Hill, (510) 935-5525.
Inside Out Health Club: 23 Orinda Way, Orinda, (510) 254-6877.
Lafayette Health Club: 85 Lafayette Circle, Lafayette, (510) 284-7732.
Medina's Gym: 6735 Sierra Ct., Dublin, (510) 829-5307.
Lakeridge Athletic Club: 6350 San Pablo Dam Rd., El Sobrante, (510) 222-2500.
Pacific Gym: 620 San Pablo Ave, Pinole, (510) 724-7195.
Club Sports: 7090 Johnson Drive, Pleasanton, (510) 463-2822.

Acknowledgments

Without the support from a lot of great people this book would have never made it to print.

Special thanks to:

Publisher Tom Todd, James Putrus & ICS Books;
Janet & Tom McKinley for getting me to California & the Bay Area;
Bill Evans & PaineWebber Investment Firm;
Editor & revision expert Tracy Salcedo at Laughingwater Ink;
My brother Andy who could always be talked into any crazy adventure.

Many thanks to those who answered all my questions and shared their local knowledge:

Kent Parker, Peter Sykes, Harry Fletcher, Jay James, Neil Gibbs, Jessica Graf, Richard Beck, Jeff Cusack, Jeff Knaus, Annie Mitchell, Stephen L Blick, Rich Luddine, Mike Carney, Aaron Mendelson, Mark McClaughlin, Nick Berg, Gloria Andrews, Stephen Jakosa, Sean Hurley, Brooks Mohrman, Neil Redfern, Wilbur Smith, Kathleen Hunt, Chuck Clarvit, Robert Higgins, Paul Yenofsky, Linda Bizzari, Map man Chris Slattery, The Pacific Bell Yellow Pages, Word 5.1 & Microsoft Inc., Computer wiz Chris Minnerly, The Mechanics, Institute Library, Alasdair Boyd & Skydance Skydiving, Ellen & Count Nick Besobrasow, Marilyn & Susan Blick, Kathryn, Sara, & Thomas McKinley, Bill & Ethel Blick, Mike & Liz O'Donnell, Joe & Liz Currier, Surfer Bill Marino, Kinko's at 201 Sacramento St., Marty Mattox & UltraHealth, Penny Wells & BASK, Dave Horning & EnviroSports, the San Francisco Lacrosse Club, Joe Oaks & Sally Bailey of the Alcatraz Challenge Group, Stuntwomen Claudia Soddeman & Trish Gooch, Physical therapist Chris Chorak, Paul Lundgren, Mike Krieger & the Bridge Bungee Company, Bungee Adventures, Andy Whitehall & Norma Jean Marsh of Chandelle SF, Inc., Dr. Jean Revere, Tom Schardt & Apple Computer Inc., Jennifer Schwegman & Rollerblade

Inc., Contributor & photographer Susi Wells-Watson, Shirwin Smith & Open Water Rowing, Kevin Campion & Marin Surf Sports, Bob Licht & Seatrek Sea Kayak Center, Dr. Dennis & Carol Hamby, Kees Tuinzing & Dave Stringer of The Schedule, David Kennedy & the Armchair Sailor, and Dr. James Burke.

Major thanks to photographers:
Ken Lee, Doug Acton, Shaw Hazen, Tara & Michael Fitz-Gerald, Greg Aston, Scott Tucker, Will Nordby, Mike Krieger, Andy Whitehall, Greta & AeroPhotographs, Christine Weaver & Colleen Levine of Latitude 38, Michael Powers, and Dan Nelson.

Selected
Bibliography

Boisver, Conrad, *Bay Area Mountain Bike Trails, SF Peninsula Bike Trails*. *East Bay Bike Trails*, Penngrove Publications, Penngrove, CA.

Boga, Steve, *RISK*, North Atlantic Books, Berkeley, CA, 1988.

Brown, Bruce, *Open Water Rowing Handbook*, International Marine Publisher, Camden, Maine, 1991.

Cheney, Peter, *Hang Gliding for Beginner Pilots*, Matt Tabor Pub., Rising Fawn, GA., 1980.

Frase, Nancy, *Bungee Jumping For Fun & Profit*, ICS Books, Merrillville, IN.

Godsey, Kast, Hughney, *Windsurfer: A Complete Guide to the SF Bay Area & Beyond,* Windnotes Enterprises, Marin, CA.

Hosler, Ray, *Bay Area Bike Rides*, Chronicle Books, San Francisco, CA., 1990.

Hudson, Michael & Mark Lord, *Mountain Biking in the Bay Area*, Western Tanager Press, Santa Cruz , CA 95060.

Jensen Mark, *Bouldering in the San Francisco Bay Area*, M&M Publishing, Hayward, CA , 1988.

Kiesling, Stephen, *The Complete Recreational Rower & Racer*, Crown Publishers, NY, NY, 1990.

Livingston, Kimball, *Sailing The Bay*, Chronicle Books, San Francisco, CA., 1981.

Lemond, Greg & Kent Gordis, *Complete Book of Bicycling*, Perigee Books, NY, NY., 1990.

Martin, Don & Kay, Mt. Tam: *A Hiking, Running, & Nature Guide*, Martin Press, San Anselmo, CA.

Peterson, Grant & Mary Anderson, *Roads To Ride*, Heydey Books, Berkeley, CA.

Soares, Eric & Jim Kakuk, *The Tsunami Ranger Anthology*, PO Box 339, Moss Beach, CA 94038.

Spangle, Francis & Jean Rushmore, *South Bay Trails*, Wilderness Press, Berkeley, CA.

Spangle, Francis & Jean Rushmore, *Peninsula Trails*, Wilderness Press, Berkeley, CA.

Thornburg, Jim, *Bay Area Rock Climbing*, Potlicker Press, San Francisco, CA., 1992.

Todd, Armor, The Marin Mountain Bike Guide, Armor Publications, 1988. Wright, Bank, *Surfing California*, Mountain & Sea Publications, Redondo Beach, CA, 1985.

Whitnah, Dorothy, *An Outdoor Guide to the SF Bay Area*, Wilderness Press, Berkeley, CA,

Young, Nat, *The History of Surfing*, The Body Press, Tuscon, AZ., 1983

Magazines:
CitySports, 214 S. Cedros, Solana Beach, CA, 92075.
The Schedule, Total Race Systems, 80 Mitchell Rd., San Rafael, CA, 94903.
California Bicyclist , 490 Second St., San Francisco, CA, 94107.
Latitude 38, P.O. Box 1678, Sausalito, CA, 94965.
WindTracks, Pistol River, Oregon.

Index

A

Achilles Wheels 98
Action Bikes 115
Adventure Cat 55
Adventure Aerosports 164
Adventure Sports Kayaking 39
air sports 152-188
Alameda Beach 67
Alcatraz Challenge Group 26
Alpine Skills Climbing School
145
American Bicycle Rentals 115
Any Mountain 98, 99
Angel Island 49
Aquatic Park 27, 28, 30
AirTime of San Francisco 169
Arete Rock Climbing Gym 148
Armchair Sailor 53
ASD Surf Designs 70

B

Bandanna Map Company 84
Bay Area bicycle shops 120-123
Bay Area health clubs 194-198
Bay Keeper 189
Bay Institute of San Francisco
190
Bay Area Ridge Trail Council 190
Bay Area Skydiving 163

bay swim 23-30
Berkeley Bicycle Club 135
Berkeley Sailboards 70
Bicycle Trails Council of Marin
190
bicycle shops of the Bay Area
120-123
Big Boat Sailing Series 52
Blanchard, J.P. 160
Blue Water Ocean Kayak 36
BodyGlove wetsuits 7
body surf 15
boogie board 15
Bolinas surf break 18
Breeze, Joe 108
Bridge Bungee Jumping Inc. 158
bungee 154-159
Bungee Adventures 157

C

Cal Adventurers 35, 37, 54, 69,
77, 147
California Bicyclist Magazine
3, 119, 125, 135, 136, 137
California Canoe & Kayak 36, 38
California Outdoor Rollerblading
Association 96
Cal Sailing Club 54, 70
Campion, Kevin 2
Case, Jan 181
CCM in-line skates 87

T

Tamal Saka Inc. 36
The Schedule 4, 106
The Surf Report 22
Thornburg, Jim 148
Tomales Bay 69
Tradewinds Sailing School 55
Triathlete Magazine 30
Tye, Scott 36

U

UCSF Bicycle Club 136
UFO Wheels 87
UltraWheels 87
US Cycling Federation 137
US Hang Gliding Association
    153, 170, 180, 181
US Parachuting Association
    163, 166
US Track and Field Association
    107

V

Valley Spokesmen 136
Vela Highwind Center 61, 70
VeloNews 138
Venture Quest Kayaking 39

W

Waddell Creek windsurf spot 69
water sports 6-82
wave skis 16
West Coast Skydiving 164
Western Hang Gliders 182
wetsuit explanation 6
Wheel Escapes 115
Wheels in Motion 99
Willows Skate & Surf 99
WindCraft Windsurfing 72
Windsurf Diablo 70
Windsurfing Lake Del Valle 70
Wind Sight 66
Windsports 70
windsurf 59-72
Windsurf Warehouse 70
Wind Tracks 3, 67
Wise Surf Shop 17, 19
Wright, Bank 19

Y

Yacht Racing Association 50, 52
Yosemite Decimal System 146
Yosemite Mountaineering School
    145
Yellow Pages 33, 99, 158, 189

Outdoor Adventures Update

The Monthly Newsletter for all the Bay Area Adventure Sports

Beginning Fall-1995 a new concept in recreational sports will debut.

OUTDOOR ADVENTURES UPDATE!

The Monthly Newsletter for all the Bay Area Adventure Sports will be premiering. The unique format will include illuminating and informative articles on all of the great local recreational sports to keep you up to date on any news and developments. Included will be equipment deals, tricks to help your learning curve, secret local spots, monthly previews and guest lecture schedule, trips, races, weather knowledge, and more on each and every local adventure sport. Each and every month you will be able to learn more about your favorite local adventure sport, or discover valuable information to easily learn a new one. This publication will be designed to save you money, fill you with inside information, and keep you from wasting time because you will always know each month what sport to play and where. So whether you live in town and just want to go play, or you're from out of town and want to know what's going on when you're here, this newsletter is for you. *For a **free complimentary copy** of the premier issue of **Outdoor Adventures Update!**, just fill out the address label on opposite page.*

Yes, send me the complimentary premier issue of *Outdoor Adventures Update!* *The Monthly Newsletter for all the Bay Area Adventure Sports.*

Just fill out & send to:
Outdoor Adventure Publications:
1001 Bridgeway #628, Sausalito, CA, 94965

NAME: _____

ADDRESS: _____

CITY: _____

STATE: _____ ZIP: _____

Sports most interested in: _____

_____

About the Author: Rick Blick grew up in New York playing the sport of lacrosse, working his way up to All-American at Hobart College and a spot on the U.S. team before escaping those freezing cold winters having to be cooped up in the house or some gym. Lucky enough to wind up in the year round outdoor sports paradise of the San Francisco Bay Area in 1981, he has been playing ever since. A stockbroker with PaineWebber in San Francisco by trade, he resides on a sailboat in Sausalito.